19 –
2131

Eucharist, Bishop, Church

John D. Zizioulas
Metropolitan of Pergamon

EUCHARIST, BISHOP, CHURCH:
THE UNITY OF THE CHURCH IN THE DIVINE EUCHARIST AND THE BISHOP DURING THE FIRST THREE CENTURIES

translated by
Elizabeth Theokritoff

HOLY CROSS ORTHODOX PRESS
Brookline, Massachusetts

Publication of this book was made possible, in part, by a generous donation from His Eminence Archbishop Iakovos of North and South America.

On the cover: *St Basil the Great*. St Sophia Cathedral, Ochrid, 11th century. Used with the permission of the Embassy of the Former Yugoslav Republic of Macedonia, Washington, D.C.

The publishers wish to thank Rev. Emmanuel Clapsis, Ph.D., of Holy Cross Greek Orthodox School of Theology for his invaluable assistance with aspects of this publication.

LIBRARY OF CONGRESS CATALOGING–IN–PUBLICATION DATA

Zizioulas, John, 1931-
    [Enotes tes Ekklesias en te Theia Eucharistia kai to episkopo kata tous treis protous aionas. English]
    Eucharist, bishop, church: the unity of the church in the Divine Eucharist and the bishop during the first three centuries / John D. Zizioulas ; translated by Elizabeth Theokritoff.
    p.   cm.
    Includes bibliographical references.
    ISBN 1-885652-51-8 (paper)
    1. Lord's Supper--History--Early church, ca. 30-600. 2. Bishops--History of doctrines--early church, ca. 30-600. 3. Church--Unity--History of doctrines, ca. 30-600. I. Title.

    BV823.Z5913 2001
    262'.1212-dc21   2001024091

To His Eminence
Archbishop Iakovos

CONTENTS

Although this work is historical in its method and content, it is not a product of historical curiosity. At a time when church unity occupies an increasingly central place in theological study, the contribution of our theology is required not simply as an academic demand, but also a fundamental debt owed to the Church.

In order to fulfil the demand and pay the debt, our theology can no longer fall back on the sources of its own confessional riches. The gradual abandonment of the confessional mentality of past generations and the recognition of the need for our theology to be an expression not of one confession but of the one, holy, catholic and apostolic Church herself, now directs the course of theological study towards the sources of the ancient undivided Church. A Church which, in spite of all the disputes and conflicts by which she was often shaken, was always well aware of what is meant by the catholic consciousness of the Church. This holds true, most especially for the study of the unity of the Church which aims to provide our divided Christian world with that supra-confessional thread which will help it to rediscover and actualize its unity through the midst of its various divisions.

For those coming from the Orthodox tradition, a reliable method of turning towards the sources of the ancient undivided Church is through study of the liturgical life of our Church. The reproach leveled at our Church that she has remained through the centuries a "community of worship" today, proves to be the best guarantee of a sure route back to the consciousness of the ancient undivided Church. For the liturgical life of our Church which is characterized by its conservatism and traditional character has not succumbed to

1

overloading with non-essential later elements, but continues to reflect in a changing contemporary world the one, holy, catholic and apostolic Church of every age, worshipping in one body.

It is within this general orientation, and encouraged by the flourishing revival in biblical, patristic and liturgical studies in our own day, that this study has been written. Without inappropriately and unthinkingly serving confessional ends, the author has taken as his starting point the fundamental importance of the Eucharist and the Bishop for the unity of the Church as this is recognized especially in the consciousness of the Orthodox Church. For it is unnecessary to stress that out of the entire Christian world, Orthodoxy alone has kept the Eucharist and the Bishop in such a central place in its own consciousness. And if this has been forgotten by certain Orthodox theologians, it has nevertheless always remained in the consciousness of the people of Orthodox piety for whom "the Church" is identified in its concrete sense with the church building in which the Eucharist is celebrated, and in the vaulted domes of which, as a distinguished contemporary Byzantinist has remarked, "the whole (of the architecture and decoration) represents the very Kingdom of God Whose 'realm' the Church is in microcosm, with the communion of saints as the subjects of Christ Pantocrator." The living and mystical depiction of the "communion of saints", i.e. of the body of the Church, in eucharistic worship, in which the bishop's throne rules as "the place of God" according to St Ignatius, reveals the "Eucharist under the leadership of the bishop" as a living symbol and practical expression of the unity of the Church.

Starting from these observations, this study aims to place in the light of the consciousness of the early Church the whole relationship connecting the unity of the Church with the Eucharist and the Bishop. Did this relationship exist in the early Church, and to what extent? Was such a relationship of decisive importance for the formation of the early catholic Church, and what specific implications did it have for that Church's consciousness concerning unity? Such were the basic questions that the present study set itself to address. It is obvious that these questions concern only one aspect of the very broad subject of the Church's unity. This must be underlined here, in order not to lay the study open to being misunderstood as "one-sided" in the position it takes towards the unity of the Church. There, certainly, remain many aspects of this very broad subject which are not covered by this study, and which await investigation. But awareness of this fact does not negate the author's conviction that at least for him, living as he does within the Orthodox milieu, it was impossible to do other than give absolute priority to this aspect of the subject.

Apart from these purely practical limitations, this study is also limited by its methodology and the chronological limits to its sources. It is natural that anything relating to the unity of the Church should touch on problems in many branches of theology and raise questions belonging to various different theological concerns. Without underrating the importance of these questions, the author has consistently distanced himself from the contemporary debate and, in conducting his research, has bypassed the theories of modern theologians concerning the unity of the Church. He has taken a purely historical vantage point and turned to the sources not only for his answers, but also for his questions. It has, therefore, been judged essential in the lengthy introduction to this book to clear the ground of our research from modern schemes within which the subject of the Church's unity has been imprisoned and which historiography, in an inadmissible betrayal of any notion of historical method, has habitually transferred to the study of the ancient Church. Confining itself to a strict examination of the sources, this study has drawn on contemporary literature only selectively and as a subsidiary source. The literature relating to the Church of the first three centuries is a veritable labyrinth out of which the scholar can find his way only by being strictly selective if he wants to avoid becoming embroiled in discussion with his contemporaries to the detriment of a correct understanding of the historical sources. But this selection requires a knowledge of the literature and demands painstaking effort. The extent of the bibliography at the end of this book and the number of footnotes show how little we have succeeded in our aim of restricting the literature used.

As to the chronological limits on the sources for this work, these have dictated themselves in the course of research. The great figure of St Cyprian and the whole period to which he belongs form a landmark in the history of ecclesiology, while the full development during this time of the axiom *ecclesiam in episcopo et episcopum in ecclesia esse* naturally presents the scholar studying the subject of this work with the first milestone of an entire period. The three parts of our study are devoted respectively to the presuppositions, the formation and the developments in our subject during this period. The continuation of this endeavor into the sources from the fourth century onwards a task which, fortunately, is infinitely easier owing to the abundance of extant sources, has yet to be accomplished.

This study owes its completion and publication to the blessing of God, which is manifested through many people. The writing of it was made possible thanks to the abundant research material available at Harvard University which gave hospitality to the author for many successive years. The presence at that university of distinguished professors, in particular G. Florovsky, G. Williams and K. Stendahl, was a font of inspiration and encouragement during the entire course of the research. Again, the submission of this study as a doctoral dissertation at my own *alma mater*, the Theological School of the University of Athens, provided the opportunity for some valuable suggestions and comments from the faculty there. The author is, therefore, deeply grateful, both for the trouble they took with him as teachers, and for all they did particularly for the present work, according it the honor of unanimous approval. Warmest thanks are due especially to my adviser Professor Gerasimos Konidaris both for his kind introduction to the School and for all his invaluable help. Finally, the original publication of this work would not have been possible but for the generous and touching financial support of Metropolitan Panteleimon of Thessaloniki and of Metropolitan Dionysios of Servies and Kozani who ungrudgingly took great trouble reading the drafts and followed the progress of the study, giving invaluable help from his rich literary and theological resources. To all of these and many others who indirectly and in various ways contributed to the appearance of this work, the expression of my gratitude repays only a small part of an unpaid debt.

J. D. Z.

Preface To The Second Edition (1990)

The reception accorded to the present work was such that it long ago went out of print. The repeated calls from various quarters for the book to be republished accorded with the author's own desire to add some chapters to the study which he considered indispensable for its completion, and to furnish the whole work with a new bibliography. Unfortunately, because of the time such an undertaking would require, it was proving ever more impracticable, and became virtually impossible after the author took on ecclesiastical obligations and duties in addition to his academic responsibilities about three years ago. There was thus nothing to be done but to reprint the work as it was, merely with the correction of some printing errors and omissions in the original edition.

Two observations contributed decisively to the decision to reprint this work. The first is *academic* in nature, and consists in the fact that even though 25 years have passed since this study was first published and many other studies relating to its subject have appeared in the meantime, the basic theses of this work are still sound and need no revision. It could indeed be said that the whole course of research internationally since this study was written has confirmed its theses with the result that they have become quite widely and internationally known and are now often regarded as commonplace. This was an encouraging factor in the decision to reprint this book even in its original form.

The second observation which contributed decisively to the reprinting of this work is *ecclesiastical* in nature. The Orthodox Church, particularly in Greece, is today going through a critical period which, if the necessary care is not taken by the Church leadership, will soon lead to a *crisis in institutions* with unforeseen consequences for the *doctrinal* purity and substance of the Orthodox Church in that country. The characteristics of this critical period could be summarized in the following points.

Firstly, under the influence of the modern spirit of so-called "democratic" tendencies, the institution of episcopacy, which had in the past been identified with "despotism" is, today, experiencing a severe crisis. Many priests, a large part of the lay faithful and many bishops, too, do not know what exactly the task and the institution of the bishop consists in, and how it is connected with the *doctrinal* substance of the Church. Unfortunately, many Orthodox have it firmly entrenched in their mind that the the bishop is in essence an administrator, and that in his liturgical function, including indeed the Divine Eucharist, he is not a person *constitutive* of the Mystery but more or less *decorative* someone who is invited to "embellish" the whole service by his presence and his vestments. Precisely because of the weakening of the ancient conception which this work demonstrates in such detail, namely, that the bishop is in essence the only president of the Divine Eucharist and that no Divine Liturgy is thinkable without reference to the bishop in whose name it is celebrated, ordination as priest has come to be regarded by many as sufficient for someone to celebrate the Divine Eucharist and transmit grace to the people without any clear dependence on his bishop. This idea can be seen at its ultimate extreme in cases where the Divine Liturgy is celebrated *without the commemoration of a bishop*! When this "presbyterianism" is permitted (a "presbyterianism" which, thanks to the influence of Orthodox theology, is starting to be questioned even by Protestants today), it threatens the doctrinal foundations of the Church as they were laid down during the first centuries. In her attempt to avoid the Scylla of "despotism", the Church is in danger of falling into the Charybdis of a sort of "presbyterianism" if the proper place of the bishop in the Church is not brought to people's awareness.

Secondly, under the influence of a revival of the "charismatic" element in contemporary Orthodoxy – or rather of the emphasis placed on it because that element had never disappeared from the life of the Church – the institutional aspect of ecclesiology tends to be relegated to second place. Orthodoxy tends to be turned into an ideology. It is forgotten that *Orthodoxy is Church*, and that the Church is a community with a specific *structure*, and that this structure is *episcopocentric*. Everything that is performed in the Church, including those manifestations considered most "spiritual" and "charismatic" (not that there is anything in the Church that is non-charismatic or non-spiritual) such as spiritual fatherhood, confession etc., all stem from the bishop and have need of his approval and permission. Never in the past, throughout the long history of the Orthodox Church, was it possible to exercise spiritual fatherhood without express episcopal permission in writing. Only in our day do we have a superabundance of "charismatics" who are active and carry on their spiritual work simply by right of their priesthood or their "gifts", without it being clear that everything in the Church is done in the name of the bishop. In this way the Orthodox laity begins to get accustomed to situations which threaten to blow up the foundations of Orthodoxy as it has been passed down to us, and we knew it only a generation ago.

The present work, grounded as it is in the sources of the first centuries, is made available in its reprinted form in fulfilment of the author's debt to the holy Orthodox Church as a bishop and as a theologian. The scholarly grounding of its conclusions seeks to persuade any sincere reader, Orthodox or not, that Orthodoxy, not as ideology but as *Church*, as founded on the teaching and the blood of a St Ignatius of Antioch, an Irenaeus or a Cyprian, is the One, Holy, Catholic and Apostolic Church because it possesses the truth not only in its teaching but also in its structure. It is the duty of Orthodoxy to bear witness to this everywhere in the critical period through which we are now passing.

+John of Pergamon

V.E.P.A.D.	*Vivliotheke Ellenon Pateron kai Ekklesiastikon Syngrapheon.* Ed. Apostoliki Diakonia, Greece, 1955 *et seq.*
D.A.C.L.	*Dictionnaire d'Archéologie chrétienne et de Liturgie,* 1907 *et seq.*
D.D.C.	*Dictionnaire de Droit canonique,* 1924 *et seq.*
D.T.C.	*Dictionnaire de Théologie catholique,* 1923 *et seq.*
E.E.Th.S.	*Epistemonike Epeteris tes Theologikes Scholes tou Panepistemiou Athenon*
E.E.Th.S.Th.	*Epistemonike Epeteris tes Theologikes Scholes tou Panepistemiou Thessalonikes*
G.C.H.G.	Konidaris, *General Church History from Jesus Christ to our own times* (in Greek), I, 1957[2],
L.T.K.	*Lexikon für Theologie und Kirche,* 1957 *et seq.*
P.G.	Migne, *Patrologia,* series graeca
P.L.	Migne, *Patrologia,* series latina
R.G.G.	Religion in Geschichte und Gegenwart, 1909[1], 1927[2], 1959[3] *et seq.*
T.W.N.T.	*Theologisches Wörterbuch zum Neuen Testament,* G. Kittel - G. Friedrich, 1933 *et seq.*
Z.N.T.W.	*Zeitschrift für neutestamentliche Wissenschaft und die Kunde der älteren Kirche,* 1900 *et seq.*
Z.K.T.	*Zeitschrift für katholische Theologie,* 1873 *et seq.*

INTRODUCTION

*The Unity of the Church in the Divine Eucharist and the Bishop as
a Fundamental Historical Question: Methodological Principles and
Scope of the Subject*

Throughout the entire period of the first three centuries,
unity was bound up at the deepest level with the faith, the
prayers and the activities of the Church. St John's Gospel
reflects this fact when it presents the unity of the Church as
an agonized petition in the prayer of the Lord.[1] The Acts of
the Apostles expresses the same reality when they emphatically stress unity as the element characteristic of the Church's
life in her first years[2] while the existence of a "theology of
unity" at a period as early as that of St Paul's Epistles[3] cannot be interpreted otherwise than as an indication of the
importance which the Church from the beginning attached
to her unity. During the years following apostolic times, the
Church regarded her unity as a matter of constant concern
and an object of vehement faith. The texts of the so-called
Apostolic Fathers present the unity of the Church as an object of teaching, and something for which they struggled
against every divisive force.[4] Around the end of the second
century, Irenaeus attempts in a work especially devoted to
the subject to show that the Church was and has been preserved as one,[5] and that unity constitutes the necessary
condition for her existence.[6] A few generations later, St
Cyprian devotes a special study to the subject of church unity[7]
while in the various credal documents, unity early assumes
the character of an article of faith.[8]

Once one sees the tremendous importance of unity for
the Church of the first three centuries, the question arises for
history – was this unity a historical reality, or was there sim-

ply an unfulfilled desire and a nostalgic quest for a unity which proved in reality a perpetually and increasingly unattainable ideal? As we shall see below, almost all modern historiography has contributed through its various theses to a picture of the Church of the first three centuries as a society from the first deeply divided in such a way as to create the impression that schism was an innate part of the Church organism.

There are thus two aspects to the overall theme of the unity of the Church. One concerns the *ideal* or the *teaching* of the early Church concerning her unity. The other concerns *what the Church experienced* as unity during the period under examination. The first theme may be characterized as *the theology of unity* as it was conceived and formulated by the early Church. The second constitutes the *history of unity* as it can be reconstructed from study of the sources with the aid of objective historical research.

It is precisely within the context of this historical problem of the existence and form of unity in the Church that the subject of the present work finds its place. If, during the highly critical first three centuries examined here, the Church experienced her unity as a historical reality, what was the significance of the Eucharist and the Bishop who led it for the expression of this reality? Church historiography in recent years has attached no importance to this question. If we follow its development, we shall be amazed at the lack of any kind of historical study of this subject even in recent years when church unity has occupied a central place in theological concerns. Why, when so much has been written about unity, has virtually nothing been written specifically about unity in the Eucharist and in the Bishop? This perplexing omission has a substantial influence on the importance of our theme. For this reason it is necessary by way of introduction to look at the reasons for this position taken by modern historiography on the subject under examination before going on to define the presuppositions underlying our own research.

If we attempt to penetrate quite deeply into the body of Western Theology in recent years, we shall discover that its writing of church history is still working within schemes and presuppositions the foundations of which were laid down in the last century without really having been revised since in the light of more recent data. These schemes and presuppositions within which unity in the Eucharist and in the Bishop can find no place might be summarized as follows on the basis of a critical review of the principal positions adopted by modern historiography.

a) Under the influence of the Tübingen School which looked at primitive Christianity through the lens of idealism, as a projection of certain ideas and values in history, the unity of the Church was placed on foundations such that it was natural for the Eucharist and the Bishop to be wholly absent. In the whole conception of the subject of church unity, it is *ideas* that dominate. Through being placed in the framework of the Hegelian scheme of the philosophy of history, the whole question of church unity was presented as a synthesis of ideological currents which had long been fighting each other. Well-known is the theory of F. C. Bauer and the Tübingen School. According to which, on the basis of St Paul's Epistle to the Galatians, early Christianity exhibited the form thesis-antithesis-synthesis. The first two elements being being represented respectively by the "Jewish Christianity" of the Church of Jerusalem and the "Hellenizing Christianity" of Paul, and the synthesis being achieved only in the person of Irenaeus.[9] This approach to the subject of unity in early Christianity has been maintained by church historians of the generations following Bauer even to this day. It is noteworthy that distinguished modern historians continue to talk about deep and unbridgeable divisions between a movement led by Paul on the one hand, and another led by the Twelve and in particular Peter and James in Jerusalem,[10] while the conclusion is emphatically drawn that "there were Christianities before there was one Christianity" – unity having appeared as the result of a dialectical development only around the end of the second century.[11] Even the strong reaction in our own day against the Tübingen theories about Paul's "Hellenism" and the "Judaism" of Peter and the others was working within just the same framework of the scheme marked out by Tübingen with its antithesis between "Judaizing" and "Hellenizing" Christianity.[12] It is Christianity were not in a position to draw the forces decisive for its formation from itself as a third agent independent of Judaism and Hellenism alike.[13]

This idealist view of the essence of Christianity misled church historiography into the antithetical scheme of Judaism versus Hellenism something which was alien to the mentality of the primitive Church,[14] while at the same time providing a point of departure for the extreme theories of the supposed original prevalence of heresy in the Church[15] and the division of early Christianity into groups which co-existed for a long time despite their fundamental differences in faith.[16] Of course, confronting such theories is not part of the purpose of this study, but they have come in for serious criticism even among Protestant historians.[17] What is of great importance for us is that behind these theories lies the notion that the unity of the Church consists essentially in a synthesis of ideas. It is precisely this assumption that explains why modern church history in its study of the unity of the Church attaches almost no significance to the person of the Lord and union with Him through the Eucharist.

b) In parallel with the idealism of Tübingen, the subject of the Church's unity also came to be strongly influenced by the school of A. Harnack, who introduced a different antithetical scheme destined, as it proved in retrospect, to have a profound effect on church historiography and one which has yet to be redressed. This scheme consists in the antithesis between *"localism"* and *"universalism"* which is another form of the antithesis between *individual* and *totality.* Thus the unity of the Church was conceived of and posed as a question within the context of these antithetical schemes. And for Harnack and the pricipal Protestant historians after him,[18] placing the question in this context led to the view that the whole evolution of the Church's unity passed first through individualism[19] and then through localism so as to end up as a world-wide organization.[20] For Roman Catholic historiography which was represented by early the great historian P. Batiffol, an author of a notable work[21] countering the views on unity of Sohm and Harnack, unity consisted in submission of the individual to the authority of the clergy on the one hand, and on the other, in the world-wide character of the Church with Rome at its center.[22]

Thus Protestant and Roman Catholic historiography alike viewed the unity of the Church through the lens of these antitheses, and have not been able to free themselves from them completely even today.[23] This has had the result that for Protestant and Roman Catholic historians alike, the unity and catholicity of the Church is essentially identified with the universality of the Church and her Romanization[24] with the further consequence that the Protestants place the "catholicizing" of the Church as late as possible, as if catholicity were something bad for the essential nature of Christianity.[25]

This view of the unity and catholicity of the Church was to the detriment of an understanding of the spirit and mind of the early Church. Oppositions between individual and totality or between localism and universality were never predominant in the mentality of the early Church,[26] but were products of modern ideals of human rights and cosmopolitanism. Harnack's transference of these schemes to the study of the early Church, and the faithful continuation of the dialogue between Protestants and Roman Catholics on church unity within this same context, have imposed on research the blinders which have not allowed proper priority to be given to the unity of the Church in the Divine Eucharist and the bishop who leads it.

c) All this happened at a time when, and perhaps *because*, the Divine Eucharist and the bishop had long since ceased to be connected either with each other, or with the essence of the Church and her unity, in the consciousness of Western theology. To believe that the bishop is an instrument of the

Church indispensable for her administration, is a different matter from connecting him with the nature of the Church and ascribing ecclesiological content to the institution of bishops. Again, it is one thing to say that the Eucharist is indispensable as one of the "seven sacraments" of the Church, and quite another to regard it as the supreme revelation of the Church herself. Only if we regard the Eucharist as the revelation of the Church in her ideal and historical unity, and the bishop first and foremost as the leader and head of the eucharistic assembly which unites the Church of God in space and time, do we recognize in each of these their profound ecclesiological content.

But Western theology, since scholasticism, had ceased to see things in this way. Relegated to the order of the "seven sacraments" the Eucharist became one means among many to human salvation,[27] being considered in an individualistic sense,[28] rather than the very expression of salvation which essentially consists in the union of man with God in Christ.[29] And the bishop, divorced from his principal task of leading the Eucharist and becoming a mainly administrative figure, was necessarily divorced also from the ecclesiological content of the Eucharist.

The state of Western theology in modern times, as set out with all possible brevity in the foregoing three points, explains, we believe, the curious fact that all modern theological study on the unity of the Church has to such an extent overlooked what ought to be the starting-point for such study: the unity of the Church in the Divine Eucharist and in the bishop.

The recognition of unity in the Eucharist and the bishop as the starting-point for any historical research on the unity of the Church follows automatically once historical research frees itself from the antithetical schemes outlined above, and looks at the unity of the Church in the light of certain basic ecclesiological assumptions whose importance is now increasingly being recognized. As to the scheme

"Judaism-Hellenism" and the relation between individual and totality, there is already evident particularly in Orthodox theology, the tendency to avoid the extremes[30] which turn these relationships into antitheses.[31] While as to the relationship between universality and localism, although the question has yet to be dealt with in its fundamentals[32] there can be seen a tendency for Orthodox theology, too to become embroiled in the dilemma placed before us when this relationship is presented as an antithesis.[33] As to the ecclesiological principles which have been given particular prominence of late and make it difficult if not impossible to view the unity of the Church through the lens of the foregoing schemes and assumptions, we shall confine ourselves to the following basic remarks.

An ecclesiological view, which is increasingly prevalent, today, holds that the first appearance and the essence of the Church – and consequently also of her unity, since Church without unity is, in principle and theoretically at least, inconceivable – should be placed not at the time when people first consciously turned to Christ and their first community was formed, i.e. on the day of Pentecost, as was once believed, but before that.[34] For, as is also strongly stressed today, the essence of Christianity and the Church should be sought in the very person of the Lord[35] on which the Church was founded.[36] But if this principle is accepted, then the revelation in Christ ceases to be a system of ideas as the Tübingen School conceived it, and becomes a truth *ontological in character.*[37] Accordingly, what is paramount in ecclesiology is not this or that doctrine, idea or value revealed by the Lord, but *the very person of Christ* and man's union with Him. In this way, the Church is described as Christ Himself, *the whole Christ* in Augustine's apt phrase,[38] while ecclesiology ceases to be a separate chapter for theology and becomes an organic *chapter of Christology.*[39]

Once *ontology* thus *takes precedence* over ideology or systems of values in an ecclesiology which is understood Christologically, this makes it impossible to study the unity of the Church within the framework of the antitheses introduced by F.C. Bauer, R. Sohm, A. Harnack etc. If the unity of the Church is seen, first and foremost, as a unity *in the person* of Christ, as *incorporation* into Him and His *increase* or *building-up,* the starting-point for studying the unity of the Church does not belong in the above antithetical schemes.

This Christological view of the mystery of the Church makes it equally impossible to study the unity of the Church within a pneumatocentric ecclesiology,[40] in which there is a risk of ecclesiology being made into "charismatic sociology"[41] and the unity of the Church becoming nothing more than a *societas fidei et Spiritus Sancti in cordibus.*[42] This observation is not to deny that in ecclesiology a fundamental position is occupied by the Holy Spirit, and indeed by the Holy Trinity as a whole, Who undoubtedly constitutes the supreme principle of the Church.[43] The question here is a different one, and concerns our *starting-point* in looking at the Church and her unity: is it correct to start from the phenomenon of the Church as "community", or from the notion of the person of Christ as the Incarnate Word who also contains within Himself the "many"? This question is of vital importance in studying the unity of the Church. For in the first case, which is where a pneumatocentric ecclesiology leads, the Church is considered as "the body of Christians" united in the Holy Spirit. While in the second case it is seen as the "body of Christ" in an ontological sense.

But if the Christological view of the Church is accepted, this automatically entails a consequence of the highest importance for the study of the unity of the Church: the necessity of considering this unity, first and foremost, *sacramentally,* i.e. as the *incorporation* of human beings *in Christ.* For historical research, this means an obligation to start with the question: *how was this incorporation of human beings into the person of Christ manifested in space and time* especially after His ascension into heaven? But precisely this question, stemming from the Christological and as such sacramental view of the Church, is in itself indicative of the need for any historical research into the unity of the Church to begin with the Divine Eucharist.

The view of the Divine Eucharist as the supreme sensible incorporation of the Church in space and time into Christ does indeed form an essential presupposition for any research on the unity of the Church. For, as has been aptly remarked, "it is only in the mystery of the Divine Eucharist that we have some perceptible portrayal of the mystical union and incorporation of Christ with the faithful who partake of Him, the members of His body."[44] Indeed, the close relationship between Eucharist and Church unity, already very widely acknowledged especially among Orthodox theologians,[45] has led some to make a complete and exclusive identification between the notions of Church and Eucharist. We see this in the so-called *eucharistic ecclesiology*[46] whose main representatives in modern times were N. Afanassieff and A. Schmemann.[47] Having reservations about placing this theory under the light of the general conclusions of this study, we shall confine ourselves here to stressing that its emphasis on the ecclesiological character of the Eucharist and also the eucharistic character of the Church[48] is an important positive element which cannot be a matter of indifference to the historian of Church unity.

But in recognizing this positive element in a eucharistic ecclesiology, we have to beware of the lurking danger of *onesidedness*[49] which can prove damaging to historical research. Undoubtedly, the unity of the Church is expressed in space and time *par excellence* by the sensible incorporation of the faithful in Christ as this is brought about in a truly unique manner in the Eucharist. But the notion of the Church and her unity, is not expressed to the full in a eucharistic unity *which lacks any preconditions*. The Church has always felt herself to be united in *faith*,[50] *love*,[51] *baptism*,[52] *holiness of life*, etc. And, it is certainly true that all this was incorporated very early into the Eucharist.[53] A fact which not only indicates the priority that the Church recognized in the Eucharist as a factor in unity, but also demonstrates that the Eucharist cannot be studied as a closed object, apart from the content of Church life as a whole and its influence on the whole of man's life in the Church and in the world.[54] If, however, we decide for methodological reasons to isolate the Eucharist as the primary factor in unity and trace it through history, as we propose to do here, we need to be constantly aware that in so doing we restrict ourselves to just *one part* of the large subject of the unity of the Church.[55] In this way, we shall avoid the danger of onesidedness inherent in the recognition, correct in principle, of the ecclesiological character of the Eucharist.

When the historian looks at the Eucharist as the supreme incorporation of the Church in Christ in space and time,[56] this necessarily leads to an examination also of the bishop as the center of unity in each Church. Historical research views the Eucharist not simply as a vertical communion of each of the faithful with God in Christ, but also as a horizontal union of the members of the Church with each other through which each person's communion with God necessarily has to pass being, thus, made into an ecclesial expression instead of an individual one. For this reason, the Eucharist is examined by the historian not so much as a thing,[57] but rather as an *action*: not so much as a communion in "holy things," but rather as a "communion of saints" (i.e. of "holy people"),[58] expressed as such through the *eucharistic synaxis* of which the visible center and head has always been the bishop, as the one who "presides" and "offers."

This connection of the bishop with the Eucharist and of both with the unity of the Church becomes even more necessary in view of the fact that the *whole canonical unity* of the Church, which, being concerned mainly with the Church's outward life on earth, is of immediate concern to historical research, cannot in principle be understood apart from the Divine Eucharist.[59] It is no accident that although the Church detached from the Eucharist many sacraments which were at one time connected with it, she never did this with entry into the priesthood. Transmission of priesthood, or *the con-*

solidation and continuation of the canonical unity of the Church outside the Eucharist was and has remained inconceivable. Thus the bishop, understood not just as the visible head of the eucharistic assembly but also as the sole transmitter of priesthood in the Church and in this way the expression and guard of canonical unity, remains for the historian indissolubly bound up with the Eucharist when this is understood principally as an assembly "in the same place" (*epi to auto*),[60] expressing in space and time the unity of the Church of God.

The foregoing remarks outline not only the fundamental significance of unity in the Eucharist and the bishop for historical research into the unity of the Church, but also the way in which our subject is to be approached. Our theme is in principle historical, since it looks at the unity of the Church not as an ideal or an object of teaching, but as something in the Church's experience, and indeed during a particular period in the past. But because history is bound up with the factor of development, the unity of the Church, looked at historically, must therefore be studied as something that is developing as a dynamic rather than a static reality operating within space and time and subject to the fundamental laws of history. In consequence, it will have to be a basic principle of methodology to examine the sources by the simple historical method of tracing development in space and time which is also the most reliable.[61]

Nevertheless, the history of the Church is not ordinary history and is not ultimately determined by the usual course of human affairs. The character of church history is composite, both theological and secular,[62] just as the nature of the Church is composite, both divine and human. As a theandric reality the Church preserves her essence unchanged even though she operates in space and time.[63] This is especially true of those aspects of her history which bear a direct and organic relation to her very essence. One such is her unity or catholicity which frequently coincides with the very concept of the Church.[64] In consequence, the historian studying the unity of the Church should not be content with establishing the facts and their developments. Behind the motion of the Church's "becoming," he needs to discover her stable being, in other words, the fundamental ecclesiological principles through which the essence of the Church is preserved unchanged.[65]

In consequence, investigation of our theme will be approached in two ways. The initial question will be: what exactly *happened*, what *events* go to make up the unity of the Church which we are examining and what *developments* have they seen during the period under investigation? To this end, the sources will be examined in strict *chronological order*. Comparisons of texts according to period and content will be essential so as to ascertain what developments may have taken place. A similar observation of events *place by place* will necessitate comparison of sources so as to ascertain whether the information they give us represents the situation in only one locality or in more. In this way, we shall attempt to determine *whether, when and in what way* the unity of the Church in the Eucharist and the bishop constituted an historical reality. But in parallel with this task and for the reasons explored above, the historical events must also be placed under the light of ecclesiological principles – they must be evaluated ecclesiologically. In particular, the fundamental burning issue facing us is whether and in what way the oneness and catholicity of the Church contained in her essence were preserved beneath the surface of the various historical events and developments. If and to what extent, for example, the forms and institutions through which unity around the bishop and Eucharist was expressed or shaped in history are constructs of passing significance serving a particular purpose, and capable of being replaced when the needs of the time require it; or whether on the contrary they are organically connected with the essence of the Church, as inescapable consequences of ecclesiological principles.

Such a linkage of historical events with ecclesiological principles makes our research exceedingly difficult because, as has already been stressed, the existing sources especially from the first centuries do not provide us with definitions and theories concerning the unity of the Church, and besides, these sources are so few and fragmentary[66] as to make the first three centuries the most difficult period of history to research. It is essential, then, to use all existing sources[67] and to make a special effort to ascertain the ecclesial consciousness at work behind events and texts which at first glance bear no relation to the unity of the Church. For this reason, the various liturgical and canonical regulations will prove exceptionally useful for our work. We must add to this that we are not examining the subject of unity dogmatically and systematically, and in consequence we should not look for answers to all our questions about the unity of the Church, but only to those which are answered by the historical sources. It is, therefore, natural that our research will often appear deficient in the eyes of systematic theology, but this will be because the sources themselves which ought not to be forced have nothing to say about our questions.[68]

The questions encompassed by our theme as they appear from the sources of the first three centuries, can be grouped under three main headings. Firstly, we must examine the general presuppositions underlying the formation of each Church into a unity in the Eucharist and the bishop.[69] The fundamental question here is this: in the consciousness of the primitive Church, how were the Eucharist and the bishop connected with the Church and her unity? In order for there to develop, in the post-Apostolic period and later, the strong consciousness expressed by Ignatius of Antioch that each Church finds her unity and fullness in the one Eucharist "under the leadership of the bishop," this must have been preceded by a consolidation of the relationship between Eucharist, bishop and Church. The first part of our study will be devoted to the investigation of precisely this relationship in the consciousness of the first Apostolic Churches. More specifically, in the two chapters of Part I we shall examine (Chapter 1) the relationship of the Eucharist to the Church, and (Chapter 2) the relationship of the bishop to the Eucharist in the years up to and including Ignatius.

The second set of questions which will be examined in Part II of our study has to do with the actual formation of the early Church into a unity in the Eucharist and the bishop, and the implications of this fundamental event for the formation of the early Catholic Church. Here we encounter many questions of an historical and ecclesiological nature. The principle, laid down by Ignatius, of one Eucharist and one bishop in each Church, gives rise to the serious historical problem of whether, in the period under examination, this principle actually corresponded to historical reality, or whether it is simply an exhortation on Ignatius' part.

This problem is compounded if one takes into account the existence of "household Churches" and of Christians in country areas. How is it possible that all the Christians of one Church came together for one Eucharist under the bishop when there existed on the one hand "household churches" usually regarded as being several semi-official eucharistic assemblies within one and the same city, and on the other, Christians in the villages who were far away from the city and could not, therefore, participate in the Eucharist under the bishop? Furthermore, it should be investigated whether this principle applied to all geographical areas, given certain indications in Eusebius' *Ecclesiastical History* that some places, such as Egypt, Pontus etc., had their own organization. These questions will be looked at in the first chapter of Part II. Following on from this, the second chapter will deal with the question of ecclesiological concern: what were the implications of unity in the Eucharist and the bishop for the emergence and establishment of the consciousness concerning a "Catholic Church"? Here the problems that arise are immense. It will be necessary first to determine the content of the term "Catholic Church" as it appears in the sources from the years we are studying, and not as it came to be defined in later times. The content of this term will have to provide the basis for examining the relation of Eucharist and bishop to the consciousness of a "Catholic Church" at that period. Thus, we shall try on the basis of the sources to throw light on the main theme of our study; the significance of unity in the Eucharist and the bishop for the formation of the early Catholic Church. Questions such as the catholicity of each episcopal Church and it relationship with the "Catholic Church throughout the world"[70] and with schism and heresy, will come up in this second part of our study.

Finally, the third set of questions is dictated by the developments over time of the initial unity of the Church in one Eucharist centered on the bishop. Because, as is obvious from the situation prevailing in the Church today, the original gathering of each Church into one Eucharist under the bishop at some point ceased to exist. Its place was taken by the institution of parishes which signalled the breakup of the one episcopocentric eucharistic assembly into many assemblies headed by presbyters. This led to the weakening of the originally indissoluble link between bishop and Eucharist. Thus the Eucharist, from being the business of the episcopate *par excellence*,[71] was later (it remains to be seen when) largely transformed into the principle task of the parish and the presbyter. While the bishop, from being *par excellence* the "president" of the Eucharist, was largely transformed into an administrator and coordinator of the life of the parishes. This event, one of the most momentous in the history of the Church, has yet to receive from scholars the attention it deserves.[72]

Thus we should look in vain for a historical study of when and how the parish arose in history. We shall have to deal with this thorny problem in the first chapter of Part III. This chapter will present the problem of the transition from one eucharistic assembly to many, as this appears from comparative study of the texts, and will go on to examine how the ground was prepared for the parishes historically and when they finally appeared. Beyond this, however, we have to touch on the delicate subject of the ecclesiological implications of this event which likewise have not been examined to date. This is to pose the question: how did the early Church receive the proliferation of eucharistic assemblies at a time when she had a firmly established sense that the one Eucharist under the leadership of the bishop unites the whole people of God in a given place "in the unity of God and of the episcopate"? Did the breakup of the one Eucharist not mean breaking up the unity in each Church? This question leads directly into the fundamental question of the relationship which exists between the parish and the unity of the diocese. Did the parish appear in history as a self-contained and ecclesiologically self-sufficient unity within the diocese? To this crucial question, we shall attempt to give an answer in the second chapter of Part III as far as the sources from the period under examination permit. Given that the fourth century marks a watershed in these developments, as will be established in the appropriate place, in conjunction with the fact that with St Cyprian the consciousness concerning the unity and catholicity of the Church reaches the stage of full and explicit maturity, our whole study will confine itself principally to the first three centuries[73] which were anyway the most decisive for the formation of the early Catholic Church.

NOTES

[1] John 17.11 and 20 f.: "Holy Father, keep them in Thy name, which Thou hast given Me, that *they may be one* even as We are one... I do not pray for these only, but also for those who believe in Me through their word, *that* they may all *be one*, that the world may believe that Thou hast sent Me." It is worth noting that St John's Gospel links the "agony" (Luke 22.4) of the prayer before the Passion with the unity of the Church as is shown by the emphatic repetition of "that they may be one".

[2] Acts 2.44f.: "And all who believed were together (*epi to auto*) and had all things in common; and they sold their possessions and goods and distributed them to all, as any had need."

[3] Paul is aptly characterized as "the theologian of the Church's unity". See V. Ioannidis, "The Unity of the Church According to the Apostle Paul" (in Greek) in *Efcharisterion, Essays in Honor of Professor H. Alivizatos*, 1958. p. 172.

[4] See *inter alia* 1 Clement 49.5; 46.5-7; 54.1-2; Ignatius *To the Philadelphians* 2; 3.2; 6.2; *To the Magnesians* 14.1; 13.2; 1.2; *To the Ephesians* 8.1, etc.; *Didache* 8.4; 10.5 etc.

[5] Irenaeus, *Adv. Haer.* I.10.2.

[6] *op. cit.* III.7.1-2; IV.31.3 etc.

[7] Cyprian, *De Catholicae Ecclesiae Unitate, passim.* One could give other examples from nearly all the writers of the first three centuries as the analysis of their work in the main body of this study will demonstrate.

[8] The first appearance of a confession of faith in *one* Church may perhaps be placed very early, in St Irenaeus' Letter to the Smyrneans (1.1-2), where the phrase "in one body of the Church" forms part of a paraphrase of a baptismal creed in the view of T. Zahn (*Das apostolische Symbolum,* 1893, p. 42f.}, A. Harnack (Appendix to Hahn's *Bibliothek*), R. Seeberg (*Zeitschrift für Kirchengeschichte,* 40 (1933) 3) *et al.* But even if we accept the opinion of J.N.D. Kelly, *Early Christian Creeds,* 1952, p. 69, according to which this is not a paraphrase of an official creed, the second century seems the most likely time for this belief to have been formulated into a confession (cf. V. Ioannidis, *op. cit.* p. 172). The expression of faith in the "holy Church," which occurs in ancient creeds of the second century such as those of the Roman Church preserved by Hippolytus and of the Alexandrian Church preserved in the Der Balyzeh papyrus also suggests the acceptance of the "one" Church. The first clear mention of the "one" Church in a creed is found in the Jerusalem Creed put forward by Macarius of Jerusalem at the First Ecumenical Council. For this see I. Karmiris, *Dogmatic and Credal Documents of the Orthodox Catholic Church* (in Greek), I, 1960², p. 64. On the theological background to the appearance of the confession of faith in "one Church," see J. Daniélou, "Mia Ekklesia chez les pères grecs des premiers siècles," in *1054-1954. L'Église et les Églises,* I, 1954, p. 129-139.

[9] F.C. Bauer first attempted to establish his theory in his article "Die Christuspartei in der Korinthischen Gemeinde, der Gegensatz des petrinischen und paulinischen Christentums in der ältesten Kirche," in *Tübinger Zeitschrift,* 1831, No. 4, pp. 61-206. For the further development of his views as they are set out here, see apart from his hermeneutical works, his writings in *Kirchengeschichte des neunzehnten Jahrhunderts,* 1862, pp. 395-9; cf. also E. Zeller, "Die Tübinger historische Schule," and "Ferdinand Christian Bauer" in *Vorträge und Abhandlungen geschichtlichen Inhalts,* I, 1865, pp. 267-353 and 354-434, as also H. Schmidt and Haussleiter in *Realencyklopädie für protestantische Theologie und Kirche,* II, 1897, p.475 and 29-31. Cf. also V. Ioannidis, *Introduction to the New Testament* (in Greek), 1960, p. 77.

The division of early Christianity into two by historians went so deep at that time that there was talk of two different religions, the religion of Jesus Christ and the "religion of Paul." See e.g. W. Wrede, *Paulus*, 1907, esp. p. 104. It is also well known that Harnack divided early Christianity into *Evangelium Christi* and *Evangelium de Christo*. The appearance of the so-called history of religion school, initially in the person of R. Reitzenstein (*Die hellenistischen Mysterienreligionen. Ihre Grundgedanken und Wirkungen*, 1910), lent support to Baur's view concerning Paul's extreme Hellenism, albeit modified on the basis of theories about the more general influence of the mystery religions on Christianity (cf. W. Bousset's classic work *Kyrios Christos: Geschichte des Christusglaubens von den Anfängen des Christentums bis Irenaeus*, 1913. Similarly A. Deissmann, *Paulus*, 1911). The first reaction against these theories on Paul's "Hellenism" can be seen with the advancement of eschatology as the characteristic *par excellence* of the early Church. On this see A. Schweitzer, *Geschichte der Paulinischen Forschung*, 1911, pp. 45-50.

[10] As typical examples we may cite H. Lietzmann, *Geschichte der alten Kirche*, I, 1937, p. 53-60, 154-6, 107-111; A. Nock, *St Paul*, 1946, pp. 52, 67, 63, 168 f., 110 f. M. Dibelius-W.G. Kümmel, *Paulus*, 1951, pp. 25, 82, 114, 131, 120. W.L. Knox, *St Paul*, 1932, pp. 64, 94, 120. M. Goguel, *Les premiers temps de l'Église*, 1949, p. 53, 68, 106 etc. The division of ancient Christianity into "judaizing" and "hellenizing" can also be observed in the work of the late Professor V. Stephanidis, *Church History* (in Greek), 1948, pp. 20f., 27f., 21 and esp. 41, where we even have the impression that there was no communion between Jewish and Gentile Christians.

[11] See M. Goguel, op. cit. p. 19: "The movement in the formation of Christianity was from diversity to unity. There were Christianities before there was one Christianity. It was only around the end of the second century with the early catholicism of Irenaeus and Tertullian that the movement towards unification reached a conclusion which was subsequently confirmed and fixed." For this writer, the unity of the primitive Church was more a "yearning for unity than the sense of its complete realization." See his study "Unité et diversité du Christianisme primitif," in *Revue d'Histoire et de Philosophie religieuses* 19 (1939), 5. The idea of a progression from division and diversity to unity is one that we constantly find as a cornerstone of Protestant church historiography. Thus *inter alios* M. Hornschuh, "Die Apostel als Träger der Überlieferung," in E. Hennecke, *Neutestamentliche Apokryphen*, ed. W. Schneemelcher, II, 1964, p. 41 f.

[12] See *inter alia* the works of G. Dix, *Jew and Greek*, 1953 and J. Daniélou, *Théologie du Judeochristianisme*, 1958 and *Message Évangélique et Culture Hellénistique aux IIe et IIIe Siècles*, 1961, which work within the same antithetical scheme.

[13] The subject is of great importance and exceptionally difficult, and has yet to be dealt with in our own history of dogma. Cf. J. Karmiris' review of a study by E. Benz in *Theologia* 30 (1559), 520 f., esp. 522f. For the present, it is sufficient here to recall the two-pronged thrust of church literature during the first three centuries taking a position opposed equally to Gentile-Hellenizing and to Judaizing.

[14] On this see the excellent study by B. Sundkler, "Jésus et les Païens," in *Revue d'Histoire et de Philosophie Religieuses* 6 (1936), 473f.

[15] As for example by W. Bauer, *Rechtgläubigkeit und Ketzerei im ältesten Christentum*, 1964² and W. Nigg, *Das Buch der Ketzer*, 1949. Cf. W.G. Kümmel, *Das Neue Testament. Geschichte der Erforschung seiner Probleme*, 1958, pp. 145-243.

[16] On the "group" theory, besides the above see also H. Schoeps, *Urgemeinde, Judenchristentum, Gnosis*, 1956, pp. 3-8. Cf. also below.

[17] For a serious critique of these theories, particularly those of W. Bauer, see H.E.W. Turner, *The Pattern of Christian Truth. A Study in Relations Between Orthodoxy and Heresy in the Early Church*, 1954; A. Ehrhardt, "Christianity Before the Apostles' Creed," in *The Harvard Theological Review* 55, (1962) 73-119 and E. Käsemann, "Ketzer und Zeuge. Zum johannischen Verfasserproblem," in *Zeitschrift für Theologie und Kirche*, 48 (1951), 292-311.

[18] For the present, see the theories on early catholicism of H. Lietzmann, *op. cit.* I, p. 234; J.V. Bartlet, *Church Life and Church Order* (ed. Cadoux), 1942, pp. 4, 40, 167-171; K. Heussi, *Kompendium der Kirchengeschichte*, 1949¹⁰, p. 25 and M. Goguel, *La Naissance du Christianisme*, 1946, p. 282. For an excellent analysis of the position of earlier modern research on this subject, see O. Linton, *Das Problem der Urkirche in der neueren Forschung*, 1932, passim. See also H. Kung, "Der Frühkatholizismus im N.T. als Kontroversstheologisches problem", in *Tübinger Theolog. Quartalschrift* (1962) 385-424.

[19] The foundations for individualism in ecclesiology had already been laid by R. Sohm, for whom, consistent as he was with the whole pietistic theology of Lutheranism (Schleiermacher etc.), the Church is in essence nothing but an invisible reality; a number of the predestined and the believers (*predestinatorum et credentium*) whose groups form parallel lines meeting only at infinity. The grav-

est misfortune in the whole development of the Church therefore took place, according to Sohm, when "through 1 Clement" the spirit of organization and law entered into Christianity, elements which he regarded as incompatible with the essence of religion (see his views on the subject set out in his work *Kirchenrecht*, I, 1892, passim and esp. p. 161). A. Harnack was certainly opposed to Sohm's extreme position on the incompatibility of religion and law (see *Entstehung und Entwicklung der Kirchenverfassung und der Kirchenrechts in den zwei ersten Jahrhunderten*, 1910, p. 149), but without disagreeing with the individualistic view of Christianity, the essence of which, as set out in Harnack's own work *Das Wesen des Christentums* (see second edition, 1950, passim), is nothing more than the inner moral renewal of each human being. Protestant theology after Harnack continued along the same lines of an individualistic view of the essence of Christianity. The "life in Christ" was regarded as an inner, psychological state of each individual (see e.g. A. Deissmann, *Die neutestamentliche Formel "in Christo Jesu" untersucht*, 1892 and eiusdem *Licht vom Osten...*, 1923, p. 257. Despite the prominence given to the communal character of primitive Christianity by the so-called eschatological school, which is first found in J. Weiss' work *Die Predigt Jesus vom Reich Gottes*, 1892 and especially in its second edition (1900), and was reinforced by the influence of supporters of the so-called "New Consensus" (cf. K. Mouratidis, *The Essence and Polity of the Church in the Teaching of John Chrysostom*, 1958, p. 145, n. 2), the individualistic interpretation of ecclesiology was never abandoned altogether. We see this from e.g. R. Bultmann's theories on the Church in *Glauben und Verstehen* II, 1958, pp. 13 and 18, and even more strongly from the work of E. Brunner, *Das Missverständniss der Kirche*, 1951, esp. Ch. 8 § 6 etc., where we come back to the extreme position of R. Sohm on the relation between religion and law.

[20] Because of the influence this view of Harnack's has had on modern historiography, we give the complete passage from his *Dogmengeschichte*, I, 1894[2] (ET Buchanan, *History of Dogma*, 1905, p. 45): "If again we compare the Church about the middle of the third century with the condition of Christendom 150 or 200 years before, we shall find that there is now a real religious commonwealth (*ein religiöses Gemeinwesen*), while at the earlier period there were only communities (*Gemeinden*) who believed in a heavenly Church, whose earthly image they were, endeavored to give it expression with the simplest means, and lived in the future as strangers and pilgrims on the earth, hastening to meet the Kingdom of whose

existence they had the surest guarantee. We now find a new commonwealth, politically formed and equipped with fixed forms of all kinds... We find the Church as a political union (*politischen Band*) and worship institute (*Kultusanstalt*), a formulated faith and a sacred learning (*Gottesgelehrsamke*); but one thing we no longer find, the old enthusiasm and individualism which had not felt itself fettered by subjection to the authority of the Old Testament. Instead of enthusiastic independent Christians, we find a new literature of revelation, the New Testament, and Christian priests."

[21] See P. Batiffol, *L'Église Naissante et le Catholicisme*, 1909[3].

[22] The idea that the unity and catholicity of the Church consist precisely in her being a worldwide body with Rome at her center, in such a way that Rome alone remains the Church of the Lord *par excellence*, is maintained by certain Roman Catholic historians even at the time of this writing. See e.g. G. Bardy, "Die Religion Jesu" in *Christus und die Religionen der Erde. Handbuch der Religionsgeschichte*, ed. DDr F. Köning, III, 1951, pp. 547-642, esp. p. 632. Cf. also the scathing critique of this by Professor L. Philippidis, "Incredible!" (in Greek), in *Orthodoxos Skepsis* 1 (1958), 51-54.

[23] See e.g J. Colson, *L'Évêque dans les Communautés Primitives*, 1951. This study concludes that the ministry of the bishop took shape under the influence of two traditions: on the one hand, the Pauline tradition which, according to the writer, emphasized the universal unity of the Church and the charismatics, and on the other, the Johannine which, according to the same writer, emphasized the local Church and the permanent ministers, the two traditions being brought together into one by Irenaeus. It is evident that this author, although a Roman Catholic, is a prisoner of the models introduced by Harnack with their antithesis between localism and universalism, and has not altogether escaped the influence of the Hegelian model of the Tügingen School as discussed above.

[24] This coincidence in the views of Protestant and Roman Catholic historians as to the essence of catholicism is revealed, we think, by the following admission by Harnack in his review of Batiffol, op. cit.: "That Roman = Catholic is something that I as a Protestant historian first put forward 22 years ago in my *History of Dogma*, with certain reservations which the author admittedly seeks for the most part to remove." (*Theologische Literaturzeitung* 34 (1909), 52).

[25] See above, note 18. Certainly things are different today, with the increasing recognition of the significance of Church unity within

the Ecumenical Movement. There is already a tendency evident in Protestantism for its churches to claim catholicity for themselves, giving the term a peculiar sense which has yet to be fully clarified. Study of the subject of the Church's catholicity is thus extremely important and useful today.

[26] See once again B. Sundkler, *op. cit.*

[27] Cf. A. Schmemann, "Theology and Eucharist" (in Greek), in *Theology, Truth and Life* (ed. Zoe Brotherhood, in Greek), 1962. It is characteristic of that kind of Roman Catholic theological position that in the valuable entries on the Divine Eucharist in the *D.T.C.*, one looks in vain for a paragraph on the ecclesiological character of the Eucharist. The same goes for the rich recent work by J. Betz, *Eucharistie in der Zeit der griechischen Väter*, I/1, 1955 who does not intend to examine the relationship between Eucharist and Church unity even in the ensuing second volume of his work judging by the preface to the first volume (p. viii). It is, however, worthy of special note that this work of Betz's revives the emphasis on the active presence (Actualpräsentz) of the *work* and also the *person* of the Lord, in place of the scholastic emphasis on the Real Presence in the *elements* of the Eucharist. This is perhaps a definite step towards an ontological view of the mystery which also leads naturally to an ecclesiological view. The only strong voice of protest in modern Roman Catholic theology against the scholastic doctrine of the Eucharist, which has, therefore, been considered revolutionary for Western theology, is the teaching of Odo Casel, who was the first to oppose the view of the Eucharist as an "object" and a mere means of salvation underlining its character as an *assembly* and an *action* of the Church. See his work *Das christliche Kultmysterium*, 1935[2], p. 27. For his teaching on the Eucharist more generally, see his works: *Die Liturgie als Mysterienfeier*, 5th ed. 1935, and "Die Kirche als Braut Christi nach Schrift, Vaterlehre und Liturgie," in *Theologie der Zeit*, ed. Karl Rudolph, I, 1936, 91-111.

[28] Cf. H. Fries, "Die Eucharistie und die Einheit der Kirche," in *Pro Mundi Vita. Festschrift zum eucharistischen Weltkongress*, 1960, p. 176. This study came to the attention of the present writer when his research had already been completed and submitted for examination. It is a noteworthy study, and its strong emphasis on the ecclesiological character of the Eucharist lends support to the present work. See esp. p. 169.

[29] Undoubtedly, a major factor in this position taken by Western theology regarding the Eucharist was the whole soteriology of the West as it developed from the Middle Ages onwards. The theo-

logical systems of the West saw man as being saved by a juridical action on God's part and did not regard as an absolutely basic necessity the "continuous, real and life-giving operation of Christ in the bodies of the faithful" (see J. Romanides, *The Original Sin* (in Greek), 1957, p. 13f.) – the operation or energy which is offered *par excellence* through the Eucharist. On the relationship between Church unity and Eucharist according to ancient and medieval church writers, see H. de Lubac, *Katholizismus als Gemeinschaft*, 1943, p. 81f.

[30] See above, note 13, and V. Ioannidis, *Introduction to the New Testament* (in Greek), 1960, p. 264 and elsewhere, and G. Konidaris, *General Church History from Jesus Christ to our own times* (in Greek), I, 2nd ed. 1957 (hereafter referred to as G.C.H.), pp. 102, 103f., 108 note 3, 109. See also *eiusdem The Formation of the Catholic Church up to the Beginning of the Fifth Century and the Three Hierarchs* (in Greek), 1955 p. 18f.

[31] Particularly, in regard to the relationship between the individual and the totality, which is essentially linked to the concept of unity, it should be noted that the presentation of this relationship as an antithesis in modern theology is frequently due to the confusion we habitually make between the notions of "individual" and "person," treating the two as identical. The crucial distinction between individual and person has been to a great extent illuminated by modern existentialist philosophy (even though this distinction occurs already, from a different standpoint, in Thomas Aquinas) developed in modern times by J. Maritain (*Du Régime temporel et de liberté*, 1933). The individual is a natural category referring not only to man but even to inanimate objects. The person is a category proper to man, a concept which is spiritual and involves a value judgement, an expression of the purpose of existence, the image and likeness of God (cf. N. Berdyaev, *Solitude and Society*, 1938, p. 168). Further, the individual is an arithmetical category, a concept relating to quantity. The person is a qualitative category which abolishes or transcends the laws of arithmetic. One person may be worth two or more individuals; and consequently the law of arithmetic according to which two men are twice one man, while true for individuals, is not applicable to persons. Still more importantly, the individual contains the idea of combination and ultimately of serving a purpose. Ten individuals added together go to make up a certain purpose (collectivism). By contrast, the person, as an image of God, cannot be a means to the realization of any end. Any exploitation of the person to achieve certain ends,

even the most exalted, turns him into an individual and degrades him from the greatness of God's image. But the paradox in this distinction between individual and person is this: it seems at first sight that the person, as an end in himself, should always be understood in himself while the individual as being subject to combination should be understood in relation to others; whereas, in actual fact the opposite is true. For, although the individual can be added to other individuals, nevertheless, he cannot be really united with others. In the words of M. Buber (*I and Thou*, 1958, p. 62): "individuality makes its appearance by its differentiation from other individualities." The person, by contrast, cannot be added and become part of a whole since, as an end in himself, he constitutes the whole. Yet not only can he be really united with others, but he cannot even exist as person without unity with others: "A person makes his appearance by entering into relation with other persons" (ibid.). An essential element in the concept of person is his reflection in the other, the discovery of the "I" within the "Thou." This creates for the person the necessity of unity. Once the individual is isolated from other individuals, it finds its justification. Once the person is deprived of its communion with others, it meets its destruction. For the person cannot set boundaries around itself (egocentricity) without automatically becoming an individual: a part instead of a whole, a means instead of an end in itself. Thus, egocentricity is the death of personhood, while denial of the "I" and its placing within the "Thou" and the "We" is its confirmation. (Cf. N. Nissiotis, *Existentialism and Christian Faith* (in Greek) 1956, p. 299: "as Christian personality, the true subject is conceived of and created in communion with other such persons who are called to salvation"). In this way, the paradox is elucidated. Individualism is the enemy of personhood and – however strange this may seem at first sight – the essential concomitant of collectivism since the latter in a mechanical unity produced by adding together units independent of each other which serve as means to common ends. By contrast, unity as communion forms the confirmation of personhood. Christianity was identified from the beginning with the second kind of unity and for this reason required the burial of the "I" as individual in order that the "I" might be found as person in the "Thou" and the "we" of the Kingdom of God. In consequence, Christianity was a religion not of the individual but of the person which means a religion of unity. This is why the dilemma of modern research between individual and collective finds so many difficulties in the texts of early Christianity, and has trouble with the paradox encountered in these texts that the many are expressed through the One and *vice versa* (see below). These texts have in view a situation of persons. In this situation, the relationship of the individual with the whole ceases to be an antithesis because through the burial of individualism, it is transformed into a relationship of the person with the unity, in which, as has been said above, the person presupposes the unity and the unity the person.

[32] To Orthodox theology, this seems at first glance a clash between two fundamental ecclesiological principles. Thus according to one of these principles, abandoned by Rome at the First Vatican Council, each bishop is absolutely equal to all the other bishops in every way as presiding over a complete Church and not a partial Church; and according to the other, equally basic principle of Orthodox ecclesiology, all the Churches in the world make up only one Church. It is evident, then, that neither the Roman Catholic concept of the unity of incomplete parts (= local churches – bishops) added together into a universal grouping (= universal Church – universal bishop), nor the Protestant concept of local Churches (= communities) entirely independent of each other, accords with the ecclesiological principles of Orthodoxy. For this reason, the usual characterization of the local Churches as "particular" (*epi merous*) Churches can introduce the notion, foreign to Orthodox ecclesiology, of a unity of "parts," i.e. a unity formed by addition. There is a manifest need to define the relationship of unity existing between the one Church in the world and the complete churches in various places from the viewpoint of Orthodox ecclesiology.

[33] The Orthodox canonist N. Milasch, *Canon Law of the Eastern Orthodox Church* (in Greek), 1906, pp. 294-298, holds that there is a purely spiritual unity on the universal level and independence in the administration of the local Churches. This position is based exclusively on the distinction between spiritual and administrative unity. But once one maintains the correct view that administration cannot be understood without an ecclesiological basis, then we have to ask ourselves: what are the facts of ecclesiology that support the administrative independence of each local Church? This is the heart of the problem.

[34] I. Karmiris, *The Ecclesiology of the Three Hierarchs* (in Greek), 1961, p. 37, note 1: "From what has been said, we may draw the firm conclusion that what happened at Pentecost was, to be precise, the official public appearance of the Church and the inauguration of her saving work, but not her rebirth or foundation, as it is less that aptly put in our Dogmatics and Catechisms...";

V. Ioannidis, "The Kingdom of God in N.T. Teaching," in *E.E.Th.S.* 1956, p. 160: "So the Church already existed and Jesus Christ was born and lived within this Church." Cf. also G. Konidaris, *G.C.H.* pp. 85 and 101. Likewise K. Mouratidis, *The Essence and Polity*, p. 68 f., and I. Kalogirou, *On the Character of the Orthodox Catholic Church according to the Basic Soteriological Principles in the N.T.*, 1961, p. 16. Roman Catholic theology, today, also recognizes the existence of the Church before Pentecost. See M. Schmaus, *Katholische Dogmatik*, III/1, 1958, p. 16 f.

[35] V. Ioannidis, "The Kingdom of God" p. 131: "The entirely new and entirely different element that Christianity has to present relative to other religions, or to the teachings of the prophets and later teachers in Judaism, is not this or that teaching of Jesus but the very person of Jesus Christ Himself." See likewise G. Konidaris, *G.C.H.* pp. 85 and 87, where the person of Jesus Christ is seen as preceding and taking precedence over His teaching from the viewpoint of the historical foundation of Christianity. Cf. also the remark by W.G. Kümmel, ("Jesus und die Anfänge der Kirche," in *Studia Theologica Cura Ordinum Theologorum Scandinavorum edita*, VII/1 1953, – 1954, p. 27): "It is not the teaching of Jesus, but the person of Jesus as the hidden Messiah-Man and the Risen One which became historically the root of the Church."

[36] A highly illuminating and original interpretation of the ecclesiological passage Mt 16:18 is given by Prof. L. Philippidis (*History of the N.T. Period*, 1958, p. 74 f.), according to which on the basis of the Hebrew term translated in Matthew's Gospel as "rock" (*petra*), "when Jesus said to Peter... [that] on this rock... He would build His Church, He meant Himself..." This interpretation agrees with the biblical understanding of the Church as the Body of Christ and as His building-up and increase (see below). It is notable that the earliest church writers who spoke of the pre-existence of the Church, such as the author of 2 Clement (2:1 and 14:1), locate this pre-existence primarily in the person of the Lord (2 Clem. 2:3 and 7).

[37] See M. Siotis, *History and Revelation...*, 1953, p. 28. Cf. also the apt remark of T.W. Manson, that Jesus taught His disciple simply by being with them. Thus, He was not only the Teacher, but also the teaching (Ministry and Priesthood, 1958, p. 8 f.). It is hence an observation of vital importance that "Christianity is not a world view or an ideology, as is commonly and inaccurately stated; it is not a sterile system of religious knowledge and moral rules... Anything that is a truth of faith and a rule of life circulates and appears

in the world *"in person"*. It is *"in the person of Jesus"* that we see God and have the Gospel...". Metropolitan Dionysios of Servies and Kozani, in *Oikodomi: weekly written sermon...*, 1965, p. 223 f. cf. ibid. p. 139 f.

[38] *Tract. on the Gospel of John* 21:8 (P.L. 35:1568. Cf. 35:1622 and 37:1679). Cf. likewise John Chrysostom, *Homily on 1 Corinthians* 30 (P.G. 61:249-253) and esp. *Homily on Ephesians* 3 (P.G. 62:29). Thus K. Adam is correct in remarking (*Das Wesen des Katholizismus*, 1927, p. 24), that "Christ the Lord is the proper 'I' of the Church." For the views of Roman Catholic theology on this subject see H. Schmaus, *Katholische Dagmatik*, III/1, p. 9 f.

[39] Cf. the fundamental remark of Prof. G. Florovsky: "The theology of the Church is nothing but a chapter, and one of the principal chapters, of Christology. Without this chapter, Christology itself would not be complete. It is within the framework of Christology that the mystery of the Church is proclaimed in the New Testament. It was presented in the same way by the Greek and the Latin Fathers." ("Le corps du Christ vivant," in *La sainte Église universelle. Confrontation oecumenique*, 1948, p. 12.)

[40] J. Mohler, *Die Einheit der Kirche*, 1824 (French translation by A. Libienfeld, *L'unité dans l'Église* in the series Unam Sanctam No. 2, to which we refer here), and A. Khomiakov, in W.J. Birkbeck, *Russia and the English Church*, 1895, Ch. 23. On a connection between Mohler's ecclesiology and that of Khomiakov, see G. Florovsky, op. cit. p.11. Cf. also the critique of Khomiakov's ecclesiology by J. Romanides, "Orthodox Ecclesiology according to Alexis Khomiakov," in *Greek Orthodox Theological Review* 2 (1956), 57-73; also Archim. S. Charkianakis, *On the Infallibility of the Church in Orthodox Theology*, 1965, p. 133 f., where in his very interesting critique of Khomiakov's theology he notes the latter's "pneumatocratic ecclesiology" (pp. 138, 152), which should however be attributed primarily to a lack of the Christological approach which characterized the Fathers in their ecclesiology (cf. the criticism of J. Romanides, op. cit. p. 73).

[41] See G. Florovsky, "Christ in His Church. Suggestions and Comments," in *1054-1954. L'Église et les Églises*, II, 1954, p.164. It is characteristic that the Pauline term "spiritual body" (1 Cor. 15:44) never took on an ecclesiological meaning as happened with the term "body of Christ."

[42] So the unity of the Church is defined in the Augsburg Confession. See Ch. Androutsos, *Symbolics from an Orthodox Perspective*, 1930[2], p. 96.

[43] See K. Mouratidis, *The Essence and Polity...* (in Greek) pp. 125-135.

[44] I. Karmiris, *Summary of the Dogmatics of the Orthodox Catholic Church* (in Greek), 1960, p. 80. Karmiris brings out the relationship between Eucharist and unity even more clearly and emphatically in his article "The Body of Christ, Which is the Church" (in Greek), in *Ekklesia* 39 (1962), 365f., where he writes: "The Divine Eucharist is the centre of the unity of Christians with Christ in the body of the Church. For it is through this *par excellence* that the Church is revealed as the body of Christ and the communion of the Holy Spirit, and the 'present' age and world is joined with that which is to come, the earthly Church with the heavenly. In the Divine Eucharist is contained the whole body of Christ..."

[45] See ibid., and *inter alia* M. Siotis, *Divine Eucharist. N.T. information on the Divine Eucharist in the light of the Church's interpretation* (in Greek), 1957, p. 69; P. Trembelas, *Dogmatics...*, III, 1961, p. 154. Cf. G. Florovsky, "Le corps du Christ," p. 36 f.; J. Meyendorff, *The Orthodox Church*, p. 22 f.; as also G. Bebis, "The Divine Eucharist according to Patristic Interpretation," in *Ekklesia* 36 (1959), 143-145.

[46] See P.B. Schultze, "Eucharistie und Kirche in der russischen Theologie der Gegenwart," in *Z.L.T.*, 77, (1955) 257-300 and E. Lanne, "Die Kirche als Mysterium in der orthodoxen Theologie," in Holbock-Sartory, *Mysterium Kirche in der Sicht der theologischen Disziplinen*, II, 1962, pp. 891-925.

[47] Unfortunately, we do not have access to the works of these two theologians written in Russian, and have, therefore, drawn our information about their theory mainly from the following articles (as far as we know, only articles exist): 1) N. Afanassieff, "L'Apôtre Pierre et l'évêque de Rome," in *Theologia* 26 (1955), 464 f.; 2) *eiusdem* "La doctrine de la Primauté à la lumière de l'ecclésiologie," in *Istina* 4 (1957) 401-20; 3) *eiusdem* "The Church which presides in Love," in *The Primacy of Peter in the Orthodox Church*, ET 1963, pp. 57-110; *eiusdem* "Le Concile dans la Théologie orthodoxe russe", in *Irénikon* 35 (1962) 316 f.; 5) *eiusdem*, "Una Sancta," in *Irénikon* 36 (1963), 436; 6) A. Schmemann, "Unity, Division, Reunion in the Light of Orthodox Ecclesiology" in *Theologia* 22 (1951) 242 f.; 7) *eiusdem*, "The Idea of Primacy in Orthodox Ecclesiology," in *The Primacy of Peter* (as above); 8) *eiusdem*, "Theology and Eucharist" (in Greek), in *Theology, Truth and Life*, (ed. Zoë Brotherhood) 1962, and 9) *eiusdem*, "Towards a Theology of Councils," in *St Vladimir's Seminary Quarterly* 6 (1962) 170-184.

[48] As Prof. I.Karmiris puts it (*Orthodox Doctrine of the Church*,

1964, p. 16), the Divine Eucharist constitutes "as it were the very mystery of the Church." Cf. G. Florovsky's comment (in *Ways of Worship*, ed. P. Edwall et al., 1951, p. 58): "The Church lives in the Eucharist and by the Eucharist."

[49] Cf. P. Trembelas, "Unacceptable Theories concerning the *Una Sancta*," in *Ekklesia* 41 (1964), 167 f.

[50] Eph. 4:5 and 13. cf. Rom. 12:16; 15:5; 2 Cor. 13:11; Phil. 2:2; 4:2.

[51] Jn 13:35; Eph. 4:16; 2 Cor. 5:14 and elsewhere.

[52] Eph. 4:5.

[53] Thus a) on faith, the confession of faith and Holy Scripture see examples in K. Federer, *Liturgie und Glaube. Eine theologiegeschichtliche Untersuchung*, 1950, p.59f.; C.F.D. Moule, *The Birth of the New Testament*, 1962, and C. Peifer, "Primitive Liturgy in the Formation of the New Testament," in *Bible Today*, 1 (1962), 14-21; b) on love and the works of mercy inspired by it, see Acts 2:42, 4:32, Heb. 13:10-16, Jn 13:29, and also the institution of the *agape* or "love-feast" which was initially connected with the Eucharist. Cf. G. Williams, "The Rôle of the Layman in the Ancient Church," in *Greek, Roman and Byzantine Studies* 1 (1958), 33f.; O. Cullmann, *Urchristentum und Gottesdienst*, 1950, pp. 102-106 and B.O. Beicke, *Diakonie, Festfreude und Zelos in Verbindung mit der alchristlichen Agapenfeier*, 1961, p. 24; c) on the connection between martyrdom and Eucharist see J. Betz, *Die Eucharistie...*, p. 184f.; d) on the connection of worship as a whole with the Eucharist, see P. Trembelas, "The Divine Eucharist in its connection with the other Mysteries and Sacramental Rites" (in Greek), in *Efcharisterion, Essays in Honor of Professor H. Alivizatos*, 1958. pp. 462-472.

[54] See N. Nissiotis, "Worship, Eucharist and Intercommunion: An Orthodox Reflection" in *Studia Liturgica* 2 (1963), 197 f.

[55] The more general question of Church unity, and the consciousness of it, in the context of the formation of the early Catholic Church, was first posed in Prof. G. Konidaris' study *The Formation...* p. 32, n. 1. The present work appears as part of this broader subject, other aspects of which have been addressed in other works by this author.

[56] Such a view necessarily belongs, of course, within the biblical understanding according to which the mystical life of the Church in time and history is a "pledge" and "foretaste" of the life in the "age to come". See S. Agouridis, "Time and Eternity (eschatology and mysticism) in the Theological Teaching of John the Theologian," in *E.E.Th.S.Th.* IV (1959), 60.

[57] The sacramental aspect of the elements of the Eucharist is a

subject in itself. On this see Professor M. Siotis, *Efcharistia* (in Greek), passim.

[58] The early Church did not see the Eucharist only as a communion in the "holy things", but mainly as a communion of the "holy ones". See the excellent work of W. Elert, *Abendmahl und Kirchengemeinschaft in der alten Kirche hauptsächlich des Ostens,* 1954.

[59] The connection of the Eucharist with the ministries in the Church (the Greek term *liturgema* is indicative in itself) was only natural, given that "the Eucharist forms the centre of all life in the Church" (G. Konidaris, *The Historian, the Church and the Content of Tradition during the First Two Centuries* (in Greek), 1961, p. 8). The connection of the origin of Canon Law with the Eucharist had already been emphasized by R. Sohm (K. Mörsdorff, "Altkanonisches Sakramentsrecht? Eine Anseinandersetzung mit den Anschauungen Rudolph Sohms über die inneren Grundlagen...", in *Studia Gratiana,* I, 1953, pp. 485-502); but because of his ideas about the relationship between Law and Church (see note 19 above), he was not able to see in the sources all those elements which give the Eucharist ecclesiological content. For this reason, the whole question still remains open for the historian who perceives in the Eucharist an ecclesiological character.

[60] See 1 Cor. 11. Cf. also below.

[61] G. Konidaris, *On the Supposed Difference in Forms in the Polity of Primitive Christianity,* 1959.

[62] G. Konidaris, *G.C.H.,* p. 20 f.

[63] The view that the Church evolves, put forward by both Roman Catholic and Anglican theologians (see e.g. L. Cerfaux, *La theologie de l'Église suivant s. Paul,* 1948, p. 140; F.M. Braun, *Neues Licht auf die Kirche,* 1946, p. 166; G. Dix, *Jew and Greek,* pp. 67 and 80), cannot be accepted without the gravest reservations. This cannot be an evolution of the Church in her essence, but rather of her outer covering even though there are aspects and "coverings" of the Church's essence which are inseparably bound up with that essence (e.g. the literary form of Scripture, the basic order of the Eucharist, the organization of the Church around the bishop, etc.)

[64] Cf. Y. Congar, *The Mystery of the Church,* 1960 and F. Heiler, *Urkirche und Ostkirche,* 1937, p. 826.

[65] We have already made a distinction in principle between the history of unity and the theology of unity (see above, p. 12f.). Yet, despite the fact that it is imperative for this reason carefully to distinguish what relates to the historical reality from what the early Church taught or aspired to, it must be admitted here that on the

subject of Church unity, history and theology often touch on one another, given that the Church is an integral reality, whether she is understood as a conceptual or an empirical state, and her unity forms an inalienable element of her essence. This is why in the present case it becomes very difficult and often impossible to isolate the evolving "becoming" of the Church from her stable "being" without the risk of misinterpreting or distorting history.

[66] Cf. G. Konidaris, *On the Supposed Difference*, p. 23.

[67] On the subject of the sources used for this study, it should be explained here that we shall mainly be using those sources which are purely Christian and ecclesial. This is not because we underrate the value of outside sources for the history of early Christianity such as the Dead Sea Scrolls, but on account of the nature of our theme which relates mainly to the Church's self-understanding which can be reflected faithfully only in her own documents. Besides, theories about a direct relationship between the Dead Sea Scrolls and the Church do not seem well-founded. On this subject see K. Stendahl, "Kirche: II. Im Urchristentum" in *Die Religion in Geschichte und Gegenwart*, 3, Aufl. III (1959), 1300. But more generally, the relationship of these texts to the Holy Scriptures will remain unknown, as Prof. V. Vellas observes, until all the texts discovered are published in full, and others perhaps come to light (V. Vellas, *Commentary on the Book of Habakkuk* (in Greek), 1958, 30,43). In consequence, it would be at least premature to place these texts alongside the already existing sources of primitive Christianity in studying the unity of the Church. On the relation of the Dead Sea Scrolls to early Christianity, the interested reader may see, inter alia, P. Simotas, *The Discoveries of Kirbet Qumran* (in Greek), 1952; S Agouridis, "Judaic Eschatology in N.T. Times" (in Greek), in *Theologia*, 1956, p. 408 n. 2; *eiusdem, The Dead Sea Scrolls and the N.T.* (in Greek), 1959; A. Chastoupis, *The Dead Sea Scrolls in relation to Holy Scripture* (in Greek), 1958; Th. Kirkasios, *The Dead Sea Scrolls* (in Greek), 1959; *eiusdem. "The Damascus or Sadokic text" (in Greek)*, in *Theologia* (1960), 151-166; M. Siotis, *The Dead Sea Scrolls. Story of their discovery and Description* (in Greek), 1961.

[68] It should be noted that many of the problems of systematic theology are later constructs of the philosophizing mind and not infrequently altogether alien to the mentality of the early Church. Allowing these problems to interfere with historical research will not only fail to serve contemporary Orthodox theology, which is trying to purge itself of alien influences, but will do it great harm.

[69] It should be noted that a full examination of the presupposi-

tions and foundations of the Church in the Eucharist and the bishop needs to go back into the history of Israel. The sources and the history of the Church demand such a connection between the Church and Israel, given that the primitive Church regarded herself as the true Israel, and saw the Old Testament and the history of Israel as her own. In this regard, it is sufficient to read carefully the beginning of Paul's Epistle to the Ephesians (1:4), the beginning of Hebrews and John's Gospel, the genealogies of Jesus included in the Gospels of Matthew and Luke etc., to satisfy oneself that the primitive Church saw herself as an organic part of the history of Israel "from the foundation of the world," or as the very "seed of Abraham" (Gal. 3-4. Cf. Jn 5:39, 46). The Church had the same consciousness in the second century: "We are the true race of Israel" (Justin, *Dial.* I 135:36 and 123:9), and also in the third: "to us the ... true Hebrews" (Origen, *On Mart.* 33). The Christological character of the O.T. was already stressed by the Fathers (Augustine, *On Ps.* 30, P.L. 36:244) and is underlined today by research (e.g. L. Philippidis, *History of the N.T. Period* (in Greek), p. 825 and V. Ioannidis, "The Kingdom of God," p. 160. For this reason, it is strongly stressed today that from a methodological viewpoint too, the correct starting point for any discussion of primitive ecclesiology consists in the question: what does the Old Testament have to say about God and His people? (See R. Newton Flew, "Jesus and the Kingdom of God," in *The Expository Times*, (1934-35), 217). While recognizing this fact, we shall not go into a detailed investigation here of the history of Israel, both because the Divine Eucharist and the Bishop make their appearance as historical institutions after the O.T. period, and also for practical reasons. This subject will therefore be treated on its own in a special study to appear shortly.

[70] See the formulation of the problem above, note 31.

[71] It is not accidental that in 1 Clement (96 A.D.) it was called "the gifts of the *episcopê*." See below for greater detail.

[72] Research for the present work had already been completed when A. Schmemann's study "Towards a Theology of Councils" was published (*St Vladimir's Seminary Quarterly* 6 (1962), 170-184). On the enormous importance of the question of the origin of the parish and the scant attention afforded it hitherto by research, he writes as follows (p. 177): "This process (which transformed the original episcopal structure of the local Church into what we know today as parish) although it represents one of the most radical changes that ever took place in the Church, remained, strange as it

may seem, virtually unnoticed by ecclesiologists and canonists."
[73] To determine what developments have occured, it will often be necessary to use sources later than the first three centuries. This is required sometimes because they throw light on earlier conditions, or else because by their contrast or agreement with the sources of the first three centuries, they either make clear what developments have taken place, or connect the later developments with the original situation. Sources later than the third century will be used in this way only insofar as this aids the investigation of problems which go back to the first three centuries. As to the unity of the Church from the fourth century on, a special study will be needed.

PART I

PRESUPPOSITIONS

The Relationship Between Church, Eucharist and Bishop in the Consciousness of the Primitive Church

Chapter One

THE DIVINE EUCHARIST AND THE "CHURCH OF GOD"

1. The connection of the Eucharist with the initial appearance of the term "church"

The ecclesiology of primitive Christianity was not abstract and theoretical but rather practical.[1] As a result, not only is there no definition of the Church in the sources, but there is not even a theoretical description of her. Out of the eighty or so passages in which the term *ekklesia* occurs in the New Testament, fifty-seven at least have in view the Church as an *assembly in a particular place*. If we try to group these passages under different headings, we have the following picture:

(a) those referring to the "Church" (singular) of a particular city;[2]

(b) those referring to the "Churches" (plural) of an area wider than a city, or without specifying a locality;[3]

(c) those containing the term "Church" or "Church of God" without specifying a locality;[4] and

(d) those containing the phrase "church in the household" (*kat' oikon ekklesia*).[5]

Out of these passages, only those of the third group can be connected with the Church in an abstract or theoretical sense. For most of these, however, this is merely a first impression. Passages such as 1 Cor. 15:9, Gal. 1:13 and Phil. 3:6, where Paul says that he persecuted the "Church of God," have in mind specifically the Church of Jerusalem, where there was a "great persecution" during which "Saul laid waste the Church."[6]

45

In consequence, the term "Church" in these ancient texts normally describes the Church as a *concrete reality in space*. This observation should serve as our basis for tackling the question, introduced by modern scholarship,[7] of whether the idea of the "universal" or of the "local" Church came first in primitive ecclesiology.[8]

But the point of altogether special importance is that it was not just any assembly, but strictly speaking, the *eucharistic assembly* that was called *ekklesia* of "Church." This is clearly shown by a careful examination of the information we can glean from the most ancient texts we have, namely Paul's Epistles. There are also other early Christian texts which concur with these, and those will be discussed later.

The Epistles of the Apostle Paul (apart from the so-called Pastoral Epistles, which are personal in character[9] and therefore do not concern us directly), which are addressed to the Christians in various regions under the term "Church," presuppose certain specific circumstances in which the recipients would be appraised of their contents.

These circumstances appear to be none other than the assembly of the Eucharist. As H. Leitzmann has observed,[10] the greetings at the end of these Epistles show that they were intended to be read at the time of the Eucharist, and for this reason they would be an excellent guide in reconstructing certain parts of the ancient liturgy.[11] So when Paul writes, for example, "To the Church of God which is at Corinth,"[12] this "Church" is first and foremost the actual assembly of the Corinthians gathered to perform the Eucharist. From certain observations on points which do not yet seem to have come to the attention of scholars, we may note the following phenomenon: while in referring to Corinth Paul uses the term "Church," when he is talking about Achaea he uses the term "saints." In other words, while he could most naturally have said: "To the Church of God which is in Corinth and Achaea," or simply "which is in Achaea" (given that this would be understood to include Corinth),[13] he makes a distinction between Corinth and Achaea, *placing the "Church" in Corinth*. This might perhaps be pure coincidence with no especial significance, if it were not corroborated by almost all the passages in which the term "Church" is used according to the categories given above.[14] Thus *whereas the Apostle uses "Church" in the singular in all cases where he refers to the Church of a particular city, in cases where he is referring to geographical areas wider than the city he uses the term in the plural.* The only possible explanation for this curious phenomenon is that for Paul, the term "Church" did not simply mean Christians in a general and theoretical sense, without regard to their eucharistic gathering at the time when the Epistle was read. Thus Corinth, as the recipient of the epistle at the eucharistic assembly, is called a "Church" by the Apostle. Achaea, by contrast, is not called a "Church," since it is not in eucharistic assembly at the time when the epistle was received. This occurs in the case of every region wider than a city. Hence Paul speaks only of "Churches" and not of a "Church" in the singular in such regions.

This is the explanation for that characteristic feature of the Pauline vocabulary, namely that we never encounter in it "the Church of Macedonia" or "the Church of Achaea" or "the Church of Judea." The Christians of these wider areas did not differ from those of a city in any other particular way that would allow us to interpret this linguistic phenomenon in some other way. They, too, were full members of the Church just like those of Corinth. But because in these earliest times to which Paul's epistles belong, the word "Church" meant principally, the faithful united in their eucharistic assembly. It was natural that for Paul and his readers the Church should be not in Achaea or some other area wider than the city, but in Corinth, i.e. in a specific city, because it was there that the assembly took place during which his epistles would be read.

Such an identification of the Church with the eucharistic assembly, can be attested more clearly from a careful analysis of the content of the First Epistle to the Corinthians and particularly Chapter 11. In this chapter, the Apostle Paul gives the Corinthians practical directions relating to their assemblies for worship. A careful examination of the terminology used by the Apostle at this point leads us to the following observations:

Although, it is evident from the whole content of this chapter that Paul is speaking here about the assembly to perform the Divine Eucharist in Corinth, he nevertheless describes this assembly as a "Church": "*when you assemble as a Church* I hear that there are divisions among you" (v. 18). Reading this phrase of the Apostle Paul's, the Christians of Corinth might be expected to have asked, "What exactly does the Apostle mean when he talks about "coming together as a Church"? Aren't we a "Church" whenever we meet, and even when we don't come together in the same place?" This question, which seems so natural to twentieth-century Christians, did not concern the Christians of the Apostle Paul's time. Indeed, from the passage it can be concluded quite naturally that the term "Church" was not used in a theoretical sense but to describe an actual meeting; and again not to describe just any sort of meeting, but the one that Paul had in mind when he wrote the words quoted above – the assembly to perform the Divine Eucharist. Paul does not hesitate in the slightest to call this assembly "the Church of God": *to despise the eucharistic assembly is to despise the very "Church of God"* (v. 22). And going on to identify Eucharist and Church in a manner which is quite astonishing, he talks about the institution by Christ of the divine Supper, linking his reference to the "Church of God" with the subject of the Eucharist by a simple explanatory "for," as if it were one and the same thing: "*For* I received from the Lord what I also delivered to you" (v. 23), namely the celebration of the Eucharist. This identification of the eucharistic assembly with the Church allows Paul to use the expression "coming together in the same place" (*epi to auto*) as a term having *at once ecclesiological and eucharistic content. "When you come together in one place* (epi to auto) it is not the *Lord's supper* that you eat" (v. 20), because, by the way you behave, "you despise *the Church of God"* (v. 22). "So then, my brethren, when you *come together* to eat, wait for one another... lest you come together to be condemned..." (vv. 33-34).[15] Thus, in the thought of Paul and the Churches which read his Epistles, *the terms "coming together" or "coming together in the same place" (epi to auto), "the Lord's* supper" (i.e. Divine Eucharist) and "the Church" (ekklesia) or "the Church of God" mean the same thing.

That the eucharistic assembly is identified with the very Church of God is also the conclusion that emerges from a study of the term *church in the household (kat' oikon ekklesia)* contained in the passages belonging to group (d) according to our classification.[16] The significance of the term *church in the household* seems to be much greater than might be suggested by the number of passages in which it occurs. At a time when the Church was gradually adopting a technical terminology and did not yet have one fixed, no technical term could be universally applicable.[17] Whereas, it seems that there were many such terms in use locally, either temporarily, or for a long time until they became fully part of the worldwide vocabulary of Christianity.[18] The term *church in the household* did not survive in the vocabulary of the Church. The epistles of Paul seem to be the only sources in which it occurs. Two things, however, clearly demonstrate its importance. Firstly, this term has the appearance of a usage already established in the Pauline Churches at the time when Paul's epistles were being written. The fact that he uses the term without any variation and never goes on to explain it presupposes a familiarity with the term on the part of those who were reading the epistles. This means that in the Pauline Churches at least, this term had acquired currency as a technical term. Aside from this, the importance of the term lies in its relationship with the term "Church" which finally prevailed. What sort of *Church* does the *church in the household* represent? Students of history are usually familiar with the *local* Church and the Church "throughout the world." Does the *church in the household* constitute a third type of *Church* for primitive Christianity? This question does not seem to have been examined in detail hitherto, so far as we know.[19] One probable reason for this is the fact that the meaning of the term is usually considered self-evident. But if we take into account the significance of this term for the history of the unity of the Church, determining its meaning through detailed study becomes a necessity.

Many of the scholars who have been indirectly concerned with this subject seem to identify the *church in the household* with the "Christian family" in general, which is presented as a special unity within the Pauline local Churches.[20] In this case, *church* is used in the widest sense of "Christianity" or "Christian community" (*Gemeinde*). Thus for example Michel, exploring the meaning of the terms *oikos* and *oikia* in the New Testament,[21] collects all the passages referring to the "church in the household" together with those referring to Christian families and gives them all the common title of *Gemeinde in Familien*. This approach is in agreement with the older understanding of *church in the household*, according to which this term denoted the groups of Christians who gathered around strong personalities such as Philemon or Priscilla and Aquila and in which, so it was believed, the Church organization and above all the bishop had their origin.[22]

This inclusion of the "church in the household" among the passages which refer to the Christian family in general is also continued by later works,[23] with the exception of the distinguished J. Jeremias, who studiously avoids using the passages which refer to the "church in the household" alongside those referring to Christian families generally.[24]

But is it correct methodology to examine all these passages together? Does the *church in the household* belong with the passages which refer to the Christian family in general? The answer is negative if we take into account the strict division St Paul makes between the house/household (*oikia*) or Christian family and Church. Referring to the celebration of the Divine Eucharist in Corinth and the social distinctions which were being made in the course of it, he asks the members of the Church of Corinth: "Do you not have houses (*oikiai*) to eat and drink in? Or do you despise the Church of God and humiliate those who have nothing?"[25] Yet it is known that at the time the epistle was written and for a long while afterwards, the Eucharist was celebrated in Christians' houses. So while *house* and *Church* are linked by the Eucharist in practice, they constitute two different realities in the faith of the Church. The *Church of God* should not be confused with the *house*; otherwise it leads to "despising the Church of God."

Another example of this firm distinction between the notions of house and Church is taken from 1 Timothy 3:4-5. This passage talks about the family of the "bishop." No other "household" or *Gemeinde in Familien* could be more Christian. Nevertheless, Paul not only refrains from calling it a "church," but clearly distinguishes it from the "Church of God": "A bishop must be above reproach... he must manage his own *household* (*oikos*) well, keeping his children submissive and respectful in every way; for if a man does not know how to manage *his own household*, how can he care for *God's church*?" These two examples from the Epistles of Paul are sufficient for us to conclude that the distinction between the notions of Christian family (*oikos, oikia, Gemeinde in Familien*) and of *church* was so sharp in the mind of the primitive Church that identifying the notion of the "Church" with that of the "Christian family" would not have been possible.

But in that case, what led these two different notions, of *house* and of *church*, to be joined together to form one term? The crucial factor is obviously the celebration of the Divine Eucharist. All ecclesial activities could be performed outside Christian houses. We know, for example, that preaching took place also in the synagogues.[26] And worship itself could in principle be performed in Jewish buildings, as we see from Acts 2:46. But there was one activity of the Church which never took place outside Christian homes: the celebration of the Eucharist.[27] That this was due to strong convictions on the part of the Church and was not fortuitous is shown by Acts 2:46: "And day by day, attending the temple together and breaking bread at home (*kat' oikon*), they partook of food with glad and generous hearts...." In this passage, the contrast should be noted: prayer could take place also in the Temple, but the "breaking of bread," that is the Eucharist,[28] took place in the Christians' homes. [28a see also Acts 20:7.] If we now take into account the identification of eucharistic assembly and local Church found in Paul,[29] the meaning of the term in question becomes clear. The terms *house* and *church* expressed two different realities: the former something secular, and the latter a purely ecclesial reality. But whenever the Eucharist was celebrated in the house of a Christian family, the *Church of God* was automatically linked with that *household*. The connection of the Eucharist both with that *house* and with the *Church of God* gave rise to the *church in the household* which took its name from the owner of the house.[30]

Thus the phrase *church in the household* refers to the assembly of the faithful for the celebration of the Eucharist.[31] If this assembly was called a *church*, this was because the assembly, *epi to auto,* for the celebration of the Eucharist was also called a *church* (1 Cor. 11). In contrast with the other terms used for the Church, the term *church in the household* was the most concrete expression of the Church, denoting the assembly of the faithful in a particular place in order to be united in the body of Christ. In consequence, the *church in the household* was not a third type of Church, different from the "local" or the "universal," but the local Church herself or *Church of God*, breaking bread at the house of one of her members.

So from an examination of the oldest texts of primitive Christianity, the Epistles of Paul, it transpires that *the eucharistic assembly was identified with the "Church of God" herself.* If we now examine those texts which are already seeing the end of the Apostolic period, such as the Revelation of John, we shall again have no difficulty in establishing the same identification of the eucharistic assembly with the Church of God. Written characteristically "on the Lord's day,"[32] which is to say the day of the Eucharist *par excellence,*[33] the Book of Revelation moves within the milieu and atmosphere of the eucharistic assembly to such an extent that scholars studying it are faced with the problem of whether the Eucharist influenced this book or *vice versa.*[34] However that may be, it should be considered that there is at least a "mutual" influence between the Book of Revelation and eucharistic worship.[35] This book transports us from the Eucharist to the throne of God and from the Church on earth to the Church in heaven in such a way that we think it is one and the same reality. Indeed, the mystical identification of the Church in heaven before the throne of God with the Church on earth worshipping before the Table of the Eucharist is such as to call to mind the connection between these two aspects of the Church which only in Orthodoxy has been preserved in such depth.[36] Chapters 4 and 5 of Revelation, to which we shall return later, make no sense without the presupposition that the eucharistic assembly incarnates on earth the very Church of God.

From this is becomes clear that from the first appearance of the term *ekklesia* there was a most profound connection, even to the point of identity, between this term and the Eucharist celebrated in each city. Each such Eucharist constituted the expression in space and time of the Church of God herself.

2. The connection of the Eucharist with the original consciousness regarding the unity of the Church.

The identification of the eucharistic assembly with the Church of God herself in the use of the term *church* would make no sense if there did not exist in parallel a very profound connection between the Divine Eucharist and the primitive Church's consciousness regarding unity. This connection, which extends beyond the terminology used for the Church into the early theology regarding the Church among the first Christians, is brilliantly expressed by the "theologian of unity" *par excellence*,[37] the Apostle Paul. Addressing the Corinthians, the Apostle writes: "Judge for yourselves what I say. The cup of blessing which we bless, is it not a communion (*koinonia*) in the blood of Christ? The bread which we break, is it not a communion in the body of Christ? Because there is one bread, we who are many are one body, for we all partake of the one bread."[38] In this highly significant passage, the dominant idea is that "the many" form "one body" identified with the bread of the Eucharist. Since this idea was to have a decisive influence on the whole formation of the Church's unity, it is necessary to look at it in more detail at this point while we are examining the presuppositions of this unity.

The connection of the Divine Eucharist with the consciousness that the "many" are united through it and in it into one
body, and not just any body but the "body of Christ"[39] – thus
forming not "one thing" in the neuter but "one" in the mas-
culine,[40] the "one Lord" Himself[41] – is deeply rooted right in
the historical foundations of the Divine Eucharist and the
Church alike. A careful examination of the texts referring to
the Last Supper with which the origin of the Eucharist coincides historically[42] shows convincingly that despite their
many differences on various points,[43] they all agree on the
connection of the Supper with the "many" or "you" (pl.),
"for" or "in the place of" (*anti* or *peri*) whom the One offers
Himself.[44] This relationship of the "many" with the "One"[45]
who offers Himself for them connects the historical foundations of the Eucharist with the Judaeo-Christian tradition of
the servant of God or servant of the Lord[46] which again is
connected with Jesus Christ's understanding of Himself[47] and
goes back to the people of Israel's consciousness of unity.[48]
In this way, the connection of the Eucharist with the consciousness that the "many" are united to the point of identity
with the One who offers himself on their behalf is shown to
be as ancient as Christianity itself.

This connection of the Divine Eucharist with a sense of
the unity of the "many" in the "One," effected through the
tradition of the "Servant of God," is already firmly established in the consciousness and life of the primitive Church
by the first century as shown by the oldest surviving liturgical texts after the Last Supper. Thus in the most ancient
liturgical prayer of the Roman Church, which certainly goes
right back to apostolic times and is preserved in 1 Clement
(96 A.D.), we repeatedly read the phrase "of Jesus Thy Servant," clearly in connection with the hymns of the Servant
of God in the Book of Isaiah.[49] The same thing can be seen
even more clearly in the eucharistic prayer of the *Didache*,
also very ancient, where we read: "We thank Thee, holy Father, for Thy holy Name which Thou hast caused to make its
dwelling in our hearts, and for the knowledge and faith and
immortality which Thou hast made known to us through

Jesus Thy servant."[50] This fact is of particular significance given that, as a rule, liturgical texts preserve very ancient traditions. If indeed this is coupled with the existence of the Servant of God tradition also in other very ancient hymns of worship, such as we most likely find included in Paul's Epistle to the Philippians (2:6-11),[51] the connection between the Divine Eucharist and the Servant tradition should be considered something very ancient in the mind of the Church. In this way the "many" of the Servant tradition, the "many" of the Last Supper and the "many" of Paul's epistles meet and are identified with each other through the synthesis achieved by the systematic thought of the great Apostle\ when he writes, "... one bread, we who are many are one body, for we all partake of the one bread."

But the connection of the Eucharist with the primitive Church's sense of the unity of the "many" in the "One" goes back to the historical foundation of the Church also by way of another fundamental tradition, that of the Lord as "Son of Man." This is especially true of the Johannine Churches, which, while not unaware of the connection of the Eucharist with the Servant of God tradition,[52] nevertheless preferred, at least on the evidence of the Fourth Gospel, to connect it with the "Son of Man" tradition. This tradition, which also goes back to Jesus' understanding of Himself[53] and through it to the Judaeo-Christian foundations of the Church,[54] has justly been regarded as the source of the idea of the Church.[55] For interwoven with this tradition, we find the paradoxical relationship of the unity of the many in the one which can be seen more generally in the Judaeo-Christian consciousness[56] taken to the point of identity.[57]

This unity of the many in the "Son of Man" is first clearly linked with the Divine Eucharist in the Gospel of John. In the sixth chapter of this Gospel, which obviously refers to the Eucharist,[58] the dominant figure is that of the "Son of Man." It is He who gives "the food which endures to eternal life."[59] In contrast with the manna which God gave to Israel through Moses, this food is the "true bread," which as that "which came down from heaven"[60] is none other than the

"Son of Man."[61] Clearly, then, it is *as "Son of Man"* that the
Lord appears in His relationship with the Eucharist in the
Fourth Gospel. Hence, communion in the Eucharist is de-
scribed there as eating not simply the flesh of the Lord, but
the flesh of the "Son of Man": "unless you eat the flesh of the
Son of Man and drink His blood, you have no life in you."[62]
In this capacity, as "Son of Man," Jesus appears in the Fourth
Gospel not only as identified with the bread of the Eucharist
("I am the bread of life"),[63] but also as the reality which is *par
excellence* inclusive of the "many": "he who eats my flesh and
drinks my blood abides in me, and I in him."[64] This abiding
in the "Son of Man," though participation in the Eucharist is
underlined in chapters 13-17 of the same Gospel, which move
within the eucharistic presuppositions of the Last Supper and
are so profoundly connected with the unity of the Church.[65]
The insistent appeal, "Abide in me, and I in you"[66] should
not be understood without reference both to the eucharistic
presuppositions of this text, and to the Lord's property of
taking up the new Israel and including it within Himself.[67]

For all these reasons, the eucharistic character of the Fourth
Gospel, which is increasingly being recognized,[68] makes it a
first class historical source for studying the presuppositions
on which the formation of the Church's unity in the Divine
Eucharist is based. Coming as an indispensable complement
to those sources which inform us about the mind of the
Pauline Churches, it proves that despite being expressed in
ways different from those we encounter in Paul's Epistles,[69]
the consciousness was the same throughout the primitive
Church: through the Divine Eucharist the "many" – the new,
true Israel, those who make up the Church – become a unity
to the point of identity with Christ.

All this demonstrates how incomprehensible the whole
ecclesiology of ancient Christianity becomes without reference to the Divine Eucharist particularly in anything to do
with the notion of the Church's unity. The principal images
used to depict and describe the Church in the New Testament[70] are based on the relationship of the "many" with the
"One," exactly as this is dictated by the eucharistic experi-

ence of the Church. This is especially true of the descriptions of the Church as "body of Christ," "house" or "building" (*oikodomê*), and "bride of Christ."

The characterization of the Church as the "body of Christ," which has provoked much discussion among modern scholars,[71] cannot be understood apart from the eucharistic experience of the Church,[72] which was most likely the source of the use of this term.[73] Neither the parallels to this term found in Rabbinic sources,[74] nor Gnosticism,[75] nor other ideas from the Hellenistic milieu[76] could have lent this term to the primitive Church, given that its content in the New Testament is *sui generis*, characterized by its emphasis not on the idea of the "body," but on the accompanying genitive "of Christ." In other words, it is not first and foremost the body of Christians, but the body *of Christ*.[77] This takes on its full meaning only within the context of the Judaeo-Christian tradition with which, as we have seen, the Divine Eucharist was connected from the beginning.

It is within this same tradition that the other ecclesiological images, too, take on their full meaning. Thus the characterization of the Church as a "building"[78] or "house"[79] does not imply something inanimate, but an organism living and *growing*[80] to "mature manhood,"[81] "to the measure of the stature of the fullness[82] of Christ."[83] This is not unrelated to the Divine Eucharist.[84] In the spirit of the unity of the "many" in the One, we can also have a right understanding of the description of the Church as "bride of Christ," through which the faithful are understood as "members of Christ"[85] in a manner analogous to the union of husband and wife "into one flesh."[86]

These ecclesiological images, of course, require special study which lies outside the scope and nature of the present work. But the point relevant to the very close connection of the Divine Eucharist with the primitive Church's consciousness of unity, is this: that all these images become meaningless outside the ontological unity of the "many" in Christ. Deeply rooted, as we have seen, in the historical foundations of Christianity, this unity found its fullest expression through the

Divine Eucharist. The ancient Church was fully aware of this when she declared, through the first theologian of her unity, "we who are many are one body, for we all partake of the one bread."

Chapter Two

THE "PRESIDENT" OF THE EUCHARIST AS "BISHOP" OF THE "CHURCH OF GOD"

1. The identification of eucharistic unity with the canonical unity of the Church.

The identification of the eucharistic assembly with the "Church of God" led naturally to the coincidence of the structure of the Church with that of the Eucharist. It is a noteworthy fact that the Church was distinguished from the world around her as a *sui generis* unity mainly by forming a eucharistic unity.[87] For precisely that reason, her organization, as will be shown below, was not borrowed or copied from the world around her, as historians have often contended,[88] but arose naturally out of the eucharistic assembly through which canonical unity is connected with the essence of the Church.[89]

The reconstruction of the image presented by the eucharistic assembly in Apostolic times in all its particulars does not concern us in the present work.[90]

As regards to the relationship of the Church's canonical unity with the Divine Eucharist, the existing sources allow us to make the following observations.

Through her worship, and especially through the Eucharist, the primitive Church lived under the influence of an absolute theocracy. The whole of her worship is performed on earth, but forms a type of the heavenly worship where the throne of God dominates.[91] In consequence, all authority in the Church is concentrated in the person of Jesus Christ. He is the one Lord, i.e. the only one who has power over all things, being exalted on the right hand of God.[92] Hence also, unity in *one Lord*[93] is manifested first and foremost in wor-

ship and especially in the Eucharist. As the one Lord, Christ
is also the one ruler, again recognized as such primarily in
the Eucharist.[94] Precisely because of this position He holds
in eucharistic worship, Christ concentrates in Himself all the
forms of ministry that exist in the Church. He is *par excellence* the minister,[95] priest,[96] Apostle,[97] deacon,[98] bishop,[99] and
teacher,[100] "in everything being preeminent."[101]

But here too, as has been remarked in another case,[102]
Christ is a great paradox in His relationship with the Church.
While He is worshipped in heaven, He is at the same time
present on earth and in the Eucharist,[103] thus transforming
the heavenly state into an earthly and historical reality. Thus
eucharistic worship on earth does not constitute a reality
parallel to that of heaven, but is the heavenly worship itself
(mystical identity).[104] In precisely the same way, the paradox
of the relationship between Christ and the Church is also
extended to the forms of ministry. The fact that the ministries in the primitive Church were always understood in
humility as "ministries of service" (*diakoniai*)[105] does not mean
that they were devoid of authority.[106] In precisely the same
way as the heavenly worship was truly represented typo-
logically in the Eucharist on earth so the authority of Christ
was truly reflected in the ministers of the Church. The Church
ministries, therefore, were not understood as existing in parallel with Christ's authority,[107] but as expressing the very
authority of Christ. As the one Lord and ruler of the Church,
Christ does not govern in parallel with an ecclesiastical administration on earth, but *through it and in it*. The ministries
that exist are antitypes and mystical radiations of the very
authority of Christ, the only minister *par excellence*. The rank
of Apostle, for example, was not understood in the primitive Church as an authority existing in parallel with the
authority of Christ, but as the very authority of Christ.[108] In a
similar manner the bishop, as we shall see shortly,[109] was
understood as occupying the "place of God" and as the "image of Christ." In this way, Christ remained the only minister
and the only one holding authority in the Church. Ministers
had no authority except as images and representatives of

Christ. This makes the Church a theocratic unity.[110] But this authority of Christ was not expressed except through the ministers of the Church; the law of which had a human as well as a divine character. This was made possible mainly because of the Divine Eucharist which identified heavenly worship with earthly and Christ with His Church in a manner that was mystical and real.

So thanks to the Eucharist and, therefore, chiefly in it, the various forms of ministry grew up in the primitive Church, and these in turn gave rise to the various "orders" in the Church and produced her law as a strictly Christocentric reality. All the ministries of Christ were reflected as historical realities in the Church in a way that created order and, therefore, "orders." In other words, while Christ was identified with the whole Church which was His body, and, therefore, *all* the members of the Church were "sharers in Christ,"[111] the powers or ministries of Christ were not expressed through all these members, but through certain ones. Thus Christ was regarded as the "apostle," but this did not mean that in His Body all were apostles.[112] Christ was the "Teacher," but in the Church there were not "many teachers."[113] He was the deacon, but this property of His was expressed through a particular order which received a special charism for this.[114] This held good for all the ministries of Christ which are mystically reflected in the Church.[115] In the same way, the unity of the Church came to be the unity of a body, but in diversity of *charismata*[116] which is equivalent to a unity in law and hierarchy.

Thus, the Divine Eucharist through which Christ was united to the point of identity with the Church, making it possible in this way for the *charismata* to be distributed, became not only the source of canonical unity, but also the chief area in which it was expressed.[117] As we know from the First Epistle to the Corinthians, the diversity of gifts was manifested chiefly in the eucharistic assembly. But it was precisely there also that unity in order was manifested – the unity which Paul tries to reinforce still further by opposing the individualism of the charismatics and making the *charismata* subordinate to the unity of the Church which for Paul meant unity in order.[118] The frequently attempted separation between spiritual gifts and order,[119] even to the point of an antithesis such that order is seen as the destroyer of the spirit in the primitive Church,[120] finds no basis in the sources of primitive Christianity. The division between charismatics and non-charismatics, introduced by Harnack, founders on the fact that the permanent ministers too received the gift of the Holy Spirit and were therefore considered charismatics.[121] The act of ordination by which the permanent ministers were "appointed" was nothing other than a laying on of hands to convey a special charism,[122] one which remained permanently with the person ordained.[123] Nor is there any serious basis in the sources for the idea, again introduced by Harnack, that the so-called "charismatics" took precedence in the early Church over the permanent ministers. Looked at in the light of the entire section of the Epistle concerning the eucharistic assemblies in Corinth, the passage in 1 Cor. 12:28 on which Harnack bases his thesis, is evidence that Paul did not have in mind a hierarchy such that the "charismatics" were placed above the permanent ministers. On the contrary, his whole purpose is to subordinate the charismatics to the "order" of the Church,[124] and this is why he places the gift of tongues, so dear to the Corinthians, right at the end of the list of gifts. The fact that Paul is not interested in that kind of order of precedence is further evident from several passages where he places the so-called "charismatics" after the permanent ministers who are regarded as "administrators."[125] The primitive eucharistic assemblies, in consequence, knew no antithesis between spirit and order, charism and hierarchy, because hierarchy and order without a spiritual charism were inconceivable at that time.[126]

2. The elevation the "president" of the Eucharist to "Bishop" of the Church.

What specific distinctions of "order" do we find, then, in the eucharistic assemblies of apostolic times? And how did they lead from the structure of the Eucharist to the permanent structure of the Church's unity? Again, the information available to us is severely limited by the nature of the sources. The actual situation in the Church of that period is known to us only from the Apostles, and this prevents us from seeing what exactly happened in the Apostles' absence. So what we discover is only the minimum of the historical reality. A fact which should make us wary of arguments from silence.[127] From Paul's description of the eucharistic assembly in Corinth, we learn that the Eucharist involved all the members of the Church,[128] but within it there were those who gave their consent and confirmation through the "Amen."[129] So in the Eucharist there was, on the one hand, the order of offerers or leaders, and on the other, the order of respondents through the "Amen." Who exactly these leaders and respondents were, 1 Corinthians does not tell us. About a generation later in the Church of Corinth, we learn that there were two orders clearly distinguished from one another, the clergy and the laity, and that – significantly enough – the substance of these two orders is based on the place each of them occupied in the Eucharist.[130] When, in about the middle of the second century, the eucharistic assembly in Rome is described by Justin (and judging from 1 Clement which links Corinth and Rome, it cannot have differed from the practice in Corinth), the "Amen" attested in 1 Corinthians is placed in the mouth of the order of laity.[131] So insofar as we can throw light on the situation in Corinth around 55 A.D. through what we know from somewhat later sources,[132] the distinction between those who led the Eucharist and those who responded with the "Amen" sprang from the structure of the Eucharist to appear clearly a short time later (1 Clement) as the fundamental canonical division of the Church herself into clergy and laity.

More particularly now on the question of the leaders of the eucharistic assembly, the apostolic period is again obscured by the shadow of the Apostles.[133] From what the book of Acts tells us, we are obliged to accept that when the Apostles were present at a eucharistic gathering, they led the Eucharist.[134] It seems that the same applied to the itiner-

ant "prophets," judging from what we are told by the
Didache.[135] But, whenever the Apostles were absent, which
was most of the time, leadership of the Eucharist naturally
belonged to the permanent ministers. Here, again, there is
an impenetrable historical problem, because the information
we have is sporadic. When the Twelve disappeared from the
historical scene in a highly obscure manner, we find leadership of the Church of Jerusalem in the hands of James and
the presbyters.[136] These presbyters may have existed in the
Church of Jerusalem before James took over its leadership.[137]
Appearing there in parallel are the "deacons,"[138] an institution not unrelated to the common tables, with which the
Eucharist too was connected at that time.[139] Thus, the Church
of Jerusalem was headed by the triad: James – the presbyters
– those who serve (*diakonountes*),[140] which probably replaced
the scheme: the Twelve (or the Apostles) – the presbyters –
those who serve. This may have formed the model also for
the organization of the other Churches which received Christianity from the mother Church of Jerusalem.[141] As we can
know, today, thanks to the research of Professor G.
Konidaris,[142] this triad was the first linguistic form under
which the Bishop appeared in history as a specific and complete rank, initially known only by the personal name of the
office-holder and implicit within the collective term "the presbyters" whenever there was no reason to single him out. It
follows that the office of Bishop exists even in the apostolic
period, overshadowed by the institution of the Apostles[143]
and linked with the presbyters and deacons, either (more
rarely) through the scriptural expression "Bishops and deacons,"[144] or (more commonly) through the everyday
expression "the presbyters."

That the Bishop, surrounded by the presbyters and deacons, was from the beginning the leader of the Eucharist is
shown by the existing texts even though they do not provide us with clear evidence as to who exactly offered the
Divine Eucharist. A careful examination of the sources leads
to the conclusion that the Divine Eucharist could be offered
principally and *par excellence* a) by the Apostles or other

charismatics such as the prophets, and b) by the Bishop, surrounded by the presbyters and deacons.

Texts such as the Acts of the Apostles, 1 Clement and the *Didache* point in the former direction. In Acts (20:11), we read that Paul celebrated the Divine Eucharist in Troas on the occasion when the youth Eutychus accidentally fell from the third floor room where the Christians had gathered to "break bread." Again, 1 Clement talks about a "ministry of the apostles."[145] What was the nature of this ministry in which the Apostles were succeeded by the presbyters of Corinth who had been dismissed? Even though the term "ministers" is used by Clement in a variety of ways,[146] as used here of the Apostles it has the specific meaning of offering the Gifts of the Eucharist. The ministry of the Apostles which had been given to the dismissed presbyters was the offering of the Gifts; this is why it was considered "no small sin" to dismiss them from it.[147] It follows that the Apostles had the right among other things to offer the Divine Eucharist whenever they were at any Church. It is possible, indeed, that each Church had a special place at the table of the Divine Eucharist which would be used by the Apostle whenever he visited; and that later, once the apostolic generation was gone, this became not simply the exclusive *locus* of the Bishop, but also the most vital symbol of his succession from the Apostles.[148] This probability stands, whether we accept the theory first put forward by C.H. Turner,[149] according to which apostolic succession was understood in the early Church as meaning that the Bishop of a local Church traced his succession back, not to the Apostles in general, but specifically to the apostle and the apostolic foundation of the local Church over which he presided – or whether we accept the opposite view upheld by A. Ehrhardt and other historians,[150] according to which the succession was seen as a succession from *all* the Apostles. In either case, it does not alter the fact which interests us here, that apostolic succession as an historical fact stemmed from the Divine Eucharist, in the offering of which the Bishops succeeded the Apostles. This becomes clear from studying 1 Clement where the meaning of succession from the Apostles revolves exclusively around the ministry of "offering the Gifts." A similar conclusion is to be drawn from studying the *Didache*. In this text, the Divine Eucharist appears as a ministry of the prophets too,[151] which permits the conclusion that charismatics generally were able to offer the Divine Eucharist when they were visiting a local Church.

Despite this, however, two historical facts should be taken into consideration before drawing more general conclusions. Firstly, it should be borne in mind that many local Churches were not founded directly by the Apostles, but by missionaries who came from other Churches. As to the meaning of apostolic succession, this fact does not change things because by tracing his succession back to the apostolic foundations of his Church, the Bishop would ultimately go back to the apostle of the Mother Church from which his own Church had received Christianity. But as regards the unity of the local Church and its relation to the person offering the Eucharist, this fact is of particular importance as we shall see. A second historical fact which should be taken into consideration here is that even in those Churches which had been founded by one of the Apostles not all the charismatics were connected permanently with the local Church. Furthermore, which is more important, that at an early date the Apostles and charismatics started to disappear and be replaced in all their ministries by the permanent pastors of the local Church.[152] In view of these facts, the Apostles and other charismatics cannot be regarded as figures connected permanently with the offering of the Divine Eucharist in the local Church and, therefore, capable of expressing her unity. This was the task and character of the permanent ministers of the local Church and in particular the Bishop.

The task of the Bishop was from the beginning principally liturgical consisting in the offering of the Divine Eucharist. This is attested in very early texts. If we combine the information Ignatius gives us about the Bishop with the image of the eucharistic assembly that the author of the Apocalypse has in mind (late first century), we see that the Bishop is described as "presiding in the place of God,"[153] precisely because in the eucharistic assembly he occupied that place, which the Apocalypse describes as "the throne of God and of the Lamb" in the heavenly assembly, the image of which the Apocalypse takes from the celebration of the Divine Eucharist in the Church.[154] The very title of "Bishop" (*episkopos*) is used by Ignatius most probably because, in keeping with his whole theology, the *episkopos par excellence* is God, Whose place in the eucharistic assembly was now occupied by the Bishop who presided over it.[155] Everything in the vision of the Apocalypse revolves around the altar which is before the throne of God. Before it stands the multitude of the saved, and around the throne in a circle the twenty-four presbyters. The metaphor is plainly taken from the eucharistic assembly at which the Bishop sat on his throne before the altar with the presbyters in a circle around him[156] and the people in front of him.[157] This was from the beginning the place the Bishop occupied as the one who offered the Divine Eucharist, and for this reason the Church saw him as the image and type of God or of Christ.[158] The basis for this vivid consciousness in the Church lay in the understanding of the Divine Eucharist as the Body of Christ in both the Christological and the ecclesiological sense.[159] In the Divine Eucharist, the Church was manifested in space and time as the body of Christ, and also as a canonical unity. In this way the unity of the Divine Eucharist became the font of the Church's unity in the body of Christ, and also of her unity *"in the Bishop."*[160] How the unity of the Catholic Church was established and took shape on the basis of this reality will be the subject of our enquiry in the chapters which follow.

To summarize the conclusions of the first part of this study, we observe that the Divine Eucharist was from the beginning identified with the Church of God. Through this link with the consciousness that in Christ the "many" are united in the One, the Eucharist appeared as the highest expression of the Church as body of Christ. Thus, in the earliest historical documents, Paul's Epistles, the eucharistic assembly is unreservedly identified with the Church of God which is in a given city. Identification of the eucharistic assembly with the "Church of God" led automatically to the coincidence of eucharistic unity with the basic canonical unity of the Church. The division of those taking part in the Eucharist into those who led and those who responded with the "Amen" appeared already in the first century (1 Corinthians and 1 Clement) as a clear and now permanent canonical division of the members of the Church into clergy and laity. At the same period the "president" of the eucharistic assembly, as occupying the "throne of God" in the altar, was elevated in the consciousness of the Church to the one who was seated "in the place of God." In this way, the unity of the Church in the Eucharist automatically became also a unity in the "Bishop."

These general presuppositions of the first three generations or so of Christianity formed the basis for the further formation of the unity of the Church in the Divine Eucharist and the Bishop.

NOTES TO PART ONE

[1] The distinction between theoretical and practical ecclesiology is intended here to underline the fact that the first theology concerning the Church did not develop as speculation about the idea or the concept of the Church, but initially appeared as an experience of a reality; a state, in which Christians were continuously living. The conscious recognition of this state and the subsequent expression of the consciousness which had been created constituted the first theology of the Church, expressed through images which described but did not define the reality which the Christians lived. Thus, the theoretical theology of the Church did not precede the historical events and institutions of the Church's life. On the contrary, the events and experiences of the Church, consciously recognized by her, led gradually to theoretical theological formulations. This has particular significance from the point of view of methodology, especially for this study, which examines the unity of the Church, starting not from the theoretical teaching on unity in the sources, but from those events, institutions and experiences,

the consciousness recognition of which led the early Church to ecclesiological formulations of a purely theoretical character.

[2] Rom. 16:1; 1 Cor. 1:2; 2 Cor. 1:1; Col. 4:16; 1 Thes. 1:1; Acts 8:1 and 11:22.

[3] Gal. 1:2 and 22; 1 Thes. 2:14; 2 Cor. 8:1; 1 Cor. 16:19; Acts 15:41 and 16:5; Rom. 16:16; 1 Cor. 11:16 and 14:33-34.

[4] Mt. 16:18 and 18:17; Acts 5:11; 8:3; 9:31; 12:1; 12:5; 11:26; 14:23; 14:27; 15:3; 15:4; 15:22; 18:22; 20:17; 20:28; 1 Cor. 6:4; 10:32; 11:18; 11:22; 12:28; 14:4; 14:12; 14:19; 14:23; 14:28; 14:35; 15:9; Gal. 1:13 and Phil. 3:6.

[5] Rom. 16:5; 1 Cor. 16:19; Col. 4:15; Philem. 2.

[6] Acts 8:1-3. The same is true of most of the passages in category (c). An exception could be made only for the passages Mt. 16:18; Acts 9:31; 20:28 (?); 1 Cor. 10:32 (?); and 12:28 (?) which are also the only ones which may not have in view the Church as a concrete local reality.

[7] It should be stressed that the problem as it is posed today does not stem from the texts but is artificial given that the antithetical scheme "localism vs. universalism" was alien to the mind of the primitive Church (see above, p. 21).

[8] The view that the "universal" Church precedes the "local" is held by (among others) P. Bratsiotis, " The Apostle Paul and the Unity of the Church" (in Greek), in *E.E.Th.S.* (years 1957-58), 1959, p. 154; R. Bultmann, "The Transformation of the Idea of the Church in the History of Early Christianity," in *Canadian Journal of Theology* 1 (1955), 73-81; and A. Medebielle in *Dictionnaire de la Bible*, Suppl. II, 1934, 660 and 668. The opposite view is taken by J.V. Campbell, "The Origin and Meaning of the Christian Use of the Word *Ekklesia*," in *Journal of Theological Studies* 49 (1948), 130 f. and 138; K. Schmidt, "Ekklesia" in *T.W.N.T.*, III, 503; and L. Cerfaux, *La Théologie de l'Église*... For a full bibliography, see K. Stendahl, "Kirche..," col. 1303 f.

[9] G. Konidaris, *On the Supposed Difference*, p. 29.

[10] *Messe und Herrenmahl*, 1926, p. 237.

[11] This reconstruction is attempted by Lietzmann (*Ibid.*)

[12] 2 Cor. 1:1.

[13] On the boundaries of Achaea at this time see G. Konidaris, *Church History of Greece*, I, 1954-60, pp. 44-47.

[14] See above, notes 2 and 3.

[15] Cf. verse 29, where "coming together unto judgement" is clearly connected with being a communicant of the Eucharist.

[16] See above, note 5.

[17] Most probably, even the term "church" had not yet prevailed everywhere as a technical term when Paul's Epistles were being written.

[18] Thus, for instance, the terms "Christianity," "Catholic Church," "Bishop," etc., which first appeared in purely local usage in Antioch and soon became technical terms for the entire Church. Cf. G. Konidaris, *On the Supposed Difference*, p. 45f.

[19] It is worth noting that one does not find an examination of "church in the household" either in H. Strack-P. Billerbeck, *Kommentar zum N.T.*, III, 1926, nor in the entry "ekklesia" in Kittel, *T.W.N.T.*

[20] E.g. "the household of Stephanas" (1 Cor. 1:16 and 16:15), of Crispus the ruler of the synagogue (Acts 18:8), of Lydia in Thyateira (Acts 16:15), of Narcissus and Aristobulos in Rome (Rom. 16:10-11). etc.

[21] *T.W.N.T.*, V, p. 132 f.

[22] See e.g. K. Hase, *Kirchengeschichte*, I, 1885, p. 210. Cf. also Winderstein, *Der Episcopat*, p. 38 *et infra*.

[23] E.g. E.A. Judge, *The Social Pattern of Christian Groups in the First Century*, 1960, pp. 30-39.

[24] Jeremias, J., *Hat die älteste Christenheit die Kindertaufe geubt?*, 1938 (1942²), and more recently *Die Kindertaufe in der ersten vier Jahrhunderten*, 1958.

[25] I Cor. 11:22.

[26] Acts 9:29; 13:14, 45; 14:1; 17:1-2, 10, 17; 18:19; 19:8.

[27] In Acts 5:42 we find Temple and house linked: "And every day in the temple and at home they did not cease teaching and preaching Jesus as the Christ." But this linkage refers to preaching. It should be noted that nowhere do we find such a linkage in connection with the Eucharist; the exclusive place for which was the Christian home.

[28] That this refers to the Eucharist is agreed by most modern scholars. See e.g. A. Arnold, *Der Ursprung des christlichen Abendmahl in Lichts der neusten liturgiegeschichtlichen Forschung*, 1932, pp. 43-47; W. Goosens, W., *Les origines de l'Eucharistie*, 1931, pp. 170-174 and J. Gewiess, *Die urapostolische Heilsverkundigung nach der Apostelgeschichte*, 1939, 99. 152-157.

[29] See above, p. 46f.

[30] E.g. "the Church in your [Philemon's] household" (Philem. 1:2) or "the Church in their [Priscilla and Aquila's] household" (Rom. 16:5). The houses from the first four centuries found in Rome by archaeologists, which had been turned into churches, bore the

names of their owners (S. Clementia etc.). On these churches, cf. J.A. Jungmann, *The Early Liturgy to the Time of Gregory the Great,* 1959, p. 13.

[31] This view is expressed, but with no reasons given, by L. Cerfaux, *La Théologie de l'Église,* p. 145 and P. Trembelas, "Worship in Apostolic Times in *Theologia* 31 (1960), 183.

[32] Rev. 1:10.

[33] Cf. D. Moraitis, *The Liturgy of the Presanctified* (in Greek), 1955, p. 12 f.

[34] See P. Bratsiotis, *The Revelation of the Apostle John* (in Greek), 1950.

[35] Ibid. p. 51.

[36] See P. Bratsiotis, "L'Apocalypse de Saint Jean dans le Culte de l'Église Grecque Orthodoxe," in *Revue d'Histoire and de Philosophie religieuse,* 42 (1962), 116-121.

[37] V. Ioannidis, "The Unity of the Church..." (in Greek), p. 172.

[38] 1 Cor. 10:15-17. Cf. P. Neuenzeit, *Das Herrenmahl. Studien zur Paulinischen Eucharistieauffassung,* 1958; K. Rahner, "Kirche und Sakrament," in *Geist und Leben* 28 (1955), 434 f. and R. Schnackenburg, *Die Kirche im Neuen Testament,* 1961, p. 41 f.

[39] 1 Cor. 10:16, taken together with 12:27 and Eph. 1:23; 4:12-16; 5:30; Col. 1:18-24.

[40] Gal. 3:28. Cf. 2 Cor. 11:2.

[41] Eph. 4:5.

[42] See M. Siotis, *Divine Eucharist* (in Greek), p. 50 f.

[43] Historical and literary differences of a liturgical character between these texts do not concern us here. On these see Lietzmann's work *Messe* etc. See also J. Betts, *op. cit.* p. 4 f. and especially D. Moriatis, *History of Christian Worship. Ancient Times (First to Fourth Century)* (in Greek), 1964, p. 56 f.

[44] See Mk 14:24; Mt. 26:28; Lk 22:20 and 1 Cor. 11:24.

[45] Cf. also H. Fries, "Die Eucharistie und die Einheit der Kirche," in *Pro Mundi Vita. Festschrift zum eucharistischen Weltkongress,* 1960, p. 165f.

[46] On this connection see J. Betz, "Eucharistie," in *L.T.K.,* III, 1959, col. 1143.

[47] The identity of the Servant of God is clearly applied by the Lord to Himself in Lk. 22:37 (= Is. 53:12), as also in all the passages concerning the sufferings of Jesus, while the correspondence between the story of the Servant and the account of the Lord's Passion is amazing (Mt. 27:38 or Mk 15:27 or Lk. 23:32 f., 39 = Is. 53:9). The view of this passage by modern exegetes as a *vaticinia ex eventu*

(e.g. R. Bultmann, *Geschichte der synoptischen Tradition*, 1951, p. 154 and *Theologie des N.T.*, I, 1953, p. 30), runs into insuperable difficulties, on which see O. Cullmann, *Die Christologie des N.T.*, 1957, p. 63f. More generally on the significance, only recently recognized, of the figure of the Servant in the Gospels, see W. Zimmerli – J. Jeremias, "?AI?," in *T.W.N.T.*, V, 636 f.; H.W. Wolff, *Jesajia 53 im Urchristentum*, 1950[2]; and O. Cullmann, "Jésus, serviteur de Dieu," in *Dieu vivant* 16 (1950), 17 f.

[48] The people of Israel appeared from the beginning as a strong unity in the formation of which strong religious and ethnic figures such as Moses and David had been a contributory factor. See V. Vellas, *Personalities of the O.T.* (in Greek), I, 1957[2], pp. 58, 66, 70, 80f. 121 etc. This unity was considered so profound and strong as to make the people of God one entity in it, relationship with its God. Hence, the repeated description of Israel in the O.T. through images of living organisms such as the vine (Is. 5:1 f., Hos. 10:1-2, Jer. 12:10, Ezek. 15:6), the cedar (Ezek. 17:22), the olive tree (Jer. 11:16), and indeed the son (Ex. 4:22-23, Hos. 11:1, Is. 49:14 etc.) and wife of God (Jer. 31:32, Masoretic text). It was within the context of this sense of organic unity that there arose the tradition of the Servant of Yahweh of which we get a clear picture in the Book of Isaiah, 40-55. The discussion of how this figure is to be interpreted belongs to others (see. V. Vellas, *op. cit.* p. 295 f.; P. Bratsiotis, *The Prophet Isaiah* (in Greek) 1956, p. 8 and N. Bratsiotis, *The Position of the Individual in the O.T.* (in Greek), I. Introduction, 1962). But regardless of whether the individualistic or the "collectivist" interpretation of this paradoxical figure is correct, the relationship to the point of identity between the Servant and the "many" whose sins he takes upon himself is a clear characteristic of this figure. This is recognized today not only by Protestant theology but by Roman Catholic theology as well, as shown by J. de Fraine's work *Adam et son Lignage: Études sur la "Personalité Corporative" dans la Bible*, 1959. This interpretation does not necessarily vitiate the individual characteristics of the Servant, which are beyond doubt, as V. Vellas proves (*op. cit.* p. 295 f.).

[49] 1 Clem. 59:2-4.

[50] *Didache* 10:2. Cf. also 9:2: "We thank Thee, our Father, for the holy vine of David thy servant (*pais*), which Thou hast made known to us through Jesus Thy servant." On the identification of both of these passages as Eucharistic texts see J.P. Audet, *La Didaché. Instruction des Apôtres*, 1948, p. 407. Cf. also D. Moraitis, *History of Christian Worship* (in Greek), p. 88.

[51] On the phrase "taking the form of a servant" as an allusion to the tradition concerning the Servant of God, see E. Lohmeyer, *Gottesknecht und Davidsohn*, 1945, p. 3 f. The same idea is also implied in Rom. 5:19 through the prominence given to the relationship of the "one" with the "many": "by *one man's* obedience *many* will be made righteous." This is a clear reference to Is. 53:11 where the Servant is presented as the one through whom "many" are justified.

[52] When the Lord is likened to the "lamb, who takes away the sin of the world" in Jn 1:29 and 36 (cf. also 19:36), this is a reference to the Servant who, in Is. 53:7, is likened to a "sheep." The same characterization is also prevalent in the Book of Revelation which is now clearly linked with the Eucharist by the fact that Christ who is offered is likened to a "lamb."

[53] The use of this title to denote the person of Jesus is so frequent in the Gospels (the term appears 69 times), occurring *exclusively* in the mouth of the Lord Himself, that many scholars consider this attribute "Son of Man" to be the most authentic expression of Jesus' understanding of Himself. (See e.g. J. Hering, *Le royaume de Dieu et sa venue*, 1952[2], p. 11 f. and S. Mowinckel, *He that Cometh*, 1956, p. 445 f. The rejection of the Christological sense of the term on literary grounds originated with H. Lietzmann, in his youthful work *Der Menschensohn. Ein Beitrag zur neutestamentlichen Theologie*, 1896, the reason being that the Aramaic term *barnasha* means simply "man" (Menschenkind); this view was later abandoned by Lietzmann himself, but found a supporter in J. Wellhausen (*Skizzen und Vorarbeiten*, VI, 1899, p. 187; cf. also P. Feine, *Theologie des N.T.*, 1934, pp. 57-70. Today, some reject the Christological sense of the term on the basis of textual criticism in those passages which refer to Jesus' activity on earth, "Son of Man" being thus seen as a property of Christ's future coming (see e.g. R. Bultmann, *Geschichte...*, 1958, pp. 124, 128, 163, 171 etc.; H.E. Todt, *Der Menschensohn in der synoptischen Überlieferung*, 1959, pp. 197-201 and J. Hering, *op. cit.* p. 142). Some scholars are also dubious about the passages referring to the future coming of the "Son of Man." So P. Vielhauer, "Gottesreich und Menschensohn in der Verkundigung Jesus', in *Festschrift für G. Dehn*, 1957, p. 51 f.; H.H. Conzelmann, in *Zeitschrift für Theologie und Kirche*, 54 (1957) 277 f. and P. Winter in *Theolog. Literaturzeitung* 85 (1960), 745 f. However, the objections of these liberal commentators conflict with the idea of a "hidden Messiah," who has an awareness of his identity as "Son of Man" but does not reveal it fully before his future coming

(see E. Sjöberg, *Der verborgene Menschensohn in den Evangelien*, 1955, p. 120 f. Cf. E. Schweitzer, "Der Menschensohn," in *Zeitschrift für die neutest. Wissenschaft* 50 (1959) 185-209). Besides, the Lord's identification of the "Son of Man" who will come in glory "on the clouds of heaven" with the humiliated Jesus on earth is clear in such passages as Mk 8:31; 10:45; Mt. 8:20 etc. On this identification see also A. Papageorgakopoulos, *The Son of Man* (in Greek), 1957, p.65 f.

[54] The tradition probably goes back to the Book of Daniel (7:13 f.). Cf. J. Coppens, "Le Fils d'Homme Daniélique et les Relectures de Dan. 7, 13 dans les Apocryphes et les Écrits du N.T.," in *Ephemerides Theologicae Lovanienses*, 37 (1961) 37.

[55] Earlier by F. Kattenbusch, "Der Quellort der Kirchenidee," in *Harnack-Festgabe*, 1921, p. 143. See also more recently Y. Congar, *The Mystery of the Church*, 1960, p. 85 f.

[56] This gave rise to the theory of "corporate personality," the chief exponents of which were J. Pedersen, *Israel: Its Life and Culture*, 1926; H. Wheeler Robinson, *The Hebrew Conception of Corporate Personality* (Werden und Wesen des A.T. Wissenschaft), 1936, p. 49 f. and A.R. Johnson, *The One and the Many in the Israelite Conception of God*, 1942. An extension of this theory to the whole of the Bible has been attempted more recently by both Protestant theologians (e.g. O. Cullmann, *Christus und die Zeit*, p. 99 f.) and Roman Catholics (e.g. de Fraine, *op. cit.*). On the O.T., cf. also N. Bratsiotis, *op. cit.*, p. 22 f.

[57] Such appears to be the relationship between the "Son of Man" and the "people of the saints" in Daniel 7:13-27. In the N.T., this same relationship is clearly presented in the depiction of the Judgement (Mt. 25:31-46) where the "Son of Man" identifies Himself completely with the group of "the least of these my brethren" (vv. 40 and 45). Cf, with certain reservations, the interpretation of T.W. Manson, *the Teaching of Jesus*, 1955, p. 265.

[58] See M. Siotis, *Divine Eucharist* (in Greek), p. 33 f. Cf. H. Fries, *loc. cit.*, p. 170 f.

[59] Jn 6:27.

[60] Jn 6:51.

[61] The principal characterization of the "Son of Man" in the Fourth Gospel is as "he who descended from heaven." See Jn 3:13, where the phrase "he who descended from heaven" is followed by the explanatory phrase "the Son of Man."

[62] Jn 6:53.

[63] Jn 6:48.

[64] Jn 6:56. One indication of the connection in the Fourth Gospel

between the "Son of Man" and the idea of the identity of Christ with the Church is the curious interchange between "I" and "we" in Jn 3:11-13: "Truly, truly, *I* say to you, *we* speak of what *we* know, and bear witness to what *we* have seen; but you do not receive *our* testimony. If *I* have told you earthly things and you do not believe, how can you believe if *I* tell you heavenly things? No one has ascended into heaven but he who descended from heaven, *the Son of Man.*" It should be noted that here again the "Son of Man" is mentioned. Cf. characteristically 1 Jn 1:1 f.

[65] Through their climax in Christ's prayer for unity "that they may all be one" (Jn 17).

[66] Jn 15:4-16.

[67] The Lord's description of Himself as the true vine in which the disciples are called to remain, comes precisely at the moment when He appeals to them, "Abide in me" (Jn 15:1-5), cannot be seen as unrelated to the idea of Israel as the "vine" (see above). For John, the Church, as comprising those who are "of the truth," is the true Israel (cf. C.H. Dodd, *The Interpretation of the Fourth Gospel*, 1953, p. 246) with which the "Son of Man" is identified. This is indicated, for example, by the way John transfers the passage from Gen. 28:12 into his Gospel (Jn 1:51) by replacing the word "Jacob" with the phrase "the Son of Man" (cf. C.H. Dodd, ibid.)

[68] See S. Agouridis, "Time and Eternity," *loc. cit.*, III, 1958, p. 114 and 150.

[69] The fact that the Pauline Churches had different ways of expressing their consciousness regarding the Divine Eucharist from those familiar to the Johannine Churches is indicated also by the different terminology they used to designate the Eucharist. Thus, for the Pauline Churches, the favored term is the "body," whereas, for the Johannine Churches, it is the "flesh" of Jesus Christ; perhaps on account of John's battle against Docetism, as was the case with Ignatius. See G.H.C. MacGregor, " The Eucharist in the Fourth Gospel," in *New Testament Studies* 9 (1963), 117. For both of these terms see J. Jeremias, *Die Abendmahlsworte Jesu*, 1949[2], p. 103 f. In the end the Pauline term "body of Christ" to denote the Eucharist prevailed in the Church as is shown by the ancient phrase "The Body of Christ" which accompanied the giving of Holy Communion, and to which the communicant answered "Amen" (see Hippolytus, *Apost. Trad.*, ed. Dix, p. 41; *Apost. Const.* VIII:13:15; and Eusebius, *Eccl. Hist.* VI:43:19).

[70] For a detailed analysis of these images see P. Minear, *Images of the Church in the New Testament*, 1960. Cf. also E. Mersch, *Le corps*

mystique du Christ, I, p. 143 f.

[71] See *inter alios* E. Schweitzer, "??MA," in *T.W.N.T.;* eiusdem "Die Kirche als Leib Christi in den Paulinischen Antilegomena," in *Theolog. Literaturzeitung,* (1961) 241-256.; D. Michel, *Das Zeugnis des N.T. von der Gemeinde,* 1941, p. 44 f.; J.A.T. Robinson, *The Body,* 1952; E. Best, *One Body in Christ,* 1955; R.P. Shedd, *Man in Community,* 1958, p. 161 f.; R. Bultmann, "The Transformation of the Idea of the Church...," in *Canadian Journal of Theology,* 1 (1955) 73-81; K. Barth, *Kirchliche Dogmatik,* IV/1, 1963, p. 741.; P. Minear, op. cit.; J. Schneider, *Die Einheit der Kirche nach N.T.,* 1936, p. 60 f. For RC views see *inter alios* T. Soiron, *Die Kirche als der Leib Christi nach der Lehre des hl. Paulus,* 1951, p. 9-32; H. Dieckmann *Die Verfassung der Urkirche, dargestellt auf Grund der Paulusbriefe und der Apostelgeschichte,* 1923, p. 107 f.; F. Mussner, *Christus, das All und die Kirche,* 1955; L. Cerfaux, *La Théologie...,* p. 150ff; and J. Hamer, *L'Église est une communion,* 1962, p. 50 f. For an Orthodox view in very general terms, see V. Ioannidis, "The Unity," *loc. cit.* p. 178 f.

[72] Cf. C.T. Craig, *The One Church in the Light of the N.T.,* 1951, p. 21: "The identification of the Church with the Body of Christ cannot be understood apart from the Eucharistic word 'This is my body'." Cf. H. Schlier, *Die Zeit der Kirche. Exegetische Aufsätze und Vorträge,* 1962³, p. 246 f. and R. Schnackenburg, op. cit., p. 158 f.

[73] For details, see A.D.J. Rawlinson, "Corpus Christi," in *Mysterium Christi* (ed. G.A. Bell and A. Deissmann), 1930, p. 225 f.

[74] See L. Strack – P. Billerbeck, *Kommentar,* III, p. 446 f.

[75] See e.g. R. Bultmann, "The Transformation...," ibid., pp. 73-81.

[76] See e.g. V. Ioannidis, "The Unity," loc. cit. p. 179, where the source of the term is regarded as being the story told by the Roman Menenius Agrippa who was trying to emphasize to the rebellious Roman plebeians that the citizens of a state are like the members of a body.

[77] This is in response primarily to the view set out in the preceding note.

[78] 1 Cor. 3:9; 14:5,12; 2 Cor. 12:19; Eph. 2:21, 4:12, 4:16.

[79] 1 Tim. 3:15; Heb. 3:6; 1 Pet. 2:5.

[80] The notion of "building" (*oikodomê*) here is not static. The Church is "being built up," i.e. she "increases." Cf. 1 Cor. 14:4; 1 Thes. 5:11; 1 Pet. 2:5 in combination with 1 Cor. 3:6-7; Eph. 2:21, 4:15-16; Col. 1:10, 2:19; 1 Pet. 2:2.

[81] 2 Cor. 11:2 and Eph. 4:13.

[82] The interpretation of the term *pleroma* presents difficulties for which see F. Mussner, op. cit. p. 46 f. Cf. also H. Schlier, *Die Zeit der*

Kirche, p. 170 f. But whether the word is given an active meaning (= the Church as complement of Christ), as favored by ancient exegetes including St John Chrysostom, or a passive meaning (= the Church is fulfilled through Christ), as favored by modern commentators, it still makes no sense without the idea of an ontological interdependency between Christ and the Church.

[83] Eph. 4:13. Cf. 1:23.

[84] This is clear at least in Hebrews 12:22-24 and 13:10, where the allusion is certainly to the Eucharist as shown by the verb "to eat." Cf. D. Stone, *A History of the Doctrine of the Holy Eucharist*, I, 1959, p. 15, and perhaps also the relevant passages of 1 Peter.

[85] 1 Cor. 6:15, 12:12, 12:27; Eph. 4:25, 5:30 etc.

[86] Eph. 5:29 f. Cf. also the whole of Paul's argument in 1 Cor. 6:15 f.

[87] Unity *per se* was not a characteristic exclusive to the Church. In the Roman Empire, the formation of "associations" was such a widespread practice that there were special laws governing the affairs of the various organizations which were known by the term *collegia* (see Tacitus, *Annals* 14.17; Pliny, *Ad Traj.* 34.97; Minucius Felix, *Octavius* 8-9 and Origen, *Against Celsus* 1.1. Cf. J.P. Waltzing, *Étude Historique sur les Corporations Professionels des Romains*, I, pp. 113-129 and Th. Mommsen, *Le droit penal romain*, II, pp. 274-8). The love and mutual support which prevailed among the members of these *collegia* was extraordinary and was organized through a common fund to which each would contribute monthly (*stips menstrua*); thus, the members would address each other as "brethren" (*fratres, sodales, socii*). Cf. F.X. Kraus, "Fraternitas," in *Realencyclopaedie der christl. Altertumer*, I, 1880, p. 540). Apart from the pagans, the Jews who lived within the Roman Empire came together in special communities under their own ethnarch (cf. E. Schürer, *Geschichte des jüdischen Volkes*, 1914, pp. 14,17). The brotherly love between them was strong, and was manifest especially in groups such as the Essenes whose life was organized on principles of common property (cf. L. Philippidis, *History*, p. 480 f.) To characterize the Church's unity as simply a "communion of love," therefore, does not satisfy the historian who sees the Church as a *sui generis* unity.

[88] E.g. E. Hatch, *The Organization of the Early Christian Churches*, 1888, p. 26 f. and L. Duchesne, *Histoire Ancienne de l'Église*, I, 1906, pp. 381-87.

[89] The connection of the Eucharist with the essence of the Church (see above, Introduction) should be especially stressed because it is precisely on this point that R. Sohm goes astray in his attempt to

connect the origin of Canon Law with the Eucharist.

[90] On this see H. Chirat, *L'Assemblée Chrétienne à l'Âge Apostolique* (ser. Lex Orandi No. 10), 1949, passim and esp. p. 188 f.

[91] This is clear in the book of the Apocalypse (see above p. 51); but also in Hebrews, where worship dominates, the "altar" of the Eucharist (see above p. 64, n. 83) is linked with "Mount Zion and the city of the living God, the heavenly Jerusalem, and to innumerable angels, and to the festal gathering and assembly of the firstborn who are enrolled in heaven, and to a judge who is God of all..." (12:22 f.).

[92] Heb. 12:2, Col. 3:1, Eph. 1:2 and esp. Phil. 2:6-11, where we most likely have a hymn used in the worship of the primitive Church (cf. above, p. 56). I. Karavidopoulos, *The Christological Hymn in Phil. 2:6-11* (in Greek), 1963.

[93] Eph. 4:5.

[94] Rev. 1:5.

[95] Heb. 8:2.

[96] Heb. 5:6; 8:4; 10:21; 2:17.

[97] Heb. 3:1.

[98] Rom. 15:8; Lk 22:77; cf. Phil. 2:7; Mt 12:18; Acts 3:13, 4:27.

[99] 1 Pet. 2:25; 5:4; Heb. 13:20.

[100] Mt 23:8; Jn 13:13.

[101] Col. 1:18.

[102] See above, p. 53 f., on the relation of the One to the "Many" united in Him.

[103] Cf. the phrase in the Liturgy of St John Chrysostom, "Who art enthroned on high with the Father, and invisibly present here with us."

[104] This is especially evident in the Apocalypse and in Hebrews, and also in Ignatius on whom see below.

[105] G. Konidaris, *On the Supposed Difference*, p. 34 f.

[106] Cf. F.M. Braun, *Neues Licht auf die Kirche*, p. 179.

[107] As is the opinion of e.g. B.O. Beicke, *Glaube und Leben der Urgemeinde*, 1957, p. 25 f.

[108] Between the Apostle (lit. "sent one") and Christ the sender there exists a mystical relationship. Christ Himself is working in and through the Apostle: "He who hears you hears me, and he who rejects you rejects me" (Lk 10:16. Cf. 1 Thes. 4:8).

[109] See p. 65ff.

[110] Cf. K. Mouratidis, *Diversification, Secularization and Recent Developments in the Law of the Roman Catholic Church* (in Greek), 1961, p. 36: "The divine factor dominates during this period (i.e.

the initial period) in the organization of the Church...."

[111] Heb. 3:14. Thus, from the viewpoint of participation in the body of Christ, the Church, there is complete equality of her members irrespective of what order they belong to. This is expressed *par excellence* in the Divine Eucharist in which from the beginning all orders of the Church had to participate. Cf. G. Dix, *The Shape of the Liturgy* p. 195 f. and I. Kotsonis, *The Place of the Laity in Church Organization* (in Greek), 1956, p. 32 f.

[112] "Are all Apostles?," asks Paul (1 Cor. 12:29).

[113] "They shall all be taught by God," indeed (Jn 6:45); but not all are teachers (1 Cor. 12:29 and Jas 3:1).

[114] Acts 6:1-6.

[115] The same should be said of Christ's priesthood. He is the Priest (see n. 96 above) just as He is the Apostle or the Teacher; and the members of His Church, as constituting His body which is offered by the priests in the Eucharist, form a "priesthood" (it should be noted that both 1 Pet. 2:5-9 and Rev. 5:10, where a royal priesthood is mentioned, occur within Eucharistic texts). But as not all partake of His apostolic or other properties, so not all are able to partake of His priestly property. A general priesthood would have been as comprehensible to primitive Christianity as a general apostolicity or diaconate etc.

[116] Cf. J. Colson, op. cit. p.49 f.: "If all the faithful are members of the same Body in Jesus Christ, not all of these members are identical and not all have the same function. The grace of God is multiform, and the gifts of the Spirit various."

[117] It is by no means accidental that although the Church separated from the Eucharist many sacraments which were once connected with it she never did this with the ordination of priests.

[118] 1 Cor. 14:40.

[119] This distinction was introduced by Harnack, *Die Lehre der zwolf Apostel...* (Texte und Untersuchungen, II, 1884, pp. 145-149), perhaps under the influence of E. Hatch's work *The Organization of the Early Church...*, as O. Linton thinks, op. cit. p. 36 f. (cf. also E. Foerster, *R. Sohms Kritik des Kirchenrechtes*, 1942, p. 51 f.). It was subsequently established in historiography by Lietzmann and Heussi through their church histories.

[120] See e.g. J. Klein, *Grundlegung und Greuzen des Kanonisches Rechtes*, 1947, p. 10 f.

[121] See 1 Tim. 3:2, 5:17; 2 Tim. 2:2; Tit. 1:9; Heb. 13:7; Jas. 5:14 etc.

[122] On the subject of ordination as the laying on of hands to convey a particular blessing see J. Behm, *Die Handauflegung in*

Urchristentum nach Verwendung, Herkunft und Bedeutung, 1911; J. Coppens, *L'Imposition des Mains et les Rites Connexes dans le N.T.*, 1925; M. Kaiser, *Die Einheit der Kirchengewalt nach den Zeugnis des N.T. und der Apostolischen Vater*, 1956, p. 104 f. Cf. also M. Siotis, "Die klassische und die christliche Cheirotonie in ihrem Verhältnis," in *Theologia* 20 (1949), 21 (1950) and 22 (1951). Especially for installation in a specific ministry, ordination was commonplace in apostolic times. So, for example, in Acts 13:1-3 (despite the doubts of J. Brosch, *Charismen und Amter in der Urkirche*, 1951, p. 163 and M. Kaiser, op. cit. p. 38), Acts 6:6 and 14:23 (Cf M. Kaiser, op. cit. p. 94). Likewise in 1 Tim. 4:14 and 2 Tim. 1:6. The term "appoint" (Ti. 1:5) must also include or presuppose an act of ordination even though it has a special meaning (see. G. Konidaris, *On the Supposed Difference*, p. 31.

[123] Cf. H. Schlier, in *Glaube und Geschichte, Festschrift für F. Gogarten*, 1948, p. 44 f. and G. Konidaris, op. cit. p. 31

[124] See 1 Cor. 14:16 and 23 f. in combination with 14:40.

[125] Thus in Romans 12:6 deacons are placed before teachers, and in Ephesians 4:11, pastors come before teachers, etc. Besides, the view that the charismatics formed a special order and organization in the primitive Church cannot be supported from 1 Corinthians 12:28 on which Harnack and subsequent historiography tried to base it. A simple comparison of the list of charismatics contained in this passage with the similar list in Romans 12:6-9 and the explanations Paul gives in 1 Corinthians 14:6 is sufficient to demonstrate that in 1 Corinthians 12:28, Paul is not in any way referring to the administration of the Church in Corinth. Nothing could justify Harnack's supposition that the "prophets" and "teachers" in 1 Corinthians 12:28 constitute special "orders" of ministers in the local Church more than the obviously groundless supposition that "he who contributes in liberality" and "he who does acts of mercy with cheerfulness," who are numbered with the prophets and teachers in Romans 12:6-9, also formed special "orders" in the Church!

[126] The separation of administration from the charism of priesthood in such a way that a distinction is created between "administrative" and "spiritual" spheres of competence is a product of Western scholastic theology. This separation was accepted and enshrined by the Roman Catholic Church which can, thus, entrust higher administrative responsibilities to church members of lower clerical rank (cardinals, for instance, may be deacons or even laymen, without this preventing them from carrying out ad-

ministrative functions superior to the bishops).

[127] Many of the Protestant historians base their views on the polity of the primitive Church exclusively on such arguments from silence. So for example, E. Schweizer, *Gemeinde und Gemeindenordnung im Neuen Testament*, 1959, 5b; 5m and elsewhere

[128] Clearly all participated through hymns, speaking in tongues etc.

[129] 1 Cor. 14:16.

[130] 1 Clement 40:3-41:4 "For his own proper services are assigned to the high priest, and their own proper place is prescibed to the priests, and their own proper ministrations devolve on the Levites. The layman is bound by the laws that pertain to laymen. Let every one of you, brethren, be well-pleasing to God in his own order, living in all good conscience, not going beyond the rule of the ministry prescribed to him..."

[131] Justin, *1 Apol.* 65. Cf. P. Rouget, *Amen. Acclamation du peuple sacerdotal*, 1947.

[132] In this case, this is not an arbitrary procedure from the viewpoint of historical method if one takes into account that the Roman Church was distinguished for its strict conservatism in the early centuries. Thus, on the basis of 1 Clement which forms a link between the Corinth we know from St Paul and the Rome known to Justin, we are justified in believing that the situation, regarding the Eucharistic assembly, did not change substantially during the period of time covered by these texts

[133] G. Konidaris, *On the Supposed Difference*, p. 70 (note): "The presidents / presbyters / bishops who took the place of the Apostles probably did not dare to emphasize the same name more strongly. They lived under the shadow of the name of the Apostles and of their authority."

[134] See Acts 20:7-12, where Paul presides at the assembly the purpose of which was to "break bread."

[135] *Didache* 10:7: "Allow the prophets to give thanks as long as they wish." It is probable that Acts 13:2, "While they [i.e. the prophets and teachers] were worshipping [*leitourgounton*] the Lord," also implies a liturgical function for these charismatics, as J. Colson thinks, op. cit. p. 31.

[136] Acts 21:18.

[137] This conclusion may be deduced from the fact that the presbyters already appear with the Apostles at the Apostolic Council (Acts 15:2, 4, 6, 22, "Apostles and presbyters." The origin of the presbyters is an obscure historical problem. On this see the theo-

ries of G. Dix, "Ministry in the Early Church," in *The Apostolic Ministry* (ed. Kirk), 1946, p.233 f.; A.M. Farrer, ibid. p. 143 f.; Bornkamm, in *T.W.N.T.*, VI, p. 655 f. and W. Michaelis, *Das Altestenamt*, 1953, pp. 35-39. The most probable view seems to be that of G. Dix, according to which presbyters go back to the Jewish tradition.

[138] Acts 6:2ff; Phil. 1:1 and 1 Tim. 3:1. Their origin, in contrast to the presbyters and contrary to the view of G. Dix ("Ministry," p. 232 f.) should be sought in the Churches of Gentile origin, according to von Campenhausen, *Kirchliches Amt und geistliche Vollmacht*, 1953, p. 84.

[139] On the close connection of the deacons with the Eucharist, see G. Dix, op. cit. p. 245 f. It is noteworthy that a similar close relation existed between deacons and bishops probably deriving from the original position of the former as assistants to the Apostles (see Acts 19:22, 13:5; Rom. 16:21; 2 Cor. 8:23 and Phil. 2:25), and the capacity of the latter as successors to the Apostles particularly in the Divine Eucharist. See below.

[140] G. Konidaris, op. cit. p. 26.

[141] ibid. p. 42 f.

[142] In his work *On the Supposed Difference*, etc.

[143] M. Kaiser (op. cit. p. 174) is right in stressing that the absence of the Bishop from the NT is connected with the presence and prestige of the Apostles there. We should make clear, however, that this absence relates only to the title of bishop and not to the institution *per se* (cf. G. Konidaris, op. cit. p. 13). The presence of the Apostles meant that the Bishop became invisible in the sources, but not in practice.

[144] Cf. G. Konidaris, *On the Regional and Chronological Limits to the use of the term "Bishops and Deacons,"* 1960.

[145] I Clem. 44:1-3.

[146] Elsewhere he speaks of Enoch and Noah as "ministering" (9:2-4); and similarly of the angels (34:5) and of the O.T. prophets as ministers of God's grace (8:1).

[147] I Clem. 44:4.

[148] Cf. G. Konidaris, "Apostolic Succession" (in Greek), in *Threskevtiki kai Ethiki Enkyklopaedia*, IV, 1964, col. 1116.

[149] "Apostolic Succession: A. The original conception. B. The problem of non-catholic orders," in *Essays on the Early History of the Church and the Ministry*, H.B. Swete (ed.), 1918, pp. 93-214.

[150] See A. Ehrhardt, *The Apostolic Succession in the First Two Centuries of the Church*, 1953 and F. Dvornik, *The Idea of Apostolicity in Byzantium and the Legend of Saint Andrew*, 1958, p. 39 f.

[151] *Didache* 10:7.

[152] This transfer of powers is attested by 1 Clement and the *Didache*.

[153] Ignatius, *Magn.* 6:1.

[154] Rev. 4-5. In linking the Apocalypse with the Divine Eucharist here, we are not making arbitary use of an apocalyptic text as an historical source. The Apocalypse was not written without relation to the Church life of its day and particularly the Divine Eucharist. There is a widespread tendency in modern scholarship to regard even the hymns of the Apocalypse (Rev. 4:11, 5:9-14 and 17 f.) as hymns from the Divine Eucharist. See e.g. F.J. Doelger, *Sol Salutis. Gebet und Gesang im Christlichen Altertum. Rücksicht auf die Ostung im Gebet und Liturgie*, 1925, p. 127 and C. Ruch, "La Messe d'après la sainte Écriture," in *D.T.C.*, X, 858.

[155] Cf. W. Telfer, *The Office of a Bishop*, 1962, p. 93.

[156] For the term "presbyter" in the Apocalypse as meaning not angels but men, see P. Bratsiotis, *The Apocalypse* (in Greek), p. 119 f. and esp. p. 122. The fact that the reference here is not to human beings in general or the faithful in their entirety, but to a particular order, is shown by the clear distinction made between the "presbyters" and the "saints" (= all members of the Church regardless of order) in Rev. 5:8. There is thus no reason to reject the interpretation according to which this passage has to do with the institution of presbyters and in particular their place in the Eucharistic assembly, especially given that, as Professor P. Bratsiotis observes (ibid. p. 122), "this heavenly liturgy [in the Apocalypse] is a type of the earthly liturgy according to the Orthodox understanding." Ignatius" phrase "the Bishop with the presbyterium" (*Smyrn.* 8:1 and *Eph.* 20:2) most likely also takes its origin from the celebration of the Divine Eucharist which Ignatius had in mind. This hypothesis is supported by the fact that this phrase appears immediately after a reference to the Eucharist and as part of Ignatius' more general effort to underline its unity.

[157] This arrangement of the Eucharist is likewise presupposed by texts such as Justin's *First Apology*, 65 and 67; Hippolytus, *Apost. Trad.* (Dix, 6 and 40f.) etc.

[158] The Johannine understanding of the Divine Eucharist was precisely theocentric: "My Father gives you the true bread from heaven" (Jn 6:32). The Bishop who occupied the throne in the Altar was therefore seen as the living icon of God or of Christ (Ignatius, *Tral.* 3:1 and *Magn.* 3:1). Anyone who does not obey the "visible" bishop "seeks to mock the one who is invisible," i.e. God (*Magn.*

3:2). Cf. likewise the connection between the "unity of God" and "unity in the *episcope*" which Ignatius makes in *Polyc.* 8:3. The conception that the Bishop is an "icon of Christ" was long preserved (see Ps-Clement, Hom. 3:62 – Syria, fourth century).

[159] See above, Introduction.

[160] Ignatius, *Magn.* 6: "Be united with the Bishop." It is worthy of particular note that Ignatius "does not hesitate to characterize union with Christ as union with the Bishop" (K. Bonis, "St Ignatius the Godbearer and His Views on the Church" (in Greek), in *Orthodoxos Skepsis* 1 (1958), 39.

PART II

FORMATION

Unity in the Divine Eucharist and the Bishop, and the Formation of the "Catholic Church"

Chapter One

ONE EUCHARIST - ONE BISHOP IN EACH CHURCH

The identification of the eucharistic assembly with the Church of God herself had as a direct consequence the preservation of *one Eucharist* in each Church under the leadership of the presiding Bishop. This appears clearly for the first time in the epistles of Ignatius who writes, "Take heed, then, to have but *one Eucharist*. For there is one flesh of our Lord Jesus Christ, and one cup for union with His Blood; one altar, as there is also *one Bishop* with the presbyterium and the deacons."[1] From this passage it is quite clear that for St Ignatius, who, as we have seen, linked the Bishop inseparably with the Eucharist and the unity of the Church,[2] unity in the Divine Eucharist and in the Bishop presupposed *one* eucharistic assembly, *one* altar and *one* Bishop in each Church.

This raises the question: was there actually only one Eucharist, "under the leadership of the Bishop,"[3] in each Church; or does this passage quoted represent merely a desire and exhortation on Ignatius' part? This question is fundamental from an historical viewpoint, and has important implications for ecclesiology which will be discussed in the following chapter.

Many scholars studying the passage of St Ignatius quoted above have maintained the view that at the time Ignatius was writing his epistles there were many eucharistic assemblies in each Church because otherwise – according to them – he would not have written in those terms. This argument cannot be taken seriously because it is possible that Ignatius had simply discerned tendencies towards the creation of

parallel eucharistic assemblies without this meaning necessarily that the gathering of all the faithful of each Church
into one Eucharist under the Bishop was not the regular state
of affairs prevailing at the time. That such divisive tendencies did exist in the Churches to which Ignatius was writing
is clear from his repeated admonitions to the Christians not
to follow heretics and schismatics. Despite this, Ignatius repeatedly stresses that what he writes about schism is
precautionary in character: "I say these things, my beloved,
not because I know any of you to be so disposed; but, being
as I am less than all of you, I want to *protect you in advance*."[4]
That his admonition to maintain one Eucharist under one
Bishop and at one altar must have the same sense, is shown
by the affirmation that comes immediately before it: "*Not
that I have found any division among you, but disintegration
(apodiylismos[5])*."[6] It is clear, then, that for Ignatius himself the
admonition to maintain one Eucharist does not necessarily
presuppose an existing state of affairs to the contrary.

But if Ignatius' exhortation to maintain one Eucharist in
each Church is seen as reflecting a corresponding historical
reality, this gives rise to two questions which are fundamental for the history of the Church's unity in the Divine
Eucharist and in the Bishop.

Firstly: if it is true, as we have seen, that the "Church in
the household" of apostolic times signified the assembly to
celebrate the Eucharist, were there not more than one of these
"household Churches" in each city, and therefore more than
one eucharistic assembly?

Secondly: what would happen with the Christians out in
the countryside if the only eucharistic assembly in each
Church was initially that "under the leadership of the
Bishop," as Ignatius would have it?

It is not easy to give an answer to these two questions
because the sources are not only incomplete, but also indif-
ferent to our historical curiosity. In consequence, the
examination of the few sources we do have will require
minute and penetrating observation.

1. The one Eucharist under the leadership of the Bishop and the "Church in the household"

The prevailing view is that the "Church in the household" (*kat' oikon ekklesia*) was a sort of semi-official gathering in various houses within the local Church. This view is prevalent not only among those who identify the Church in the household with prominent Christian families,[7] but also among those who accept it as an assembly to celebrate the Eucharist.[8] If this view is accepted, it then follows that the "Church in the household" did not bring together the whole of the local Church, but formed a sort of smaller ecclesial unit within it, more than one of which could exist in each city. This view automatically comes into conflict with the fact that, as we have seen, Paul knows of only one Church in each city. So either the "Church in the household" is a "church," in which case there should not be more than one of them in a city; or else it is not a full "church," in which case the existence of more than one in the same city would be justified. It is, therefore, of cardinal importance for the present study to examine whether the prevailing view outlined above has any basis in the sources.

Of all the passages containing the term "Church in the household," Rom. 16:4 appears to be the only one capable of throwing light on our problem. If we take a look at the section of the text in which the term appears, we shall see that the "Church in the household" of Priscilla and Aquila is not the only group Paul refers to. "Greetings" are sent not only to individuals, such as Epaenetus, Mary etc., but also to groups and families in Rome. Thus, we find "those who belong to the family of Aristobulus" (v. 10), "those in the Lord who belong to the family of Narcissus (v.11), "Rufus, eminent in the Lord, and his mother" (v. 13), "Asyncretus, Phlegon, Hermas, Patrobus, Hermes and the brethren who are with them" (v. 14), and "Philologus and Julia, Nereus and his sister, and Olympas, and all the saints who are with them" (v. 15). These groups clearly show that at that time within the local Church certain Christians stood out who, it seems, had come to know Christianity and had perhaps spread it not as individuals, but as groups (cf. the baptism of whole "households," i.e. families, such as that of Stephanas in Corinth, etc.). But it is noteworthy and interesting that although a great number of such groups are referred to in Romans 16, *only one of them, that of Priscilla and Aquila, is called by the name of "Church in the household."* All the other groups are either not described at all, or else they are called "brethren" or "saints" – names common to all Christians. This highly significant detail, which has gone unnoticed by those who hold that there existed many "Churches in the household" within the local Church, forces us to ask: *Why does Paul use the term "Church in the household" for only one of these groups?* The answer cannot be that it is pure chance because the number of groups among which the "Church in the household" appears in the text under discussion is such that it would be natural to expect another instance of "Church in the household." Nowhere in the sources, however, do we find more than one "household Church" in each city. In Rome, we have the "Church in the household" of Priscilla and Aquila singled out amidst many other groups and families, none of which is described as a "church."[9] In Colossae, we have that of Philemon during the period of Paul's imprisonment in Rome (Philem. 2); in Laodicea that of Nymphas (Col. 4:15); in Corinth that of Priscilla and Aquila while they were living there (1 Cor. 16:19).[10] In which of the sources do we find support for the prevailing view that there were many "Churches in the household" in each city?

But there are also more explicit pieces of evidence against the prevailing view. In Rom. 16:23, we read about a certain Gaius who is called "host to me [Paul] and *to the whole church.*" This is undoubtedly a reference to the "Church in the household"[11] in Corinth from where Paul is writing to the Romans. As this passage informs us, Gaius used to offer his house to Paul whenever the latter was in Corinth, and also to the whole Church of Corinth for her eucharistic assemblies, which, in keeping with the spirit of 1 Corinthians,[12] expressed the very Church of God. If, then, as is usually believed, the "Church in the household" signified a semi-official assembly of Christians, and if there were many such "churches" in each city, how are we to understand the fact here that Gaius is called host to the *whole Church*? The phrase "the whole Church" is used by Paul also in 1 Cor. 14:23: "if therefore the whole church comes together in the same place." That this passage too refers to the eucharistic assembly identified with the "whole Church" is shown by the verb "come together" (*synelthê*), and by the fact that the eucharistic gathering or "church" in Corinth of 1 Corinthians 11 continues to be implied here.[13] It follows that the eucharistic gathering, which at the time of the Epistle to the Romans was hosted in Gaius' house in Corinth, included "the whole church," i.e. all the Christians in Corinth. Therefore, the "Church in the household" of Gaius was not a "semi-official" church or one of the many in Corinth, but the full and catholic[14] Church of Corinth. Only when one "household Church" has ceased to exist should we look for another within the same local Church. As long as a "church in a household" existed, it constituted the *whole* Church of God in that city.[15]

These conclusions follow from the passages which refer clearly to the "Church in the household." The same conclusions can also be drawn from an examination of the passages which refer to the Church in the household without using that term. Thus, in Acts 2:46, we read that the Eucharist was celebrated "in the house" or "at home" (*kat' oikon*).[16] Despite the difficulties this passage presents to commentators, one detail should be underlined: the term "house" is used in the singular. We are unable to comprehend how it is possible to interpret this passage as meaning "breaking bread from house to house" or "in their houses."[17] This not only makes the text, incomprehensible – how is it possible for the Eucharist to move from house to house[18] or to be celebrated by each family at home? – but it also goes against the sense of the text which may be paraphrased roughly as follows: The prayer of the first Christians was performed in the Jewish temple, but not the breaking of bread; this took place in the house and not in the temple. If the phrase *kat' oikon* is kept strictly within its context, then the meaning of the passage

becomes clear. The fact that the breaking of bread took place
kat' oikon (singular) and not *kat' oikous* (plural) implies that
the Eucharist was not celebrated at several houses simultaneously but only in one. This conclusion becomes more
certain if it is taken into account that the author of Acts is not
unaware of the plural form *kat' oikous*, as can be seen from
Acts 8:3[19] and 20:20,[20] *but he never uses it in connection with the
Eucharist*. The question inevitably arises: why could other
ecclesial activities, such as preaching, be performed "from
house to house," whereas the Eucharist was celebrated "in
the house"? The answer would perhaps be difficult were it
not for the fact that all the texts we have looked at point in
the same direction: to the existence of only one Eucharist in
each city. Thus the "Church in the household" did not fragment the Church, but expressed in a quite real way the unity
of each Church in one Eucharist.

If the "Church in the household" as a term appears exclusively in the Epistles of Paul, its content, as the "whole
Church" united in one Eucharist in each city, should not be
restricted either to the Pauline Churches or to apostolic times.
It is, of course, a fact that the Epistles of Paul form our only
source, but we are able to recognize a broader character in
the information the Apostle gives owing to the fact that it
seems he was aware of the prevailing situation in all the
Churches as regards the Eucharist. This at least is the indication of his express conviction that he knows the traditions
and "practices" of all the Churches,[21] to which, besides, he
extends his care.[22] Besides, the Church of Jerusalem – the most
powerful in terms of its influence on the other Churches
around the world [23] – does not seem to have differed from
the Pauline Churches in respect of the "Church in the household," as is shown by the passages of Acts examined above.

In the post-apostolic era the "Church in the household"
no longer existed as a term,[24] but it continued to exist in practice up till the time when the Christians acquired special
church buildings of their own for the celebration of the Eucharist.[25] The existence of the one Eucharist equally continued

beyond the apostolic period as an expression of the oneness of the local Church, and despite the increase in the number of Christians. The earliest text of the post-apostolic era, 1 Clement, hints at the existence of *one* Eucharist[26] while St Ignatius insists that the faithful of Philadelphia should come together into "one Eucharist."[27] But a clear and noteworthy testimony to the preservation of the single Eucharist right up to the middle of the second century, or at a time when the number of Christians must have increased significantly, especially in Rome, is given by Justin. When in 163/5 Justin was facing a martyr's death, he tried to evade the prefect's questions. But, when asked again insistently, he replied that he knew only one place in Rome where the Christians gathered and that was the house of a certain Martinus by the Timiotinian Baths.[28] This information does not of course tell us whether the gathering Justin refers to is for the Eucharist. But if this is assumed, then this information becomes highly significant. Apart from this vague piece of information, however, Justin gives us another *quite clear* indication, strictly historical in character, of the fact that in Rome around the middle of the second century the Christians (and this is still more significant) not only of Rome but also of the surrounding villages would come together for one sole Eucharist: "and on the day called Sunday, there is a gathering *in the same place* of *all those living in cities or country areas.*"[29]

If this was what happened, then, in the large and diverse[30] Church of Rome, we can imagine not only how much more naturally it would have happened in the other Churches, but, above all, how important the Church must have considered it to preserve the integrity of the Eucharist in each city. The conservatism of the Roman Church, known also from other areas,[31] preserved the primitive ecclesiology unadulterated, at least up to the middle of the second century: where there is one Church, there is one Eucharist under the leadership of one Bishop, who presides over both.[32]

Let us see now how this principle was preserved when Christianity spread outside the cities into the country areas.

2. The one Eucharist under the leadership of the Bishop and the Christians in the countryside.

Christianity made its appearance as a religion of the cities.[33] We find the first evidence for the spread of Christianity into the countryside around the beginning of the second century or end of the first.[34] Already around the middle of the second century, Justin tells us that there were Christians in the villages around Rome.[35] As regards civil organization, these Christians came under the rural prefectures know in the Roman empire as *pagi* (country areas) or *vici* (villages) as opposed to the cities (*civitas, urbs, oppidum*) which alone enjoyed full self-government as *respublicae*.[36] But while for the pagans these "country areas" and "villages" formed independent religious communities united around the worship of the gods and often having their own *genius pagi* or local deity,[37] the Christians of the country areas were from the beginning attached to the worship performed in the city. This is of great importance for history, and shows that it was wrong to seek the model for the rural parish and its origin in the political division of the Roman state.[38] The organization of the Church appears to have developed in a manner of its own, dictated by the fundamental ecclesiological principles which we have seen. Appearing from the beginning as one eucharistic assembly under the leadership of one Bishop, the Church developed her organization in a manner consistent with this original form of hers which, as we have seen, was inextricably bound up with serious theological presuppositions. Thus, as far as the sources allow us to discover, at least until the middle of the second century (composition of Justin's *First Apology*), the Christians of the villages formed *one* ecclesial unity with the Christians of the city near which they lived. This was true at least for Rome where Justin was writing without however excluding the Churches of the East whose life was not unknown to this writer and which he seems to have included in his description of the eucharistic assemblies.[39] In consequence, any investigation into the detachment of the village Christians from the city to form their own eucharistic assembly has to begin after the middle of the second century.[40] This coincides with the rapid spread of Christianity and increase in the number of Christians. Around the middle of the second century, the West saw the establishment of many new Churches. It was no longer easy to serve the rural areas through the religious assembly in the city, and for this reason the setting up of a special church community *(paroikia)* in the country became a necessity. How was this done, and what consequences did it have for the unity of the Church?

At this point in the question, an institution comes into the picture which is basic to the early Church, and the significance of which has not been adequately studied: that of the *chorepiscopus*. Examination of this institution reveals both the time at which the villages started to be formed into special ecclesial unities, and the way in which the early Church preserved her original understanding of unity. As to the time when *chorepiscopi* appeared, and therefore, when the villages became detached from the ecclesial unity of the city, scholars have put forward different views. In a valuable study,[41] F. Gillmann considers that the beginnings of the institution should be sought actually in the first century because even then Christianity had begun to spread into the countryside. But apart from the fact that we do not get our first clear evidence for Christianity in the countryside before the beginning of the second century,[42] Gillmann's view seems incorrect also because it presupposes that the *chorepiscopi* appeared automatically with the Christians of the villages which cannot be reconciled with the fact that initially the Christians from the villages congregated around the Bishop of the city.[43] But if the first or even early second centuries provide no evidence of *chorepiscopi*, then, immediately after the middle of the second century, the institution appears clearly, especially in the West.[44] Thus in the reign of Antoninus (138-161), a country area in Italy (a place called *vicus Baccanensis*, in Tuscany) had a Bishop called Alexander.[45] A little later, around the end of the second century, evidence from the *Acta Caeciliae* (the historical core of which there is no reason to doubt) refers to a certain Bishop with the phrase *urbanus papa* which is accepted[46] as meaning Triopius, Bishop of the *pagus Appiae* in Italy. Thus in the second half of the second century, we have two specific examples of Bishops of a *pagus* or a *vicus* in Italy, in other words *chorepiscopi*, even though they are not known by that title. After this, *chorepiscopi* in Italy appear in increased numbers. There is a reference to Novatian being ordained in Rome in 249 by Bishops of "villages,"[47] in other words by *chorepiscopi*. Similarly, at the same period, we hear of the convocation of a synod of the Bishops in Africa who numbered 71, a number far exceeding the number of cities then existing in that area. In the East, we learn of *chorepiscopi* for the first time from Eusebius. Recounting the events concerning Paul of Samosata, Bishop of Antioch (267-70), he quotes a letter from the Council of Antioch which deposed him in which we read about Bishops "of the adjacent country areas and cities" who surrounded Paul and supported him.[48] Although, of course, this information goes back only to the middle of the third century, this institution had certainly existed for a long time in the East[49] as evidenced by the fact that the fourth century saw not its beginning, but its end.[50]

What exactly were the *chorepiscopi*? Did they have full episcopal jurisdiction, or were they rather presbyters? Both hypotheses have been put forward.[51] Unfortunately, our earliest information as to the nature of the institution of the *chorepiscopus* comes only when it had already begun to decline. Our sources on the subject are the following Canons of local Councils: 13th of Ancyra (314), 14th of Neocaesarea (314-325), 10th of Antioch (341), 6th of Sardica (343-344) and 57th of Laodicea (343-385). Because the nature of the institution of *chorepiscopi* is of such importance for the history of the Church's unity, we shall attempt here to throw some light on it through a comparative study of these few sources.[52]

The Canon of the Council of Ancyra, despite the numerous variants in the manuscripts[53] and the difficulties it presents in interpretation,[54] undoubtedly treats the *chorepiscopi* in a different way from the following Canons and especially the last two listed. In general terms, what emerges from comparative study of these Canons is a steady diminution in the rights and importance of the *chorepiscopi*. Thus while the Canon of Ancyra is concerned, on the one hand to confine the episcopal rights of the *chorepiscopus* within his own territory (*paroikia*), and on the other to place these rights in close dependence upon the Bishop of the city,[55] the Canon of Antioch about a generation later goes still further through a slight alteration which is of particular importance to history.[56] In this Canon, we observe two points: a) It is clearly recognized that the *chorepiscopi* belong to the rank of Bishop ("although they have received the ordination of Bishop"). This is a link with the past. On the other hand, b) they are explicitly told to confine themselves to ordaining lower clergy only ("to appoint readers and subdeacons and exorcists and not go beyond these appointments").[57] This is a preparation for the future. The attitude to *chorepiscopi* which had formed in the meantime is expressed by the Council of Sardica (344): in the country and the villages, a presbyter is sufficient where a presbyter is sufficient because of the small number of inhabitants,[58] the appointment of a Bishop would be to degrade his name and his authority.[59] The following generation, represented by the Council of Laodicea (381),[60] takes the next step of making the institution completely obsolete ("bishops should not be appointed in country areas").[61] From this we may conclude that a) the depreciation and disappearance of the institution of *chorepiscopi* happened gradually, the *chorepiscopi* having originally been full Bishops ("having received the ordination of Bishop"), and b) this movement from many bishops to fewer[62] gathered pace during the fourth century,[63] and was historically bound up with the increasing liturgical jurisdiction of the presbyters as evidenced by the 60th Canon of Sardica, which we have just looked at, and the 57th Canon of Laodicea, which abolished the *chorepiscopi* and replaced them with *presbyters acting as visitors* (*periodeutai*).[64]

From these conclusions about the development of the institution of *chorepiscopi*, it becomes clear that when the Christians of the countryside were detached from the ecclesial unity in the city, they formed their own Churches under their

own Bishops with their own Divine Eucharist. In consequence, when the Christians of the villages were detached
from the Church of the city there was no question of breaking up the unity of each Church in the Eucharist. This
detachment did not create parishes, but new full local
Churches with their own Bishops.[65] In this way, the principle
that each Church is united in one Eucharist under one Bishop
was preserved even after Christianity spread into the countryside.

*3. The application of the principle of one Eucharist and one Bishop
in all geographical regions. Some problems with Eusebius'* Ecclesiastical History.

The application of the above conclusions to all regions
during the period under discussion seems at first sight prob-
lematic on account of certain passages in Eusebius'
Ecclesiastical History. These passages call in question the existence of *one* Bishop in each Church in the regions of Pontus,
Gaul, Palestine and Egypt, and therefore, need to be looked
at.

Regarding Pontus, Eusebius writes that in the second century Dionysius of Corinth sent a letter "to the Church
sojourning in Amastris together with those in Pontus... men-
tioning their Bishop Palmas by name."[66] Some[67] have seen in
this passage, the existence of only one Bishop in the whole
region of Pontus, even given that at the time Eusebius is referring to, Christian numbers had risen significantly in
Pontus.[68] Eusebius does indeed give such an impression in
this passage as he does elsewhere when he is referring to the
region of Crete: "Writing also to the Church sojourning in
Gortyna together with the other *paroikies* in Crete, he com-
mends their Bishop Philip."[69] But the question arises of
whether these passages ought to be regarded as precise historical sources testifying to the existence of only one Bishop
in such extensive areas, or evidence of confusion created by
Eusebius when he allows later situations to find their way
into his synthesis of the sources. On this question, it should
be observed that in both the above passages it is implied that

there are several *paroikies* in the regions of Pontus and Crete
("together with those in Pontus..." and "together with the
other *paroikies* in Crete"). During the period in question, the
term *paroikia* as we shall demonstrate in more detail below
did not mean "parish" in the later sense, but a full local
Church with her own Bishop.[70] That the passages cited are
not talking about *paroikies* without Bishops of their own, is
evidenced by the fact that during precisely the years Eusebius
is referring to there, apart from Gortyna in Crete there was
also the Bishop of Knossos, Pinutus, whom Eusebius himself knows of and mentions a little later.[71] It is therefore not
legitimate to make the above unclear passages of Eusebius
the basis for the view that in extended territories such as
Pontus and Crete, there were in the second century *"paroikies"*
without Bishops of their own, which all came under one
Bishop. With the phrase "their [i.e. the *paroikies'*] Bishop"
(which, it should be noted, belongs to Eusebius and not to
his sources), it is obvious that Eusebius' familiarity with the
later metropolitan system is creeping in.

Eusebius' *Ecclesiastical History* presents similar problems
in regard to Gaul during the time of Irenaeus. The obscurity
of the passages *Eccl. Hist.* V.23.3 and V.1-4 has given rise to
the opinion that Irenaeus was the only Bishop in the whole
region of Gaul,[72] and perhaps Bishop not only of Lyons, but
also of Vienne at the same time.[73] This gives the picture of an
entire region with only one Bishop under whom was more
than one Church. This, however, conflicts with the following points:

a) In the inscription to the letter of the martyrs in Lyons,
the phrase "those in Vienne and in Lyons in Gaul" (*Eccl. Hist.*
V.1.3), on which Nautin bases his conclusions, does not necessarily mean that Lyons and Vienne formed one diocese;
because in that case the parallel which follows, "to the brethren in Asia and Phrygia," would have to be interpreted in
the same way, despite that fact that, as we well know, there
were many dioceses in the regions of Asia and Phrygia at a
very early date.[74] But apart from that, in the same letter, it is
made absolutely clear further on (V.1.13) that Lyons and

Vienne formed *two different Churches*. The fact that Irenaeus composed the letter in the name of those in Vienne and Lyons does not mean that he was Bishop of both of these cities, but simply that because of what had happened to Pothinus, who was in prison, he was representing the Church of Lyons which was host to the martyrs from Vienne. Besides, the purpose of this letter is known: Irenaeus was interested in using the authority of the martyrs in order to persuade the conservative brethren in Asia to abandon their extreme position on the matter of penitents. It is obvious that this purpose would be better served if the letter were written also in the name of the martyrs from Vienne. The fact that Irenaeus does not put his name to the letter as author reveals not only the purpose of the letter, but also the fact that he did not represent the Churches of both Vienne and Lyons.

b) The tradition knows of absolutely no Bishop of Vienne by the name of Irenaeus even though it knows of a whole series of Bishops of other names.[75]

c) It is doubtful whether Irenaeus was a bishop at the time when he composed the letter from the martyrs of Vienne and Lyons. Eusebius calls him "presbyter."[76] And while it is true that in Irenaeus' time this term was understood to include bishops, we cannot unquestioningly take this fact, as Nautin does,[77] as support for the view that Eusebius was misled by the terminology and thus placed Irenaeus in the rank of presbyter. For even if we accept that the terminology was of such decisive importance in this case, we should not overlook the terminological distinction that was made between *a* presbyter and *the* presbyter, the latter referring to the "presiding-presbyter," i.e. the Bishop.[78] It would consequently be more natural for Eusebius to have written "as *the* presbyter of the Church" rather than "as *a* presbyter of the Church," as we have in the text.[79] But apart from that, as is evident from the letter of the martyrs, Pothinus was still living, and was, therefore, the canonical Bishop of Lyons. In order to accept that Irenaeus was Bishop at the time when he composed the letter in the name of the martyrs of Vienne and Lyons, we have to suppose either that this letter was written after the martyrdom of Pothinus (which would be incompatible with the purpose and content of the letter), or that when Irenaeus wrote the letter he was Bishop of Vienne, and was later transferred to Lyons which would conflict with the existing ancient tradition which, as we have seen, knows no Bishop of Vienne by the name of Irenaeus. There remains no choice, then, but to accept that Irenaeus was simply a presbyter at the time when he wrote in the name of the brethren in Vienne and Lyons, and succeeded Pothinus in the see of Lyons – and only Lyons – after the latter's martyrdom.

d) In consequence of the above, Eusebius' obscure statement that Irenaeus "oversaw" (*epeskopei*) the *"paroikies* in Gaul," does not imply that he was the only Bishop in that region in charge of more than one Church; instead, it should be regarded as a transposition of the concept of the rights of the metropolitan, already well developed in Eusebius' day, to the time of Irenaeus when such rights had not yet been definitively formed. Such anachronisms are common in Eusebius as we saw in the case of Pontus and Crete.[80]

If in the foregoing cases, Eusebius' *Ecclesiastical History* gives the mistaken impression that one Bishop headed more than one Church, in reference to Palestine, Eusebius gives the opposite and, as will be shown, equally mistaken impression that more than one Bishop was heading one and the same Church. Thus referring to Alexander of Jerusalem, he writes that he "was thought worthy of that bishopric, while Narcissus, his predecessor, was still living," and therefore describes the episcopacy of Jerusalem as "the presidency of Narcissus with him [i.e. Alexander]."[81] As was natural, this led certain ancient[82] and also more recent[83] historians to speak of Alexander and Narcissus serving jointly as Bishops of Jerusalem for a time.

But if we leave aside once again the comments introduced by Eusebius and confine ourselves to the sources he has in view, the conclusion will be different. Thus the passage of a letter of Alexander's which Eusebius preserves,[84] and which plainly forms the basis for his impressions set out above, reads: "Narcissus salutes you, who held the episcopate here before me, and is now reckoned with me through prayers, being 116 years of age; and he exhorts you, as I do, to be of one mind." The phrase in this letter "now reckoned with me through prayers" (*synexetazomenos moi dia ton euchon*) gave rise to the view that these two Bishops shared the episcopacy, among historians who interpreted it as meaning "holding the same position in prayers as I do." But the true meaning of *synexetazesthai* (translated above as "reckoned with") at that period was "to be present" or simply "to be [somewhere]," as is shown in texts preserved by Eusebius himself.[85] In consequence, the meaning of this phrase is "who is present here with me through his prayers." This is supported by a more unequivocal reason why the theory of co-episcopacy is completely ruled out. In the passage of the letter cited, Narcissus is clearly described as "having held the episcopate here before me [sc. Alexander]." This phrase would not have been used if Narcissus and Alexander were leading the same Church jointly.[86]

But the region over which the greatest problems arise is Egypt owing to the total lack of relevant sources for the first three centuries. In regard to this region, the mistake has repeatedly been made of filling in the gaps in the sources from the first three centuries by transposing onto that period states of affairs which we know of from the fourth century and later. Thus as to the position of the Bishop in Egypt, the view was formed, and became generally accepted that there was originally only one Bishop for the whole of Egypt, and that as a result, the presbyters there showed themselves especially powerful.[87] As to the power of the presbyters, this view prevailed because in the fourth century such power is indeed to be seen, particularly as a result of the Arian controversies; but this does not mean that the same situation also obtained earlier, when, as we shall see later, presbyters nowhere enjoyed such independence and power. As to the existence of only one Bishop in Egypt, this view is again due to certain obscure and misleading passages in Eusebius. Thus in *Ecclesiastical History* V.22, Eusebius writes: "in that year, when Julian had completed his tenth year, Demetrius received the

charge of the *paroikies* at Alexandria;" and further on (VI.2.2)
he comments: "Laitus was governor of Alexandria and the
rest of Egypt, and Demetrius had lately taken on the episcopacy of the *paroikies* there [sc. in Alexandria and all Egypt] as
successor to Julian." The problem with these passages lies in
their reference to several *"paroikies"* and one Bishop in Alexandria and Egypt in the late second century. If the word
paroikia is taken to mean "parish" here, then in Egypt, at least,
the principle of the assembly of all the Christians into one
Eucharist did not apply around the end of the second century. If, on the other hand, the term is taken to mean the local
Church, then it appears that the Bishop of Alexandria is in
charge of more than one Church. It is consequently essential
to see what the term *"paroikia"* means in Eusebius, so that
we can go on to clarify the position of the bishop of Alexandria.

The term *paroikia* occurs about forty times in Eusebius'
Ecclesiastical History, but in none of these cases does it mean
"parish" in the modern sense. The meaning of the term is
always that of a whole local Church or bishopric. Thus he
writes of the Church of Corinth, "First of all, it should be
said of Dionysius that he held the throne of the *paroikia and
bishopric (episcopê) of Corinth.*"[88] Similarly of the Churches in
Crete: "among these is included another letter to the people
of Knossos, in which he exhorts Pinutus *the Bishop of the
paroikia...*"[89] and "Philip, whom we know from Dionysius'
words as *Bishop of the paroikia in Gortyna.*" Similarly, he writes
of Lyons that "Irenaeus succeeded to the *episcopacy (episcopê)
of the paroikia* in Lyons, which had been headed by
Potheinus;"[90] and of Rome and Carthage, that "[Cornelius]
made a list of the names and what *paroikia* each headed,"
and "first of all Cyprian, *pastor of the paroikia in Carthage.*"[91]
Eusebius uses the word in the same sense of other bishoprics[92] and also of Alexandria of which he writes: "About the
twelfth year of the reign of Trajan the above-mentioned *Bishop
of the paroikia in Alexandria* died, and Primus, the fourth in
succession from the Apostles, was chosen to the office."[93] The
common and noteworthy characteristic of all these passages

is that the term *paroikia* which occurs there is used inter-
changeably as a synonym for, or added as an explanation of,
the terms "church," Bishop," "bishopric/episcopacy"
(*episkopê*), "pastor," "ministry" (*leitourgia*) etc., which denote
a full local Church with its own Bishop.[94]

If, then, the term *paroikia* has this sense in Eusebius, it is
clear that in the case of Alexandria and Egypt it cannot mean
"parish," but "bishopric." In consequence, we have several
bishoprics in Egypt during the second century not just one.

Unequivocal evidence for this comes from the statement
of Eusebius himself that right at the beginning of Christianity in Egypt the Evangelist Mark established many
"churches" there.[95] Specifically, indeed, we know that early
in the fourth century it was possible to talk about many Bishops "around Egypt" serving "the *paroikies* around the country
and the region."[96]

The existence of several bishoprics in Egypt already from
the second century precludes the view that the Bishop of
Alexandria was initially the only Bishop in that region. How
do we then explain what Eusebius has to say about the leading position of Alexandria in relation to the *paroikies* around
Alexandria and Egypt? First of all, it should be pointed out
that in the first centuries the Christians in Egypt made a distinction between the Church of Alexandria, as the Church of
the chief city, and the Churches around Alexandria which
belonged to the countryside.[97] The superiority of the Bishop
of Alexandria in relation to the other Bishops in Egypt was
evident from the beginning. In addition, it is noteworthy that
even up to the time of Demetrius of Alexandria (189),
Eusebius speaks of *a paroikia,* in the singular, in Alexandria,[98]
and only after that does he talk about "paroikies" around
Alexandria. This timeframe fits in with the spread of Christianity outside the cities and the establishment of the
institution of *chorepiscopi* as we have said above.[99] It is, therefore, not improbable that the *paroikies* around Alexandria with
which the Bishop of Alexandria is linked from Demetrius
onwards were *chorepiscopates.* This probability accords both
with the meaning of the term *paroikia*, which, as we have

seen, presupposes a Bishop of its own, and with Alexandria's position of superiority vis-à-vis the other *paroikies*, which gave Eusebius cause to write, again under the influence of later situations, that the Bishop of Alexandria had "taken on the episcopacy of the *paroikies* there."[100] In consequence, the region of Egypt too appears not to have ignored the principle of the unity of all the faithful in each *paroikia* – Church under the leadership of one Bishop.

In the light of this, we are able to conclude that Ignatius' exhortation to the various Churches to remain united in *one Eucharist* only, under *one Bishop* and at *one altar*, was a reflection of a corresponding historical reality. Throughout the first three centuries and, so far as we can tell, in all regions, the principle of the unity of each Church in one eucharistic assembly under one Bishop was faithfully observed. Hence around the beginning of the fourth century, when developments take place which will be looked at the Part III, the principle was being passed down that in each Church there was only *one single* altar (*monogenes thusiasterion*),[101] while the First Ecumenical Council explicitly lays down, despite the existing practical difficulties, that there can be only one Bishop in each city.[102] Here is the section of this Canon in which the consciousness of the Church of the first three centuries concerning one Bishop only in each Church reaches its climax: "Wherever, then, whether in villages or in cities, these [i.e. clergy of the "Cathari" returning to the Catholic Church] are the only people found to be ordained, let those who are in the clergy remain in the same rank. But if some of them come over where there is a Bishop or presbyter of the Catholic Church, it is clear that the Bishop of the Church will have the Bishop's dignity; he who was named Bishop by the so-called Cathari shall have the rank of presbyter, unless it shall seem fit to the Bishop to admit him to the honor of the title. If this should not be satisfactory to the Bishop, let the Bishop provide a place for him as chorepiscopus or presbyter, in order that he may be evidently seen to be of the clergy; *that there may not be two Bishops in the city.*"

This insistent effort by the First Ecumenical Council to

arrange things "so that there may not be two Bishops in the city" cannot be understood apart from the principle which already appears clearly from the time of Ignatius according to which the unity of each Church is necessarily expressed through *one* Eucharist and *one* Bishop. The preservation and application of this principle is an historical fact, as we have seen, until at least the beginning of the fourth century. The effects of this historical situation on the formation of the Catholic Church during the same period will be considered directly.

Chapter Two

THE DIVINE EUCHARIST, THE BISHOP AND THE UNITY OF THE
"CATHOLIC CHURCH." THE IMPLICATIONS OF UNITY IN THE
EUCHARIST AND THE BISHOP FOR THE FORMATION OF THE
CATHOLIC CHURCH

The fact that each Church was united in one Eucharist "which is under the leadership of the Bishop" had a decisive influence on the formation of the Catholic Church during the first three centuries. Already from its first appearance in the sources, the term "Catholic Church" is inseparably bound up with the Divine Eucharist and the Bishop who led it. This is attested by the well-known passage from St Ignatius' Epistle to the Smyrneans:

> See that you all follow the Bishop, as Christ does the Father, and the presbyterium as you would the apostles; and reverence the deacons, as a command of God. Let no one do anything connected with the Church without the Bishop. *Let that be considered a certain (bebaia) eucharist which is under the leadership of the Bishop,* or one to whom he has entrusted it. *Wherever the Bishop appears, there let the multitude of the people be; just as wherever Christ Jesus is, there is the catholic Church.* It is not permitted without the Bishop either to baptize or to celebrate an *agape*; but whatever he shall approve of, that is well-pleasing also to God, so that everything that is done may be assured and certain.[103]

The connection to be observed in this fundamental passage between the term "Catholic Church" and the Eucharist "under the leadership of the Bishop," gives rise to the following question: what is the relationship between unity in

107

the Eucharist and in the Bishop and the catholicity of the Church in the first three centuries of the formation of the Catholic Church? In order to give an answer to this question, it is necessary, first, to define the content of the term "Catholic Church" on the basis of the sources from the first three centuries. This content is usually taken by scholars to be self-evident, and this perhaps accounts for the fact that at least so far as we know no one has yet fully examined the history of this term on the basis of the sources. But any conclusions as to the formation of the Catholic Church which are not based on the history of the term "catholic church" cannot be reliable. This is why we need to look closely at the influence of unity in the Eucharist and the Bishop on the formation of the Catholic Church on the basis of the history of the term "catholic church." This will oblige us, more particularly, to examine the relationship of the unity of the Church in the Eucharist and in the Bishop to:

a) the catholicity of each local Church,

b) the position of the Catholic Church viv-à-vis heresies and schisms, and

c) the unity of the "Catholic Church throughout the world."

These three themes cover all aspects of the "Catholic Church," as will be shown in our investigation of the history of this term.

1. The Divine Eucharist, the Bishop and the catholicity of the local Church

It is the prevailing view that the term "Catholic Church" denotes principally the universal or world-wide Church, and refers to the local Church only secondarily and by extension. This view, which has become established in recent years when cosmopolitan ideals have formed in people's consciousness the scheme of "locality" versus "universality,"[104] has its roots in the time and the theology of the Blessed Augustine who was the first to give the catholicity of the Church the sense *par excellence* of "universality."[105] But if we examine the sources of the first three centuries carefully, we shall see that the catholicity of the Church did not make its appearance as a geographical or quantitative notion, and should, therefore, not be tied in principle to the world-wide or universal character of the Church.[106] In order to define the exact content of this term, we must begin with the supplementary question of the ancient Greek language from which church literature borrowed this term and the primary question of the ecclesiology of St Ignatius in whose work this term first occurs. Thereafter we shall need to compare the meaning given to the term by St Ignatius with the ecclesiology of the generations preceding him from whom he draws his conceptions of catholicity and also with that of later times in which his influence was decisive especially as regards the connection of the term "Catholic Church" with each local Church.

1. The adjective *katholike* in Greek comes from the Aristotelian sense of *kath' olou*, which is used by Aristotle sometimes in contradistinction to *to kata meros*[107] and sometimes to *kath' ekaston*,[108] understood not only as an adverb but also as an adjective of manner so that it can mean the same as the adjective *katholikos*.[109] Aristotle did not give *katholou* a geographical sense so as to mean "world-wide" or "universal" nor a quantitative sense which would take it to mean a *sum or total of the "particulars" (epi merous* or *kath' ekaston)*. It is notable that whenever he defines it he gives it a *qualitative* sense denoting what is *full, whole, general* or *common*: "That which is true of a whole class and is said to hold good as a whole (which implies that it is a kind of whole), is true of a whole in the sense that it contains many things by being predicated of each, and by all of them (e.g. man, horse, god) being severally one single thing, because all are living things."[110] Aristotle precludes the geographical or quantitative sense of *katholou* still more clearly when he uses the example: "As 'man' belongs to the general (*kath' olou*) and 'Kallias' to the particular (*kath' ekaston*)."[111] Through the comparison of the "general" (*katholou*) with man in a generic sense and of the particular (*kath' ekaston*) with the particular human being, the meaning of the term *katholikos* becomes clear. The *kath' ekaston* is in no way a segment of the *katholou*, but

constitutes its actual concrete form. Each actual man is as much full man as is man in a generic sense (*katholou*), which he encompasses in himself, constituting the only actual, personal expression it has in space and time.

This sense of the term *katholou* or *katholikos* was preserved after Aristotle, as its use by Polybius,[112] Dionysius of Halicarnassus[113] and Plutarch[114] testifies. Philo who had a decisive influence on the world which surrounded the early Church does not deviate from the Aristotelian sense of the term. Thus, for him too, the word *katholikos* does not have a geographical or quantitative meaning, but denotes what is complete, full and general.[115] As a distinguished specialist on the subject observes,[116] in all these cases Philo follows Aristotle. Such was the prevailing sense of the term *katholikos* in secular literature. The Aristotelian sense of *katholou* survived and was preserved up to the time of early Christianity. How far the ecclesiastical literature of the first three centuries preserved the Aristotelian sense of this term is the question that will concern us next.

2. Of Christian literature, neither the New Testament nor the Septuagint uses the term "Catholic Church." The Church of Antioch, in which other basic technical terms such as "bishop" and "Christian" were first used,[117] is the first to use this term in the passage from Ignatius' Epistle to the Smyrnaeans quoted above.[118] The precise meaning of the term "Catholic Church" in this passage has repeatedly been a bone of contention. The main question that has been posed is whether the distinction here is between the universal and the local Church, or the invisible and the visible Church. Funk saw in this passage a distinction between the visible and the invisible Church, the term applying to the invisible,[119] while Lightfoot equated "catholic" with "universal."[120] Roman Catholic historians such as P. Batiffol,[121] and more recently G. Bardy,[122] also consider that "catholic" here means "universal."[123] This view presupposes that in the text of Ignatius the "Catholic Church" is in contradistinction to the local Church. It is assumed, in other words, that Ignatius' thinking involved the scheme "locality-universality," through

which he conceived of and expressed the unity of the Church in his time as revolving around two centers: the Bishop for the local Church, and Christ for the universal Church. In keeping with this interpretation, catholicity is applied here not to the local Church, but to the "universal" Church.

In parallel, there developed the view that *katholou* and *epi merous* in the consciousness of the early Church were used express not so much as an opposition between locality and universality, but mainly as an opposition between the Church and the heresies or schisms: the Catholic Church represents the whole, in contrast with the heresies and schisms which represent the part. Thus "catholicity" can also be applied to the local Church. The assumption underlying this view is that the term appears in the texts from the beginning in a sense of opposition to heresy and schism, and its ultimate conclusion is that for the early Church catholicity meant orthodoxy.[124]

Beginning with an examination of these presuppositions, we observe that the scheme of an antithesis between locality and universality, often used to interpret the early Church's self-awareness, represents, as we have already observed,[125] a later, cosmopolitan outlook foreign to the mentality of the early Church. For precisely this reason, it is very risky to begin an investigation into the origins of catholicity with the scheme "locality versus universality." The other idea, according to which the consciousness regarding catholicity was born out of the Church's polemic against heresy and schism, makes an equally risky starting-point for research, because there is nothing to convince us that Ignatius – our most ancient reliable source – uses the term to make a distinction between the "catholic" Church and the heresies. As the whole of the eighth chapter of the Epistle to the Smyrnaeans testifies, Ignatius is referring to those within the Church not those outside. It is necessary, then, to pose anew the question: what content has the catholicity of the Church according to Ignatius?

In the text where the term "Catholic Church" first occurs, we observe that it is talking about being devoted to the Bishop as Christ showed Himself devoted to the Father, and to the presbyters as to Apostles, and to the deacons as to a "command of God." Nothing relating to the Church can exist without the Bishop. The only assured (*bebaia*) Eucharist is that which is performed by the Bishop or his representative. Wherever the Bishop appears, there should the local Church ("the multitude of the people")[126] be, exactly as where Jesus Christ is, there is the "Catholic Church." It is not permitted either to baptize or to "celebrate an *agape*" without the Bishop. But whatever he approves, this is well-pleasing also to God so that whatever is done may be assured and certain. It is quite obvious that the whole text refers to the unity of the local Church which revolves around the Bishop.[127] It is he that sums up and incarnates the entire unity of the local Church. Whatever takes place, and above all those elements which are expressions *par excellence* of unity, namely baptism, the *agape* and the Divine Eucharist, acquire ecclesial substance (they are "assured and certain") only when they are expressed through the Bishop. This is summed up in the phrase: "where the Bishop is, there is the multitude," i.e. the local Church. But Ignatius also adds to this conclusion the comparison: "just as wherever Jesus Christ is, there is the Catholic Church." What is the meaning of this "just as" (*hosper*) placed between the local Church and the "catholic" Church? Does it introduce a relationship to a reality different from what precedes, or is it an expression of the same thing in another form? Linguistically, either sense is possible. The "just as" can mean either that the local Church is united around the Bishop whereas the Catholic Church is united around Christ, or that the local Church constitutes a reality exactly the same as that of the Catholic Church. Therefore, no definitive conclusion can be drawn from the narrow hermeneutic method. This passage has to be placed in the more general context of Ignatius's thought (broader hermeneutic method) and then within the historical reality of its period (historical method) in order for definite conclusions to be drawn.

We begin with the question: how does Ignatius under-

stand the local Church and its relation to the Church generally? First of all, we observe that he, too, uses the Pauline
phraseology[128] and speaks of the Church "which is" in a certain city,[129] and, as we have seen, refers clearly to *one* Eucharist
in each city. It is, however, striking the way he describes each
local Church at the beginning of his letters. In the Epistle to
the Ephesians, for instance, he writes: "Ignatius who is also
called the God-bearer, to the Church which is in Ephesus in
Asia, deservedly most happy, being blessed in the greatness
and fullness of God the Father, and *predestined before the ages*
for an enduring and unchangeable glory, *united* and *chosen*
through the true passion and through the will of the Father
and of Jesus Christ our God."[130] The Church of Philadelphia
he calls the *"Church of God the Father and of the Lord Jesus
Christ."* He uses the same style to describe the Church of
Smyrna.[131] Unless these epithets are taken as empty rhetori-
cal hyperbole, which is altogether improbable, their use by
Ignatius shows that the local Church is the very Church of
God, predestined before the ages, chosen and glorified. If,
then, we allow a conceptual distinction between the Church
of God and the local Church in Ignatius's consciousness, the
Church of God is to be found fully and in all her glory in
every place. The Church of God which "is" or "sojourns"
somewhere does not merely reside among the faithful of the
local Church as a special sort of invisible state, but *is identified with the faithful*, i.e. the local Church. This is why Ignatius
calls the Ephesians "all God-bearers and temple-bearers,
Christ-bearers, bearers of holiness" (9:2). This is why *these
very Ephesians are identified* by Ignatius *with the "Church re-
nowned unto the ages"* (8:1). Here, then, is the first fundamental
conclusion: the local Church, according to Ignatius, is the
very Church of God, the eternal, full, and whole Church.
Why?

Having just described the unity of the local Church as the
unity of the Church with Christ and of Christ with the Father,[132] Ignatius writes: "Let no one deceive himself: if anyone
is not within the altar, he is deprived of *the bread of God*. For if
the prayer of one or two possesses such power, how much

more does *that of the Bishop and the whole Church?* Therefore he who does not *come into the same place (epi to auto)* has already shown pride and passed judgement on himself, for it is written, 'God opposes the proud'. Let us be careful, therefore, not to oppose *the Bishop*, that we may be subject *to God*."[133] This passage is of great importance because it is so comprehensive. Coming immediately after the description of the unity of the local Church as expressing the unity of the Church with Christ and of Christ with the Father, in a certain sense it provides an analysis of the elements which make up this unity by virtue of which the local Church is identified with the whole Church. We should, therefore, take these elements one by one and examine them.

At the center all Ignatius' thinking, lies the Divine Eucharist. Coming together, *epi to auto*, is the usual expression to indicate the Divine Eucharist,[134] and here it is quite clear that this is what it means. The Divine Eucharist is Ignatius's passion.[135] He advises the faithful to come together frequently to celebrate it.[136] This insistence on Ignatius's part seems to stem from his ecclesiology.[137] The Divine Eucharist is the body of Christ, the very flesh of the historical Christ which suffered and is risen.[138] The unity of the Church should be not only spiritual, he says, but also physical.[139] Through this physical unity which is realized in the Divine Eucharist, the local Church takes on historical substance. This is also why he identifies the local Church with the gathering for the Divine Eucharist, and not simply the local Church, but the "Church of God": the deacons, being ministers of the Divine Eucharist, are ministers of the Church of God.[140]

Both the local Church and the "Church of God" are expressed historically (in space and time) through the Divine Eucharist. We find ourselves confronted once again with the Pauline ecclesiology.[141] The Church is the body of Christ.[142] Ignatius is quite clear on the justification for this consciousness which he interprets fully: the Church is the body of Christ because the body of Christ is *the historical Christ Himself*[143] and the historical Christ is *the flesh of the Divine Eucharist*.[144] The local Church, then, is the whole Church for no other reason than because *the whole historical Christ* is made incarnate within her through the Divine Eucharist. Precisely because of the Divine Eucharist, the local Church can be regarded as the Church of God, the whole Church, and can be addressed as such through the epithets that we have seen. Because through the unity of the body of Christ, she "partakes of God."[145] This leads Ignatius to stress another element in this passage.

The Divine Eucharist is closely bound up *with the Bishop* as he is in turn with "the whole Church." These elements are so deeply bound up with one another that they are not clearly distinguished in Ignatius' thought. Thus, when he is talking about the Altar, he suddenly introduces the prayer of the Bishop and of the whole Church. And when he is saying that one who does not participate in the Divine Eucharist is showing pride, he immediately adds that in order to avoid pride we should be subject to the Bishop. He indicates the same connection of the Altar with the Bishop more clearly when he says that anyone who does something "apart from the Bishop and the presbyters and the deacons" is the same as one who is outside the Altar.[146] This most profound bond between Bishop and Eucharist in Ignatius' thought has as a consequence another, more striking identification: *the Bishop is identified with the entire local Church.* Thus, we reach the classic passage "where the Bishop is, there is the multitude..." Judging from the whole of Ignatius' theology, it appears that this passage does not have a merely hortatory sense – or if it has such a sense, it is no more than an expression and affirmation of a reality which is understood ontologically. Ignatius does not hesitate to say that the *whole multitude,* i.e. the whole local Church, appears before him in the person of the Bishop.[147] The "whole multitude" of the Church of Ephesus is present for Ignatius in the person of her Bishop Onesimus.[148] This incarnation of the local Church in the Bishop – the result, as we have seen, of the connection between the Bishop and the Divine Eucharist – leads to further consequences for the position of the Bishop in the Church. In these consequences, the characteristics of the "catholicization" of the Church find their completion.

"Where the Bishop is, there let the multitude be," because according to Ignatius the Bishop incarnates the multitude, the local Church. But the local Church is a full, complete entity, the whole Church of God, because the whole Christ is to be found in her and makes her a unity, the one body of Christ, through the Divine Eucharist. In consequence, Ignatius does not hesitate to go on to link the Bishop with Jesus Christ. The Lord is called "Bishop."[149] Whatever happens to the visible Bishop of the Church is transmitted to the invisible Bishop, Jesus Christ. The Bishop forms a "type" and icon of Christ or of the Father Himself, an icon and type not in a symbolic but in a real sense: "It is fitting to obey in no hypocritical fashion; since one is not deceiving this visible Bishop, but seeking to mock the One who is invisible."[150] This realist view of the relationship between the Bishop and the Lord allows Ignatius easily to interchange these two persons:[151] when he is being led to martyrdom and is away from Antioch, the Lord is the Bishop of that local Church.[152] Two different worlds are thus created: God with the Bishop, and those who are apart from the Bishop with the devil.[153] Unity around the Bishop is a unity around God and in God.[154] "For as many as are of God and of Jesus Christ, these are with the Bishop."[155] In the same way, union with the Bishop constitutes union with Christ, and *vice versa*.[156]

What we have said already sets out the essence of the "catholicization" of the Church. The further consequences of these statements are drawn out by Ignatius himself. The unity of the Church is not simply eucharistic, but because of the relation of the Bishop to the Eucharist it becomes hierarchical as well. The Church of the Philadelphians realizes her "oneness" when she is "with the Bishop and the presbyters and deacons who are with him."[157] Not only that, but *the community cannot even be called a church without the clergy*, i.e. the Bishop, presbyters and deacons: "without these, it cannot be called a church."[158]

The further consequences now follow naturally: whatever is accomplished in the Church is valid only when it is approved by the Bishop.[159] The Bishop is not from men or through men, but from Christ.[160] And unity around the Bishop is not the will of man, but the "voice of God."[161] The Bishop, in other words, is appointed as such by divine law, and unity around him is recognized as the will not of man but of God. Thus the "catholicization" of the Church leads to the sequence: will (*gnomê*) of the Father – will of Jesus Christ – will of the Bishop.[162] The Catholic Church, as the whole Church, is such by virtue of the fact that she has the whole Christ. *But the local Church too is likewise catholic, because she has the whole Christ through the Divine Eucharist. The Bishop as being directly connected with the Divine Eucharist* represents the local Church in the same way as the whole Christ represents the generic (*katholou*) or catholic Church. *But given that both the whole Christ and the Bishop are connected with the Church in the Divine Eucharist, the* kath' olou *or Catholic Church is to be found where the Divine Eucharist and the Bishop are.* Thus the Bishop, as it has been most aptly observed, comes to be *"the center of the visible and also the true Church,"*[163] *and the local Church comes to be the "Catholic Church" herself.*

Thus, neither universal consciousness nor polemic against heresies can explain the origin of the "Catholic Church." Its presence in history follows the line which Ignatius presents to us in such a remarkably concise and comprehensive way, and which, curiously, has been overlooked by scholarly research: one Church, one Eucharist, one flesh and one cup, one altar, one Bishop with the presbyterium and the deacons.[164] Thus, in conclusion, the "Catholic Church" is identified according to Ignatius with the whole Christ, and the whole Christ is to be found and is revealed in the most tangible way in the eucharistic synaxis and communion of all the members of each Church under the leadership of the Bishop. In consequence, the local Church is catholic not because of her relationship with the "universal" Church, but *because of the presence within her of the whole Christ in the one Eucharist under the leadership of the Bishop.* In this way, each local Church having its own Bishop is catholic *per se*; that is to say, it is the concrete form in space and time of the whole body of Christ, of the "generic" (*kath' olou*) Church.

From all this it is clear that the Aristotelian sense of the *kath' olou* which is inherent and takes its concrete form in the *kath' ekaston*[165] has been preserved in Ignatius' use of the term. Just as for Aristotle, each actual human being is the full incarnation of man as a whole, so for Ignatius each local Church forms the incarnation of the whole Christ and the Church as a whole. This incarnation is full and real, so that it cannot be understood in terms of Plato's or Philo's philosophy,[166] and is expressed *par excellence* in the one Eucharist "under the leadership of the Bishop." But if Aristotle's sense of *kath' olou* has been taken up and preserved by church literature, this happened because this term adequately expressed a consciousness which already existed prior to the use of the term "Catholic Church." What was this consciousness which Ignatius had inherited, and for the expression of which Antioch chose the term "Catholic Church"? Our information on this will come from the ecclesiology of the generations immediately preceding Ignatius or contemporary with him to which the few surviving sources bear witness.

3. In our investigation of the origins of the unity of the Church, we saw that the Church first made her appearance as Jesus Christ Himself. By virtue of the inclusion in Him of the "many" for whom He was crucified and raised up, the Church constituted the unity of the very body of Christ in which the "many" become One person. This unity was expressed historically in its fullness through the Divine Eucharist. There the One and the "many" meet regardless of their numbers because Christ was regarded as being present even if only "two or three" were gathered together (Mt. 18:20). The full presence of Christ, the whole Christ, was not tied to numbers or quantity, the indifference to which is expressed in the conjunction "or." This was manifested from the beginning as a reality in the local Church. From the moment when the Church was united around the Divine Eucharist, which means from the beginning, she believed that she constituted the whole Christ and therefore the whole Church. Thus, Paul calls the local Church of Corinth during the synaxis of the

Divine Eucharist *the whole Church.*[167] *With the consciousness of oneness* (one Lord – one Divine Eucharist) *there developed also the consciousness of wholeness, of the* kath' olou (the whole Christ – the full and certain Divine Eucharist – the whole or Catholic Church). Paul is a clear witness to the connection between the oneness and the *katholou* of the Church through the Divine Eucharist. The early Church had a sensitivity about dismemberment of the whole which deserves our attention: "let us not tear the members apart."[168] This shows that she understood herself not only as one, but also as wholeness and fullness. Hence, there arose the consciousness of the Church as the fullness of Christ which is manifested in Paul's letters to the Ephesians and Colossians.[169] How should the "fullness" (*pleroma*) and the recapitulation of everything in Christ be understood in these Epistles? The opinions of commentators differ.[170] At any rate, it is highly doubtful whether they can be understood quantitatively, as Christ being "complemented" by the Church. It is more likely and more accurate, even where the language is that of Christ being "complemented" by the Church, that this should be understood not as a matter of addition but as an expression of *the full presence of the one within the other.* The Church is the fullness (*pleroma*) of Christ because she constitutes Christ in His fullness.

The same applies to recapitulation (*anakephalaiosis*). Although the term is used by Paul in a cosmological sense, it is not devoid of ecclesiological significance. The term seems to be used in the sense of the new Adam.[171] The human being *par excellence* includes within Himself the whole of humanity[172] and recapitulates all things in Himself.[173] The "many" are united in Him, and through the many He constitutes not only the one Adam *par excellence*, but also the full and completed new Adam, in other words his fullness. But as the Apostle Paul himself explains,[174] recapitulation in Christ applies above all to the Church, "which is His body, the fullness of Him who fills all in all." Therefore, however, much these two Epistles show tendencies to interpret the body of Christ in a cosmological rather than a strictly ecclesiological sense (and for this reason are considered deutero-Pauline by some scholars), the fact that the "fullness" refers *par excellence* to the Church is quite clear. This fullness of the body of Christ is recognized both by the Epistles mentioned above and by those to the Corinthians as existing in each local Church. The Church of Ephesus is regarded as "one body,"[175] and the Colossians are likewise called to be one body.[176] Thus, the consciousness that the local Church constitutes the full body of Christ, the catholicity of which does not need complementing by the other local Churches, appears widespread in the Pauline Epistles certainly on the evidence of those which are addressed to local Churches. Hence, the Church of Corinth is called by Paul "the whole Church" (Rom. 16:23 and 1 Cor. 14:23). Thus *from the "whole Church" of Paul, we have arrived naturally at the "Catholic Church" of Ignatius.*

Going on to examine other texts belonging to the period prior to Ignatius, we have no difficulty in drawing the same conclusion from the first epistle of Clement. There too, the Pauline and Ignatian idea that the local Church is identified with the Church of God is widespread. The Church of Rome and the Church of Corinth are each separately called the "Church of God,"[177] and their faithful are "elect and sanctified." There was a "full outpouring of the Holy Spirit" on all the Christians of Corinth[178] so that the Church of Corinth can without hesitation be called a "portion of the holy" (*meris agiou*). As variations in the codices attest, it is not impossible that this is an indirect reference to participation in the Divine Eucharist.[179] But 1 Clement gives clearer expression to the consciousness that the local Church forms the whole body of Christ when in reference to the disturbances in Corinth it develops the Pauline idea of the body of Christ.[180] From the viewpoint of consciousness, then, the antiquity of the Church's catholicity goes back to the earliest texts, and from Paul's time to that of Ignatius continues to be understood as the fullness of the body of Christ in each Church. What can we say about the outward marks of this catholicity?

Exactly as in Ignatius, so in 1 Clement, unity in the Divine Eucharist is the expression *par excellence* of the catholicity of the Church. First Clement does not of course develop this theme as broadly as Ignatius does because this epistle represents a period which is facing different problems, specifically the major problem of transition from the apostolic to the subapostolic age through the link of apostolic succession, something that does not appear as a problem in Ignatius. But, it is noteworthy that in confronting with this problem too, 1 Clement reveals a consciousness that the "catholicization" of the Church is accomplished on the basis of the "gifts of the *episcopê*" which is to say the Eucharist. Thus while the Bishop is absent from this text, for linguistic rather than substantive reasons,[181] the institution of the *episcopê* is present, and is connected in a notable way *with the Eucharist.* "Their" ministry (i.e. that of the Apostles) or of those appointed by them consists essentially *in offering the Eucharist.* Although the term *leitourgia* ("liturgy" or "ministry") is used by Clement in various different ways,[182] (it is noteworthy that in the case of the "presbyters" who had been deposed and those whom they had succeeded) it is used *par excellence* in the sense of "offering the gifts."[183] The dismissed "presbyters," then, had as their main task the offering of the Gifts. This alone is mentioned in connection with their dismissal which for this reason is considered "no small sin" (44:4). In its concern to preserve the characteristics of catholicity in the Church of Corinth, 1 Clement, like Ignatius, links her Bishop and clergy with the Lord through the Apostles;[184] not in any abstract way or for any other reason, nor on a theoretical and theological level, but in relation to the Divine Eucharist which is offered by them. And, even if it is supposed that with 1 Clement certain Roman categories creep into the way the characteristics of catholicity are interpreted of (see for instance the use of the term "legitimate" in 40:4), this does not give the historian the right to speak of catholicity *appearing* with 1 Clement. On the contrary, from what we have maintained here, it is clear that there is no conceivable relationship, let alone identity, between the Roman spirit and catholicity around the time of Ignatius because catholicity arises out of the local Church's consciousness of constituting the whole Christ. The external marks which express this consciousness are essentially and primarily the Divine Eucharist as the body of Christ, and the Bishop who offers it ("with the presbyterium and the deacons"). These form the indisputable historical expressions of catholicity which 1 Clement does not invent, but *upholds* at a period which was, as we have seen, highly critical for the history of the Church. In consequence, 1 Clement is not innovating and does not, as has been maintained, introduce the Roman spirit into the teaching about catholicity. But in response to the urgent historical needs of its time, when the Apostles were starting to disappear, it connects two generations through an *existing link*, that of the Divine Eucharist with which the Bishops or "presbyters" who offered it had always been inseparably connected. Without a doubt, in doing so, it is making an interpretation and speaking theologically. It develops teachings such as those of a priesthood which exists by divine law and is understood iconically,[185] obedience to the clergy as to God,[186] a clear distinction between clergy and laity[187] etc. But this theology does not create either the consciousness of catholicity or new external characteristics of catholicity. These already existed: 1 Clement merely interprets them. Thus, the "presbyters" and apostolic succession were recognized as characteristics of the Catholic Church before Ignatius during the crucial generation when the Apostles were disappearing; and for that generation as for Ignatius, the recognition came from the Church's consciousness shaped in the celebration of the Divine Eucharist that she constitutes the whole and full body of Christ.

Similar conclusions can be drawn from study of another text which probably represents the same period as 1 Clement. Judging from the fact that both these texts are gravely concerned with the same problem: the transition from the apostolic age to a situation where the Apostles were gradually disappearing, but had not yet all gone. This is the *Didache*.[188]

In regard to two points of the greatest interest for our study, the way this problem in addressed is common to both these texts. Just as 1 Clement recognizes the fullness of the local Church on the theoretical level, identifying her with the very Church of God, so the *Didache recognizes the fullness of the local Church on the practical level setting her as judge over the itinerant charismatics and thus in essence above them.* We find the same in another text from about the same period: the third Epistle of John. This text speaks of a certain Diotrephes "who loves to have preeminence" who clearly presided over a local Church and did not "acknowledge the authority" of the Apostles.[189] The fact that this is condemned by John does not alter the situation from an historical angle. The question of whether we have here a clash between "spirit" and "hierarchy" is of only secondary importance for history. The reality is that at the time of 3 John the local Church was able, through the Bishop who represented her, to judge the charismatics and decide whether or not to receive them. In the same way, all that the *Didache* says about the charismatics being judged by the local Church should be understood not as a mere desire on the part of its author or compiler, but as a reflection of a certain state of affairs that did exist and was widely spread. In keeping with this, every charismatic had to be subject to approval by the local Church,[190] and she would judge whether he was a genuine apostle or prophet and should be received. This is the first point that testifies to the fullness of the local Church.

The other problem for this transitional generation, namely the succession to the ministry of the apostles who were no longer there, is solved as in 1 Clement: a) "Bishops and deacons" are ordained, that is "presbyters" or "Bishops – presbyters – deacons"[191] and b) – most importantly for us here – the transition or "succession" from the apostolic to the subapostolic age take place *through the Divine Eucharist.* When 1 Clement speaks of the succession of the Apostles, it refers to the "offering of the gifts" as their "ministry." The *Didache*, also speaking about the ordination of the "Bishops and deacons," says, "for they also serve for you the ministry of the prophets and teachers" (15:1). What is this "ministry of the prophets and teachers"?[192] Previously, when speaking about the Divine Eucharist (chs. 9-10), the author of the *Didache* has clearly alluded to the prophets offering the Divine Eucharist whenever they were present in the local Church: "allow the prophets to make thanksgiving (*eucharistein*) as much as they want." It is precisely this ministry that he seems to have in view also when he speaks of the ordination of the "Bishops and deacons." This is apparent from the fact that immediately before this (ch. 14) he has spoken at length about the Divine Eucharist, and still more from the conjunction "therefore" with which he links what has been said about the Divine Eucharist with the passage concerning ordination of "Bishops and deacons" as ministers to serve the ministry of the charismatics. It is also noteworthy that this is done not by introducing a new institution to replace one which was disappearing, but simply by emphasizing and reinforcing an office which already existed but was often overshadowed by the Apostles and other charismatics. This is indicated clearly by the passage: "Do not therefore despise them" (literally "overlook," *hyperidete*). For they are your honored ones, together with the prophets and teachers" (15:2). The phrase "do not despise them" testifies to their preexistence. Thus, the connection of the subapostolic age to the apostolic is achieved here too through the *already existing* link that expressed *par excellence* the catholicity of the local Church namely the Divine Eucharist and the ministers who led it. The Eucharist is of tremendous ecclesiological significance also for the *Didache* because according to this text too it is inseparably bound up with the unity of the Church.[193] Thus in confronting, with 1 Clement and 3 John, the gradual loss of the Apostles and other charismatics, the *Didache* preserves the conviction that despite the lack of Apostles and charismatics, the existing Eucharist and the permanent ministers who lead it represent the local Church in her fullness as the "Church of God."

From study of these texts, it can be concluded without difficulty that the three generations known to Ignatius, which go back to the apostolic age itself, believed that through the one Eucharist "which is under the leadership of the Bishop" each local Church is revealed in history as the full body of Christ and, therefore, as "the whole Church," as the Apostle Paul puts it. It was precisely this consciousness that Ignatius gave expression in his use of the term "Catholic Church." Derived from the Aristotelian sense of *kath' olou*, this term provided with the greatest precision the verbal form required to express this consciousness given that the *kath' olou* is understood as being fully incarnate and made concrete through the *kath' ekaston*. Thus each local Church has come to be the concrete form in history of the *katholou* Church, the Catholic Church herself.

4. The historical conditions in which the generations following Ignatius lived obliged the Church to connect her catholicity with the element of Orthodoxy as we shall see at greater length shortly. Nevertheless, even at that period, the term "Catholic Church" did not cease to refer principally to each local Church. The following examples from the history of the term are sufficient to demonstrate this:

a) In the *Martyrdom of Polycarp*, which belongs to the first or second generation following Ignatius,[194] the term "Catholic Church" now appears clearly as a technical term, but again used of the local Church. Thus in 16:2, we read that Polycarp was Bishop of *"the Catholic Church in Smyrna."*[195] This is in accordance with the whole ecclesiology of this text, in which the local Church, just as in Paul's Epistles, 1 Clement and Ignatius, is identified with the very "Church of God."[196]

Each local Church constitutes a *"paroikia of the Catholic Church."*[197] As a *paroikia*, the local Church does not constitute a segment of the Catholic Church, but *the place in which the whole Catholic Church dwells.*[198] The meaning of the term, in consequence, is no different from that given it by Ignatius: in each place the Church *kath' olou*, the whole Christ, is made a concrete historical reality. Thus, the Church in Smyrna is called in the *Martyrdom of Polycarp* the "Catholic Church."[199]

But in the *Martyrdom of Polycarp*, we also find the phrase: *"of the Catholic Church throughout the world"* (8:1). This passage is usually adduced as proof that the "Catholic Church" was identified in Polycarp's time with the "universal"

Church.[200] On the contrary, however, this passage proves that the phrase "Catholic Church" did not mean "universal Church." This is shown, we consider, by the position of the phrase "Catholic Church" alongside the designation "throughout the world." For if it is accepted that "catholic" is to be interpreted as "universal" (*oikoumenike*) then we are confronted with a curious tautology which would yield the meaningless phrase "and of all the universal (*oikoumenike*) Church which is throughout the universe (*oikoumene*)![201]

b) The first or second generation after the *Martyrdom of Polycarp* continued to apply the term "Catholic Church" to each local Church. Thus, Tertullian uses the term in the plural, writing of "Catholic Churches,"[202] which obviously precludes the identification of this term with the "universal" Church.

c) Even in the third century, the term "Catholic Church" continues to refer to the local Church. This is shown by two typical examples.

The first comes from Cyprian's well-known work *De catholicae ecclesiae unitate*, which by "catholica ecclesia" means the local Church of Carthage;[203] the unity of which Cyprian was trying to protect by this work. This becomes highly significant for the history of the term "Catholic Church" if we take into account the fact that the title most likely belongs to Cyprian himself.[204] In consequence, there is no basis for the view[205] that Cyprian was the first to formulate the idea of church organization on the basis of the Roman empire; in other words as a world-wide unity of which the local Churches form parts complementary to one another.

The second example comes from other texts of Cyprian's time. Thus, the Roman confessors of whose declarations Cornelius informs Cyprian use the term "Catholic Church" as follows: "Nor are we ignorant of the fact that there should be one Holy Spirit, *one bishop in the Catholic Church.*"[206] If in this passage *catholica* is translated "universal," it automatically yields the impossible sense "there should be one Bishop in the universal Church"![207] It is clear that here "catholic" refers once again to the local Church. The evidence of this passage takes on special significance for the historian because it comes not only from Cyprian but also from other Churches of the West (Rome and Africa), and is linked also with the Churches of the East as is shown by the exact translation of the passage in Cornelius' letter to Fabius of Antioch.[208] A similar use of the term "catholic" is to be found in other texts of the same period.[209] Thus, the identification of the "Catholic Church" with the episcopal diocese, and indeed with the Bishop, is more than clear in Cyprian's words to Antonianus: "You also wrote that I should pass on a copy of this same letter *to Cornelius* our colleague, so that he may put aside all anxiety and know at once that you are in communion with him, *that is, with the Catholic Church.*"[210]

The declaration of the confessors of Rome "that there should be one Bishop in the Catholic Church" combined with Cyprian's fundamental ecclesiological principle which prevailed at that time: "the Bishop is in the Church and the Church in the Bishop,"[211] ties in Cyprian's time fully with that of Ignatius from the viewpoint of consciousness concerning the catholicity of the Church. Just as for Ignatius, the Bishop forms the center not only of the visible "but also of the true Church," so also for the Church of Cyprian's time, the whole Church (this is the meaning of the term *ecclesia*) is present in the Bishop. And just as for Ignatius there is "one Bishop" in the Church, so also for Cyprian's time "there should be one Bishop in the Catholic Church." Only one difference is evident between these two periods which is a difference not of substance but of emphasis: whereas in Ignatius' time, the local Church united in the person of the one Bishop was "the whole Church" herself by reason of being united in one Eucharist, this latter element – although, as we have seen, not absent as an historical fact in the period after Ignatius – had faded in the consciousness of later generations as an element in catholicity. Thus in Cyprian's time, the one Bishop is no longer emphatically connected with the one Eucharist. Such changes in emphasis which do not affect the substance of things are normal in history. And this change occurred because, as we shall see below the dangers from heresies and schisms obliged the Church to concentrate her attention on other elements of her catholicity.

2. The Eucharist, the Bishop and the position of the "Catholic Church" vis-à-vis heresies and schisms.

1. From the time of the *Martyrdom of Polycarp* onwards, the attentive student of the sources will observe that the catholicity of the Church is now emphatically connected not so much with the Eucharist as with the orthodoxy of the Church. This change is attested mainly by the way in which the texts refer to the institution and function of the Bishop. While, as has been observed,[212] "curiously, Ignatius does not consider preaching an indispensable attribute of the Bishop (*Philad.* 1:2),"[213] a generation or two later the emphasis is placed precisely on the Bishop's teaching work. The *Martyrdom of Polycarp* (16:2) refers to the Bishop Polycarp in the following terms: "The most wonderful martyr Polycarp, who became in our times *an apostolic and prophetic teacher*, Bishop of the Catholic Church in Smyrna." As this passage shows, the Bishop already concentrates in himself all the properties of the charismatics (he is "apostolic" and "prophetic"); but while these properties include the offering of the Eucharist, the emphasis is placed heavily on his teaching authority: "for every word that went out of his mouth has been and will be accomplished." [214]

The same emphasis on the teaching authority of the Bishop can be seen in the rest of the texts from the latter half of the second century. In the fragments of Hegesippus (*c.* 175 AD), preserved in Eusebius' *Ecclesiastical History* (IV.22), each local Church appears united in her Bishop who is regarded as the authoritative bearer of the true apostolic tradition: *"in every succession* and *in every city* that is held which is preached by the law and by the prophets and by the Lord."[215] From historical research and also his own personal knowledge,[216] Hegesippus goes on to give the names of Bishops going back to the Apostles themselves through a continuous succession. A few years later (around the year 185), Irenaeus continues Hegesippus' line of argument.[217] True *gnosis* consists in the teaching of the Apostles and the agreement existing from the beginning in the Church throughout the whole world and the extension of the body of Christ through the succession of the Bishops to whom the Apostles had entrusted the various local Churches.[218] Furthermore, according to Irenaeus, the Bishop is the authoritative teacher not simply by virtue of his apostolic succession, but also by virtue of his ordination. This element, appearing in the sources for the first time, serves to combine teaching authority with charismatic authority in general in the Bishop. In contrast to the heretics who maintain private assemblies, the "presbyters" of the Church were not, like them, merely teachers, but had the infallible *"charisma"* of truth.[219]

What caused such prominence to be given to the teaching authority of the Bishop, and what implications did this have for the history of the term "Catholic Church"? Once we have given an answer to these questions, we shall examine how unity in the Eucharist and in the Bishop relates to this new stage in the consciousness of catholicity during the first three centuries.

It is not an accident that this emphasis on the teaching authority of the Bishop coincides with the time of Polycarp's martyrdom. With the death of Polycarp, the last living bearers of the memory of the apostolic teaching disappear. The final, rather modest attempt at referring back to apostolic times by way of memory is to be found in Irenaeus who speaks of his own and Florinus' shared recollections of what Polycarp had told them of his contact with the Apostles in his youth.[220] But, as we have seen, Irenaeus by no means confines himself with this sort of argument, and subsequent generations no longer use living memory at all as a proof of the orthodoxy of the Church. The disappearance of the living and immediate bearers of this memory created of itself the clear need to stress the teaching authority of the Bishop, just as at another time (see 1 Clement and the *Didache*), the disappearance of the Apostles had required stress to be laid on the lifelong and permanent priesthood of those who offer the eucharistic Gifts.

But apart from this reason, the stress on the teaching authority of the Bishop also became imperative as an answer to the challenge of the Gnostic heresy. If the heresies of those times can be regarded as anti-historical,[221] then Gnosticism more particularly can be said to constitute the most intellectualized form of religion. For the history of the notion of catholicism, it is a fact of especial importance that it was the Gnostics and not the Orthodox who first introduced the idea of apostolic succession. This indicates that the expression of the consciousness of catholicity did not have orthodoxy as its focal point from the beginning. The first reference to apostolic succession is to be found in the Gnostic epistle of Ptolemy to Floras (165 AD)[222] who appears again reiterating the claim of his teacher Valentinus to apostolic succession. This is explained if one takes into account that the Gnostic heresiarchs remained within the Church for a long time while they were already preaching their heresy.[223] Rome was full of teachers and philosophical schools in the second century AD; and heresiarchs such as Marcion, Basileides and Valentinus contrived for years to be in contact with the Church while they were teaching heretical doctrines. Why did the Gnostics claim apostolic succession? The reason should be sought in the fact that the primary and most grave accusation against them was that they were teaching "new things." In order to refute this accusation, they maintained that they possessed a secret and "hidden" tradition going back to the Apostles.[224]

But what is characteristic in the present instance is that they understood this succession as a succession of *teaching*, (the type of succession that existed from the teachers of the Greek philosophical schools) which forced the Church to stress the already existing, but not greatly emphasized, capacity of the Bishop as teacher and of the Church as the storehouse of truth.[225]

This prominence given to the teaching authority of the Bishop, combined with the central place that he held in the Church's consciousness regarding catholicity, brought with it corresponding developments in the notion of the "Catholic Church." Previously, as we have seen, the Church saw herself as "catholic" in the sense of the full presence within her of the whole Christ through the Divine Eucharist and the Bishop who offered it. Now, because of the increased emphasis in the meantime on the teaching work of the Bishop who expressed the Church's unity, "catholic," little by little, took on the meaning of the orthodox Church. Characteristic examples of such a development are the conceptions of the "Catholic Church" in Irenaeus, Tertullian, the author of the Muratori Canon, and Clement of Alexandria, who all lived around the end of the second century.

According to Irenaeus, "the Church of God" is usually understood as contrasted with the heretics.[226] The Church is presented as possessing her own *system* of teaching,[227] and furthermore, which is more important, as supported by her teaching mission as by a "pillar."[228] For this reason, wherever there is a reference to the Church as a whole, this is always done almost exclusively in order to emphasize her preaching and teaching.[229] "The whole Church" (*tota ecclesia*) in Irenaeus' time is used as an expression and proof of orthodoxy in contrast with heresy. Thus the college of the Apostles was not only the Church *par excellence*, but also the whole Church (*tota ecclesia*) "from which every Church had its origin."[230] It is characteristic that "the whole Church" is not connected here in any way with the concept of universality. But it is equally characteristic of the development which had taken place in the meantime that it does not appear as in Paul and Ignatius in reference to the synaxis of the Divine Eucharist but as proof of the Church's orthodoxy: the whole Church was incarnate in the college of the Apostles, free of heretics, because "there was no Valentinus there then, nor any of the others who destroy themselves and their followers."[231] Similarly the understanding of the external marks of catholicity takes on a new emphasis as we believe is shown in the following example. Irenaeus mentions 1 Clement at one point[232] and refers incidentally to apostolic succession. But the interpretation of it that he gives is noteworthy and forms a clear picture of the development that had taken place in the understanding of the marks of catholicity. Whereas Clement, as we have seen, connects apostolic succession with the offering of the Gifts, meaning the Divine Eucharist – the dismissal from which of the Apostles' successors had prompted the composition of the letter – this is overlooked by Irenaeus who sees the purpose of 1 Clement as being instead *the renewal of apostolic faith* in Corinth. The disturbance in Corinth which 1 Clement attempts to quell is for Irenaeus a matter of *faith* rather than of *liturgy*. Because apostolic succession, for the Church of his time, meant principally the guarantee of orthodoxy and the transmission of the apostolic tradition.

In Tertullian, it is equally clear that "Catholic Church" is a technical term denoting the "Orthodox Church" in contradistinction to the heresies.[233] The term "Catholic Church" also has the sense of "orthodoxy" in the fragments of the so-called Muratori Canon. In this text, a distinction is made between those books of the New Testament which the "Catholic Church" accepts and uses and those which the heretics accept and which, therefore, "cannot be accepted by the Catholic Church."[234] Here, too, the term "Catholic Church" means the true and Orthodox Church which possesses the correct canon of Holy Scripture in contrast to the heretical groups. It should be noted that the term does not indicate the "universality" of the Church in this text either, given that, when it is a matter of her "universality," the Church is described as "one Church, spread over all the world."[235]

After Irenaeus and at the beginning of the third century, the term "Catholic Church" continues to be connected mainly with the notion of orthodoxy. Thus according to Clement of Alexandria, the "Catholic Church" means the true and Orthodox Church in contrast with the heresies.[236] The heresies are later human assemblies.[237] The "Catholic Church" is the true and ancient Church whose walls the heretics have "clandestinely" dug through[238] and which they "are eager to cut asunder into many [churches]."[239] But in contrast with the divisive efforts of the heretics, the unity of the Catholic Church is stressed: "We say that the ancient and catholic

Church is one only."[240]

Such was the history of the term "Catholic Church" from the middle of the second century to the beginning of the third. The threat of heresies and of Gnosticism in particular obliged the Church to give increased emphasis to the element of orthodoxy, in such a way that the "Catholic Church" was contrasted with the heresies, and the Bishop was seen as the successor of the Apostles not so much in leading the Eucharist, as was the case earlier, but rather in apostolic teaching. This gives rise to the question: what was the meaning of unity in the Eucharist and the Bishop during this period in the history of the "Catholic Church"?

Despite the increased emphasis on the component of orthodoxy, the Divine Eucharist continued even in this period to be inseparably bound up with the catholicity of the Church. This connection appears in the sources under two aspects. Firstly, *orthodoxy is unthinkable without the Eucharist*. This is expressed emphatically by Irenaeus who more than anyone else stresses the element of orthodoxy at this period. Connecting orthodoxy with the Eucharist, he writes, *"our doctrine* (i.e. the orthodox faith) *is agreed on the Eucharist, and the Eucharist confirms our doctrine...* For we offer Him [God] His own, consistently proclaiming communion and union and confessing the rising of flesh and spirit."[241] Besides, it is well-known that Irenaeus attributes immense importance to the Eucharist in the Church's struggle against heresies especially against the dualism of the Gnostics. According to Irenaeus, the Eucharist constitutes the strongest affirmation of the value of creation and of the material world,[242] and also the expression *par excellence* of the unity of the Church in the body of Christ.[243]

The second aspect under which orthodoxy appears in connection with the Eucharist in the sources of the period under examination is expressed clearly in these sources through the principle that *the Eucharist without orthodoxy is an impossibility*. This principle requires particular examination because it is the most decisive factor in the position of the Catholic Church vis-à-vis heresies.

Orthodoxy had of course always been a precondition in the Church for participation in the unity of the Eucharist as shown by the confessions of faith incorporated into liturgical texts which are known already from New Testament times.[244] The same precondition was preserved insistently in the early Church especially in the East.[245] But the most decisive period for the establishment of this principle in the Church's consciousness proved to be the second half of the second century and the beginning of the third. A contributory factor in this was the development in the phenomenon of heresy itself which took place in the meantime.

Heresy appears as a threat to the unity of the Church even from New Testament times (Acts 20:29-30).[246] But during the second half of the second century, heresy starts to be characterized by a tendency to take on an ecclesial shape. From the notion of a personal opinion or choice, which was the original meaning of the term *hairesis*,[247] or that of a "school of thought" which it took on subsequently on the model of the Greek philosophical schools,[248] during the period we are looking at heresy began to develop into organized groups on the model of the Catholic Church. Rome, for example, was the scene of an historically unprecedented coexistence of heretical groups[249] which did not content themselves with a teaching mission, but, perhaps in order to counter the arguments of the Catholic Church, sought to obtain ecclesial status themselves. Thus, an effort can be observed on the part of heretical groups at this period to put bishops at their head, as shown by the case of the Theodotians at the time of Pope Zephyrinus (199-217), who persuaded the confessor Natalius to become their Bishop in return for a salary.[250] This effort on the part of the heretical groups occasioned further clarification of the Church's catholicity in her consciousness and thus brought about the following very important development: the catholicity of the Church now began clearly to take shape as an expression of that Church which in the person of her own Bishop, who preserved the historical and charismatic continuity of her being, combined at once right liturgical life and right faith. This consciousness which forms one of the most decisive stages in the development of ecclesial catholicity begins with Hippolytus and comes to completion with Cyprian.

Of Hippolytus's works, the *Philosophoumena* or *Refutation of All Heresies* shows that the "Catholic Church" of the beginning of the third century saw herself as *one* in each city, distinguished from the other groups in that they were simply "schools" or places of teaching, while the Catholic Church was a liturgical community, centered on the Divine Eucharist which preserved strictly defined boundaries around itself. Thus Hippolytus, being unable to accept more than the one Church in Rome, calls Callistus' group a "school" which is outside the communion of the Church[251] and cannot be called a "Catholic Church."[252]

Thus at this period, the consciousness was clearly formed that the "Catholic Church" was a notion necessarily including, apart from orthodoxy, a strictly ecclesial or liturgical communion. This is why Origen speaks in his writings of two groups in Christianity which he contrasts with one another: one is called "churchmen" (*ekklesiastikoi*) and the other "those from the heresies,"[253] and he prides himself on belonging to the group not simply of "Christians" but of "churchmen."[254] One who belongs to the groups of the heretics calls himself a "Christian" (*"professione quidem christianus est, intellectu fidei haereticus et perversus est"* – "he is professedly a Christian, but in his understanding of the faith he is a heretic and perverse"), while on the contrary the "churchman" is not called simply "Christian" but also "catholic": *"fidei credulitate et professione nominis christianus est et catholicus"* ("by belief in the faith and profession of the name he is a Christian and a Catholic"). "Churchman" and "catholic" are identified and the one explains the other. The "heretic" fighting against the "churchman" is fighting the "catholic," as once, the Egyptian who was an Israelite only on his mother's side fought against the true Israelite: *"adversus ecclesiasticum, adversus catholicum litigat."*[255] This identification of "churchman" with "catholic" is a characteristic mark of the way the term "Catholic Church" is now used to indicate "ecclesial communion" not only in faith, but also in the Divine Eucharist. As is shown by a later text which, however, reflects an earlier state of affairs, in order for strangers to gain entry into a *paroikia*, it was not enough to ask them whether they were "believers"; they also had to be asked whether they were "churchmen"[256] meaning in regular communion with the Catholic Church.

A typical example of the connection between Eucharist and orthodoxy at the beginning of the third century is the Greek text in the Toura papyrus, of great interest for the history of dogma and liturgy, entitled "Discourses of Origen to Heracleides and the Bishops with him [on the Father and the Son and the Soul], published in 1949 by J. Scherer.[257] This is the major part of the Acts of an episcopal council including the discussion between Origen and a certain Bishop, Heracleides, whose ideas had precipitated the calling of the council. What is of importance for us here is that in the course of the discussion about the Son's relationship to the Father, Origen refers to the eucharistic prayer in order to stress that the content of prayer and the content of faith should be in total harmony. The relationship of the Son to the Father is one of unity in nature in a distinction of persons, and hence "the offering [of the Eucharist] is to God Almighty through Jesus Christ as He who offers [or is offering[258]] His divinity to the Father; not twice, but let the offering be to God from God..." (2.24; *loc. cit.* p. 62). Thus the orthodox faith and the eucharistic offering, which most likely occasioned discussion, are mutually dependent, and the unity of the Church depends on the harmony between the two in such a way that whoever disagrees, be he a Bishop or a presbyter, "is not a Bishop nor a presbyter nor a layman. If he is a deacon, he is not a deacon nor a layman. If he is a layman, he is not a layman, nor does he come together" (*synagetai*, i.e. take part in the eucharistic *synaxis*) (5.5; *loc. cit.* p. 64).

The way the consciousness of the Church's catholicity was shaped by the now decisive joining of eucharistic communion with orthodoxy is clearly illustrated by the manner in which the Church in the period under discussion accounted for the institution of the episcopate. Earlier, as we have seen, the institution of episcopacy was connected in the beginning chiefly with the Divine Eucharist (Clement of Rome, Ignatius) and, later on, chiefly and emphatically with its teaching function (*Martyrdom of Polycarp*, Hegesippus, Irenaeus). At the beginning of the third century, these two elements are joined into one, and the Bishop is clearly the expression of both simultaneously. This is illustrated in the *Apostolic Tradition* of Hippolytus,[259] a text of great value for the history of this period. A careful examination of the evidence this text gives concerning the Bishop tells us that the Bishop, who was *alter Christus* and *alter apostolus* for his Church,[260] concentrates in himself the power both to "shepherd the flock" of his Church, that is to teach her members with authority, and to "offer to Thee the gifts of Thy holy Church," that is to perform the Divine Eucharist.[261]

Thus, around the beginning of the third century and under pressure from heresy, which already showed a tendency to clothe itself in ecclesial garb, unity in the Divine Eucharist is combined with unity in orthodoxy while the Bishop through his ordination is clearly made the successor of the Apostles both in the offering of the Eucharist and in the preservation of orthodoxy. In the same way, this period sees a synthesis of the elements which earlier expressed the notion of the "Catholic Church." This synthesis is expanded and matures still further in the time of Cyprian and under pressure from another negative factor, that of schism.

2. "Schism" occurs as a term even in the earliest texts of the New Testament, but the meaning it has there is simply that of a temporary disagreement[262] or of quarrels between individuals, not between organized groups.[263] Later "schism" is confused with "heresy," in place of which it is often used, and this ended finally in the definition of heresy as wrong belief, and schism as a division of an adminstrative or moral kind.[264]

Under pressure from schism, which was a most acute problem in the third century, the consciousness concerning the Church's catholicity was clarified still further. This clari-

fication was passed down to history mainly through the personality of St Cyprian who for this reason represents a
milestone in the history of the unity of the Church.

Continuing the tradition and mind of the Church of the
time of Hippolytus and Origen, the Church of Cyprian's time
inherited the consciousness that her catholicity consisted in
unity in right faith and sacramental communion, expressed
through the Bishop of each local Church. But going beyond
what it had inherited, Cyprian's generation further clarified
the components of this catholicity both for itself and for history in general, because thanks to Cyprian and the
controversies of his time, the history of ecclesiology in this
period can be studied easily. Thus we receive on the one hand
an almost complete description of the composition and organization of the local Church, and on the other, a clarification
and an ecclesiological expression of the catholicity of each
local Church.

The local Church comprises two basic components bound
together in complete unity and order: the people (*plebs*) and
the clergy (*ordo* or *clerus*).[265] The clergy consists of various
degrees. Among the laity, by contrast, there are no degrees.[266]
Within the clergy, we find clearly distinguished the three
hieratic degrees (bishop, presbyter, deacon) and also the
lower clergy[267] with the responsibilities of each defined. All
are dependent on the Bishop and owe obedience to him. In
his absence, both the clergy and the deacons can be given a
mandate to represent him in his responsibilities and his
work.[268] When he is present, however, they may only be in
obedience to him.[269] The laity similarly owes obedience to
the clergy and in particular to the Bishop. This obedience
does not preclude their participation in church affairs mainly
in the form of giving an opinion on serious issues[270] and electing clergy.[271] But as in antiquity (1 Clement – Ignatius), this
participation was approbatory in character and not by way
of a precondition: while from the other clergy the Bishop
seeks *consilium* (advice), from the laity he merely seeks *consensus* (consent).[272] These are two different things.[273] It is
possible for the rest of the clergy and the laity to participate

in the election of a Bishop, but the election depends on and receives its validity from the participation of the Bishops.[274]

All this is a consequence of the ancient consciousness that the catholicity of the local Church is expressed by the Bishop. It is he that incarnates the local Church (as we have already seen in Ignatius).[275] When, therefore, Cyprian writes to a particular Church, he addresses her Bishop alone (*Cyprianus Cornelio fratri, Cyprianus Jubaiano fratri*, etc.). If the episcopal throne is vacant, he addresses the clergy (*Cyprianus presbyteris et diaconis Romae consistentibus*). Only when he is addressing his own Church, because of course he is not addressing her entirety, does he write to her clergy and laity (*Cyprianus presbyteris et plebi universae*). Cyprian gives an ecclesiological explanation of this position of his. For him it is a fundamental and inviolable principle that the Church has been founded upon the Bishop:[276] for the Church is nothing other than the people united around their Bishop and the flock bound to their shepherd (*Ecclesia plebs sacerdoti adunata et pastori suo grex adhaerens*). The Bishop is in the Church and the Church in the Bishop, and if anyone is not with the Bishop, he is not in the Church.[277] Whoever separates himself from the Bishop, separates himself from the Church.[278] Such are the essential and inviolable ecclesiological principles of Cyprian's time.

One might reiterate here that this period presented nothing essentially new from the viewpoint of ecclesiology. This can be seen from a careful examination of what has been said up to this point. But as has been done, hitherto, in the course of our investigation, so now, too, we have to compare the period we are looking at with earlier times and establish what shifts of emphasis or interpretations ecclesiology may have undergone in the consciousness of the Church. In the present case, historical conditions contributed to the following developments which were highly significant and of decisive importance.

The schism occasioned by the "lapsed" which rocked the Church of Cyprian's time, and which arose after only the first year of Cyprian's episcopate (249 AD – persecution of Decius), had brought up for discussion the problem of the

jurisdiction of the Bishop of each local Church, and the relationship of this jurisdiction to the authority of the martyrs
(another form of the very ancient problem of the relationship between the charismatics and the permanent ministers).
The problem had been posed in the form of the question: did
the martyrs have the right and the authority, on the basis of
their sacrifices for the faith, to pardon those who had lapsed,
releasing them from the penance imposed by the Church?
The right to pardon those who were in a state of penance
belonged to the Bishop. There was a belief in some circles
that the martyrs had within them the Holy Spirit who had
strengthened them in the hour of martyrdom.[279] As Spirit-
bearers, then, did they not have the authority to act at least
as the Bishop did? The answer from Cyprian and the other
Western Bishops was negative. Only in the case of those on
their deathbeds could the lapsed be given such pardon by
economy (and anyway this presupposed the knowledge and
approval of the Bishop). Others were obliged to await the
return of the Bishop to his see. Yet again, the "Catholic
Church" showed a consciousness that her unity and catholicity rested on the Bishop. It should be noted that this took
place before the schism of Novatus which Harnack makes
the ground and starting-point for Cyprian's conviction that
"ecclesia super episcopos constituatur" ["the Church is founded
on the bishops"].[280] This is evidence that Harnack is wrong
because the above-mentioned decision by Cyprian and the
other Western Bishops came before Novatus, and reflects very
ancient beliefs which we have already looked at. This, then,
was the first historical event of Cyprian's time which led to
the clarification of episcopocentric catholicity.[281]

After Cyprian's stance against the martyrs pardoning
those who had lapsed, there followed the schism of
Felicissimus around whom a part of the laity (*"portio plebis"*)
had gathered. Such a group of Christians living apart from
the Bishop was not even called a Church by Cyprian. When
the lapsed sent him a letter "in the name of the Church"
(*"ecclesiae nomine"*), Cyprian described them as impudent for
wanting to call themselves a "Church" (*"ecclesiam se volunt*

esse..."). There was a strong consciousness that the Catholic Church could not be found outside the Bishop. But in the meanwhile and before Felicissimus was condemned and unity in Carthage restored (251 AD – Council of Carthage), Rome was faced with the Novatianist schism in which Novatus, a presbyter from Carthage belonging to the faction of Felicissimus, took part, having an interest in seeing Novatian made Bishop of Rome, since the latter would support Felicissimus' faction. The election of Cornelius as Bishop of Rome was supported without hesitation by Cyprian, and this contributed to the further clarification of his ecclesiology through letters and through his work *De catholicae ecclesiae unitate*. The notion of catholicity is used repeatedly by Cyprian: the election of Novatian took place *"contra ecclesiam catholicam"*[282] (again, the Church of Rome is meant, and not the universal Church). The "Catholic Church" in Rome was not that with Novatian, but that with Cornelius, from which those with Novatian had detached themselves.[283] Writing to the confessors of Rome, who supported Novatian, he reminds them that confession during persecutions is not a sufficient duty for the Christian, and that devotion to the unity of the Catholic Church and her Bishop is an equally serious duty. By electing a Bishop over against the existing Bishop, the confessors had acted contrary to the catholicity of the Church ("contrary to the unity of the Catholic institution, they plotted to make another bishop"), and in this way had tried to found another Church, outside that which the Lord had founded – "something that is neither lawful nor permissible to do."[284] For the Catholic Church founded by the Lord is one, and her unity rests on the unity of the episcopate (*"episcopatus unus est"*).[285] Thus, in a way reminiscent of Ignatius, the Bishop, the Catholic Church, Christ and God form an unbreakable sequence. Cyprian, therefore, has no difficulty in drawing the conclusion: whoever does not have the Church as his mother cannot have God as his Father (*"habere non potest Deum patrem qui ecclesiam non habet matrem"*). And he who is not with the Church is not with Christ ("He who gathers eleswhere than in the Church, scatters the Church of Christ")[286] just as he who is not with the Bishop is not with the Church[287] and in consequence is with neither Christ nor God.

What understanding of the Catholic Church underlies these convictions? This is elucidated for us by (a) the work *De catholicae ecclesiae unitate,* and (b) the texts written in response to the events which took place towards the end of Cyprian's life.

According to the *De Unitate,* the Catholic Church is that which concentrates in herself of all the means of salvation. The emphasis is not placed only on her orthodoxy or only on the celebration of the Divine Eucharist or simply on these two as happened in the times before Cyprian. The consciousness concerning catholicity had now matured considerably, and under pressure of historical events, it reached the fullness of its expression. The Catholic Church is that which incarnates orthodoxy, the Divine Eucharist and every other means of salvation, every sacrament: Priesthood and Baptism. These will be developed more clearly towards the end of Cyprian's life in response to the controversies over baptism. But they are already expressed in principle and in a negative way in *De Unitate*: outside the Catholic Church there is no baptism ("*non abluntur illic homines*"), nor Eucharist ("*falsa sacrificia*"), nor Bishop ("*episcopi nomen*") nor indeed a "cathedra" of right teaching.[288] Can someone maintain that he has a right faith, asks Cyprian, if he is not connected with the *cathedra* of Peter which is occupied by the Bishop in each local Church?[289] Faith and orthodoxy for Cyprian are ecclesiological concepts: right faith cannot form a self-sufficicient means to salvation, but is a component in the believer's more general dedication to the Catholic Church. He clarifies these principles still further when, around the year 255, the issue arises of the validity of baptism by heretics. This issue first appears in a letter of Cyprian's to a certain distinguished layman named Magnus who had asked, at Cyprian's own instigation, whether the Novatianists were able to perform valid baptisms. Cyprian answers in the negative: heretics and schismatics do not have the right and the power to baptize.[290] This position of Cyprian's and the way he justifies it reveal much about the then prevailing consciousness as to what exactly constitutes the Catholic Church which is our immediate concern here. Why are heretics and schismatics unable to perform valid baptisms? For Cyprian there is one answer: because they are outside the Catholic Church. To the question of whether the Novatianists do not have the same faith as the Catholic Church, he replies in the negative: their Creed is not the same as ours because in our Creed there is a reference to belief in the Church whereas the Novatianists do not have a Church. Similarly there is a reference to remission of sins, but the Novatianists do not receive this through the Church.[291] As to faith in the Holy Trinity in the name of Whom they baptize, he asks: did not Korah and Dathan and Abiram have the same faith as Moses, but were punished by God nonetheless?[292] This line of argument of Cyprian's bears witness that right faith is not sufficient to constitute the "Catholic Church." Orthodoxy no longer forms the criterion for the "Catholic Church," but the "Catholic Church" is the criterion for orthodoxy: belief in the Church forms an essential and necessary element in orthodoxy. The catholicity of the Church, then, is a wider concept than orthodoxy: it includes orthodoxy, without being coextensive with it. What does this broader reality consist in? This is the climax of our investigation on this subject. As a result of the baptism issue, Cyprian gives the first full expression in history to the catholicity of the Church. An expression which is, therefore, of decisive importance, summing up the consciousness of previous generations of Christians on this subject not by adding together various points, but as a flowing and organic whole. Here is what he says.

Heretics and schismatics, being outside the Catholic Church and not obedient to her, do not have the Holy Spirit. Even supposing, then, that they could baptize, they could not bestow the Holy Spirit. But this is not enough; for one who does not have the Holy Spirit cannot even baptize.[293] Baptism forgives sins, and sins are forgiven only by those who possess the Holy Spirit in accordance with Jn 20:22. But it is precisely this that those outside the Catholic Church lack: "all of these, heretics and schismatics, do not confer the Holy Spirit."[294]

What then is the deeper reason for this inability on the part of schismatics and heretics to perform "valid" sacraments? At this point, the unity of the Church comes into play as a factor of decisive importance in the relationship of the Catholic Church to schism and heresy.

For Cyprian, just as for Paul and Ignatius (see above), the Eucharist constitutes the sacrament of Church's unity in such a way that the Eucharist acquires ecclesiological content. We see this chiefly in the remarkable letters 63 and 69; the basic ideas in which are characteristic of the whole of Cyprian's ecclesiology. Interpreting the symbolism of the mingling of the water and the wine in the eucharistic Cup, and of the grains of wheat from which the eucharistic Bread is made, he observes that just as Christ bears all of us in Himself so in the mingling of the water and the wine in the cup the multitude of the faithful (*populus*) are united into one indissoluble unity. Therefore, the Church too, united in the Eucharist, is inseparably united with Christ in such a way that the two become one being. When the holy Cup is consecrated, it is necessary that neither wine alone nor water alone should be offered. For if we offer the water alone, the people appear without Christ. The same goes for the union of the grains of wheat for preparing the bread. Just as the multitude of grains of wheat are collected together and ground together and mixed so as to become one loaf of bread, so also in Christ, who is the heavenly bread, there is but one body in which our multiplicity is joined together and united.

Precisely because the Eucharist posseses this ecclesiological content, the schismatics and heretics who do not participate in it cannot perform "valid" sacraments. For Cyprian, this is the basis for the "validity" of the heretics' baptism: if they participated in the unity of the Eucharist, they would participate also in the whole charismatic life of the Church. This understanding, which sets up eucharistic unity as the fullness of ecclesial unity in general, is clearly expressed by Cyprian:

> If Novatian were united in this bread of the Lord, if he
> were mingled with the others in the people of God, then
> he could maintain that he possessed the grace of the one
> baptism, because he would be within the unity of the
> Church... How indivisible is the mystery of unity and how
> hopeless the destruction of those who provoke the wrath
> of God by creating a schism and making another bishop
> in place of their own Bishop, is described by Scripture in
> the Book of Kings, in connection with the ten tribes who
> separated themselves from Judah and Benjamin and
> foresook their king in order to enthrone another.[295]

This important passage reveals that for Cyprian who broad-
ens the concept of the catholicity of the Church by making a
synthesis of all the elements he had inherited from previous
generations that unity in the one Divine Eucharist and the
one Bishop[296] forms the criterion for the catholicity of the
Church. A second Eucharist and a second Bishop in the same
geographical area constitute a situation "outside the Catholic Church." Here too, the supreme mark of remaining within
the Catholic Church is unity in the one Eucharist "under the
leadership of the Bishop." Such unity describes the bounds
of catholicity which in the synthetic exposition given by
Cyprian means that living fullness of the body of Christ in
which through the sovereignty of the Holy Spirit, doctrinal
life (orthodoxy), and sacramental life (Eucharist, Baptism,
Priesthood) form mutually dependent elements and an unbreakable unity which defines the boundaries and the
substance of the Church. This fullness subsists in each Church
which is led by a canonical Bishop.

Was this understanding of catholicity Cyprian's consciousness only, or that of the Church in general around the middle
of the third century? This is difficult to answer, because at
that period there did not yet exist the criterion through which
the consciousness of all the Churches around the world could
be expressed at the same time, namely, the ecumenical council. We do, however, know that many Churches became
involved in the discussion about baptism, and this helps us

to know their views relative to Cyprian's position. First of all, we note that all the Churches of Africa had sided with Cyprian's views in two Councils, one in the autumn of 255 and one shortly before Easter in 256. Present, at the latter, were 71 Bishops from Africa and Numidia who had endorsed the decisions of the 255 Council. These decisions are a precise reflection of Cyprian's views summarizing his teaching on the "Catholic Church" as set out above: the "Catholic Church" is the sphere of operation of the Holy Spirit, and therefore, she alone is able to possess right teaching and sacraments.[297] Thus, we can say that what has been said above regarding Cyprian's ecclesiology can be taken by historical research as a reflection of the consciousness of the Churches in Africa and Numidia.[298] What was the understanding of the Churches of the East in this matter? Judging from those that took part in the discussion on baptism, we may say that the eastern Churches wholeheartedly shared the ecclesiological views of Cyprian. Writing to Cyprian (in 256) in the name of the Churches of Cappadocia, Cilicia and Galatia, obviously after a council had been convened there, Firmilian of Caesarea in Cappadocia concurs with Cyprian's ecclesiology without hesitation. Firmilian's letter[299] is a notable historical document because it vigorously proclaims the fullness and catholicity of every local Church which has a Bishop at her head,[300] and declares that the ecclesiological views on catholicity of the Churches he represents are identical with those of Cyprian.[301] As for the other eastern Churches, we have indications that the Church of Alexandria, although in practice following Rome, was theoretically in her ecclesiology more in agreement with Cyprian,[302] and if we believe Firmilian, the Church of Jerusalem too had many disagreements with Rome.[303] Anyway, the fact is that throughout the East councils were convened in the autumn of 256 which decided unanimously to follow Cyprian in his ecclesiology.[304]

It remains to examine the position on this subject of the Church of Rome which in the person of her bishop Stephen was strongly opposed to the views of Cyprian. On what exactly did Stephen disagree with Cyprian? Our concern here is to see whether and to what extent Rome shared Cyprian's views on the "Catholic Church" which should not be precluded *a priori* by the great impression made by the controversy between Rome and Africa. Unfortunately, Stephen's arguments are known to us only in part and perhaps in distorted form because they have come down to us through the letters of Cyprian and others of his opponents. We should not, then, give Cyprian's letters the status of an historical source in this matter. Fortunately, however, there is preserved a contemporary work by an anonymous African Bishop entitled *De Rebaptismate*, written probably around 256,[305] which sets out in detail the arguments against Cyprian's views on baptism. This text expounds not so much the teaching on the Church as that on the sacraments, but it reveals the writer's ecclesiological principles. The writer accepts that there is only one Church outside which the Holy Spirit is not. But he maintains that baptism is performed by Christ at the invocation of His name. Starting from this premise, this writer holds that when the name of the Lord is invoked, even by those who are outside the Catholic Church, in the course of a baptism, the invocation operates in such a way that the baptism which thus takes place is authentic. Exactly what value such a baptism has is not defined by this author. It seems, however, that he too retains many doubts as to its efficacy, since he says that if someone thus baptized outside the Catholic Church dies a schismatic, in other words before he repents and returns to the Catholic Church, his baptism is of no significance for his salvation.[306]

These views can be taken as those of the Church of Rome and her Bishop Stephen because they come to the conclusion that the rebaptism of those returning to the Catholic Church is not required which is exactly as Stephen of Rome maintained. The point which interests us here, however, is not that of rebaptism, but that of the ecclesiological presuppositions behind it. On these both the treatise *De Rebaptismate* (and Stephen of Rome) and Cyprian seem to be in essential agreement; for both accept that the Holy Spirit is not given to those who are baptized outside the Catholic Church.[307] We can in consequence accept that the consciousness of the "Catholic Church" which Cyprian formulated as a result of the schisms did not differ in essence from that of those who disagreed with him on the issue of baptism. And, therefore, that, insofar, as the sources allow us to know, this consciousness was that of all the Churches of the middle of the third century.

Summarizing the information we have, we observe that the clarification in the Church's consciousness of catholicity, which took place as a result of the acute problem of schism and with the help of the great figure of Cyprian, consisted in the following basic principles:

(a) In contrast to the schismatic group, the Catholic Church possesses the fullness of the body of Christ (original meaning of catholicity) which, however, is manifested not simply as unity in the Eucharist or in orthodoxy and in the Bishop, but as fullness and self-sufficiency in every saving operation of the Holy Spirit expressed through the unity of each Church around the Bishop in whom the Church resides (*ecclesia in episcopo*).

(b) Schismatics are outside the Church, and in consequence, there can be no question of their participation in the sphere of the body of Christ. Hence, there is no essential distinction from an ecclesiological viewpoint between schism and heresy. What interests Cyprian is that both are outside the Church. Given that the Church is the one and only body of Christ, anyone who is outside the Church is outside Christ and outside salvation.[308]

It is not hard to see that such an "ecclesiology of schism" arises out of the ancient identification of the Church with the eucharistic synaxis and the oneness of that synaxis in each Church. A basic presupposition of Cyprian's position is *the coincidence between the canonical boundaries of the Church and her essential boundaries*. This coincidence was achieved, as we have seen, through the unity of each Church in one

Eucharist under one Bishop. Hence anyone who does not participate in this unity and establishes a second Eucharist under a second Bishop within the geographical boundaries of a given Church (the creation of a schism) is establishing a second Church not only in a canonical sense but also in an essential dogmatic sense. Given, however, that the Church according to Cyprian's basic understanding is one only, any communion in another Eucharist and under another Bishop bears no relation to the body of Christ. To have two or more eucharistic communities under two or more Bishops in each city is unacceptable. Without this presupposition, the "ecclesiology of schism" developed by Cyprian would not be possible.

Was the problem of schism solved through this ecclesiology of Cyprian's? From an historical and perhaps also from a theological viewpoint, the answer is negative.[309] The coincidence between the canonical and essential boundaries of the Church was not accepted by Stephen of Rome, and was later rejected totally by Augustine. After him, this negative position towards Cyprian's ecclesiology was followed almost unanimously by the West which preferred to make a distinction between the charismatic and canonical spheres of the Church, and to accept the possibility that even those who by reason of schism did not participate in the latter, might participate in the former. The East, apart from a very few exceptions, seems to have followed Cyprian without yet having solved this fundamental problem from either a theological or an historical viewpoint. The final answer as regards history will be given only once the sources after Cyprian in both East and West have been examined. Cyprian's position, which we have examined here, covers the situation regarding the relation of schism to the unity of the Church only in the first three centuries.

3. The Eucharist, the Bishop and the unity of the "Catholic Church throughout the world"

We have seen above that the term "Catholic Church" was not identified with the "worldwide Church" in the sources of the first three centuries. The connection of the catholicity of the Church with her universality can be seen only from the fourth century onwards although the connection between these two concepts was not formed into a full identification until the time of the Blessed Augustine.[310] In order, however, for this connection to have taken place in the fourth century, the way must certainly have been prepared for it during the first three centuries. We propose to look at this preparation here because of its direct relationship with the unity of the Church in the Eucharist and the Bishop.

The consciousness that all Christians form *one* Church despite being scattered "throughout the world" is evident from the first days of the Church. This consciousness should be connected with two basic factors. The first factor is external to the Church, and consists in the fact that when Christianity first appeared, it was confronted with a widespread "universal" unity – the unity of the *oikoumene* – the idea of which was cultivated by the Greeks of Christ's time.[311] During the first three centuries, the Church never lost the consciousness of living within this *oikoumene*, and her sacred mission, as carried out indeed by the Apostle to the Gentiles, very early revealed her universal spirit.[312] The second factor contributing to the unity of Christians all over the world is internal to the Church and consists in the Church's self-awareness of forming a people, the Israel of God, which is scattered to the ends of the earth. In the same way, there was formed very early the consciousness of a *Church of the diaspora*, which is clearly expressed in the first Epistle of Peter,[313] and which, later, through the sharp differentiation of Christianity from both Judaism and Hellenism, took on the form of characterizing the Church as a *third race*.

The consciousness of the unity of the Church throughout the world was connected early with the Divine Eucharist. We see this in the *Didache* which preserves in the original eucharistic prayers the image of the unity in the Eucharist not only of each Church, but also of the whole "Catholic Church throughout the world": "Just as this loaf was scattered all over the mountains and was brought together and made one, so *let Thy Church be gathered from the ends of the earth* in Thy Kingdom."[314] It repeats the same prayer a little later (10.5) with the petition: "*...and gather her together from the four winds...*" We see this connection of the Eucharist with the consciousness of the unity of Christians all over the world also in the *Epistle to Diognetus*. In this text, the spread of the Church all over the world is heavily stressed.[315] The concept of the Church in this epistle is that of the new Paradise in the midst of which is the tree which is Christ, and in which, the faithful are gathered together to perform the Eucharist under the leadership of the ministers.[316]

In the second half of the second century and arising out of the Paschal controversies, we are confronted with a particular emphasis on the consciousness that the Churches all over the world form a unity.[317] At the same period, and as a result both of these disputes,[318] and of Montanism,[319] the first councils of Bishops make their appearance, an event which brings into history once and for all a concrete external criterion for expressing the unity of the Catholic Church throughout the world.

It is a notable fact that even at this period the unity of the Catholic Church throughout the world is combined with unity in the Eucharist and in the Bishop. The institution of councils, as it appears during the years we are looking at, has in view in the final analysis nothing other than "communion," i.e. the unity of the Churches in the Eucharist. This is evident from a careful reading of the first text to give us any information about councils: "The faithful in Asia came together often and in many parts of Asia to consider this subject, and examined the novel utterances and declared them profane and rejected the heresy; thus [the heretics] were expelled from the Church and *debarred from communion*."[320] But the Paschal disputes too were closely bound up with unity in the Eucharist: "Victor, who presided over the Church of the Romans, immediately tried to cut off *from the common union* as heterodox all the *paroikies* of Asia with the Churches bordering them, and publicized this through letters, proclaiming all the brethren there totally *excommunicate*."[321] From this passage, it becomes obvious that the supreme expression of the "common union," i.e. of the unity of the Church throughout the world, lies in the *communion* of the Eucharist. Thus, Irenaeus, writing to Victor of Rome on the same subject, uses as his principle argument the fact that the bishops of Rome prior to Victor "sent the Eucharist" to "those who did not observe" the same manner of celebrating Easter as Rome did.

On the universal level too, this unity in the Eucharist was a unity *through the Bishop.* This was shown in various ways. The communication of members of one Church travelling to another required them to be provided with a special letter from the Bishop confirming their position in their own Church[322] to the end that they should be received into eucharistic communion. This is shown even more characteristically in the practice, which appears also in the canonical sources, whereby each Bishop "concedes" the Eucharist to the Bishop of another Church who is visiting him.* We know that this took place in Rome when Polycarp went there to deal with the question of Easter[323] while the Syriac *Didascalia* around the beginning of the third century presents it as a normal practice at least in that area.[324]

In this way, it was demonstrated in the most graphic manner that there was essentially *one Eucharist* and *one episcopate* in *the whole world.* Thus, the differences over the manner of performing the Eucharist were very few and of secondary importance while the basic structure of the Eucharist was amazingly the same in all geographical regions, as we see from a comparison between the outline of the liturgy in Justin's *First Apology* and the eastern liturgies of the fourth century. The fact that the Eucharist in Rome could be performed with no difficulty by Polycarp from Ephesus, and the evidence of Egeria's account of her travels in Jerusalem and elsewhere, together with that of Abercius of Hierapolis who travelled through almost all the then known world, finding everywhere the same "infinitely great and pure fish from

---

* Trans. note: i.e. he allows the visiting bishop to take his place as celebrant.

the spring, whom a pure virgin caught and gave to His friends to eat forever, having a mixed wine that is good and giving it with the bread."[325]

But if, as appears from the above, there was but *one* Church in all the world according the consciousness of unity in the first three centuries, how is the existence of *many full* and *Catholic Churches* around the world to be understood? How, in other words, could the Christians of those days conceive of the one "Catholic Church throughout the world" despite the multiplicity of Churches in various places especially when they regarded the latter as *full Churches*? Here we come up against *the most fundamental problem of all*. This is the problem of how the Catholic Churches in various places relate to the Catholic Church throughout the world in the consciousness of the Church of the first three centuries. On this question, the existing sources permit the following observations.

If the information in the sources is examined carefully, it shows that the strong unity among Christians all over the world was necessarily manifested *through the local Church*. No Christian believer could participate in the unity of the Church throughout the world if he did not first belong to the unity of a particular local Church. This raises the fundamental problem of the relationship that existed, both ecclesiologically and canonically, between the unity of the local Church and that of the Church throughout the world. What has already been written about the catholicity of the local Church precludes an understanding of the Catholic Church throughout the world as a unity of *parts* complementing each other, given that each local Church, having her own Bishop as a genuine successor to the Apostles both in the leadership of the one Eucharist and in orthodox faith, was a *full* and *complete* Church which had no need of any complement. In this case, how are we to understand the unity of the particular Churches in the one Catholic Church throughout the world?

Already from the beginning of the second century, as Ignatius testifies, there was the consciousness that *"the Bish-*

ops who are at the ends of the earth *are in the mind (gnome) of Jesus Christ.*"[326] This is of particular importance for the unity of the Church throughout the world and the expression of this unity through the institution of councils.[327] But if this is placed in the light of Ignatius' ecclesiology, according to which, as we have seen, the whole Christ is revealed in the unity of each Church, the unity of the Bishops who are at the ends of the earth can mean nothing other than mystical *identity*: given that according to Ignatius' ecclesiology the Church under each Bishop is united and presented in him as the body of Christ, then all the Bishops, coinciding in the same center, are "in Jesus Christ." Universal unity, therefore, consists not in a mutual complementarity of parts or in a democratic "majority" but in the *coincidence* of the local Churches with each other in the same place, i.e. "in the *gnome* of Jesus Christ."

A similar understanding of the unity of the Churches throughout the world in one Church is also expressed by St Cyprian. In agreement with the entire tradition before him, he regards the Bishop, as we have seen, as the center of the Church's unity as the one *on whom* the Church is based. How does he view the unity of the "Bishops who are at the ends of the earth," however? Here we should observe, with E. Mersch,[328] that it is not possible to find in Cyprian any external criterion for the unity of the local Churches. While he keeps on talking about the unity within each Church, especially in the *De Catholicae Ecclesiae Unitate*, he does not by any means speak clearly about the unity of all the Churches in various places. It is mainly negative conclusions on this subject that can be drawn from a careful examination of his works. Thus is it perfectly clear that, despite his recognition of the primacy of Peter, he does not recognize in any of the Bishops the right to express the unity of all the Bishops. This is demonstrated, besides, by his constant struggles against Rome's view on baptism. If the texts in his works which have provoked so much discussion[329] had even the slightest sense of acknowledging in the Roman Church the property of expressing the unity of all the Churches throughout the world, these struggles of Cyprian's would be inexplicable. Besides, on the positive side, the only principle governing Cyprian's theology of the unity of the local Churches is *that of the unity of the episcopate*: *"episcopatus unus est."*[330] This means that each of the Bishops participates in the same episcopate, not as a part of a whole, but as an expression of the whole. Hence the full equality of the Bishops all over the world forms a fundamental ecclesiological axiom for this Father too. It is not only all the Bishops together, but also each one of the Bishops who is the successor of all the Apostles.[331] The unity of all these Bishops and of the Churches under them in the one Catholic Church throughout the world is described by Cyprian with the term *unanimitas*.[332] This shared consciousness and unanimity is ascertained through all the communication between the Bishops but in a quite special way through the Councils. In this way, the unity of the Bishops in different places is not a unity by addition as in a modern democracy but *a unity of identity*. St Cyprian underlines this more than clearly when he writes to Antoninus (*Epist.* 52): "Hence also the unity of the Bishops, who, though they are many, form a *unity through the identity* of their minds." In consequence, it is only as a unity in identity that the unity of the episcopate according to Cyprian can rightly be expressed.

The concept of *unity in identity* is the underlying basis for the consciousness of universality in all the Churches during the first three centuries. This was the spirit behind both the insistent rejections of any intervention by Rome in the Churches of Asia in the second century about which we have spoken already and the institution of Councils itself. In Irenaeus' famous passage about tradition,[333] the dominant idea is that of the identity of faith: the Church scattered throughout the world is one in faith and speaks with one voice because there is an identity of all the local Churches confirmed by the identity of mind of their Bishops.[334] For Tertullian, similarly, the unity of the Catholic Church around the world is nothing other than the *coincidence* and identity of the Churches in different places *with the content and life of the first apostolic Church*; an identity which makes each one of the Churches fully apostolic and catholic: "For this reason," he writes, "these Churches (i.e. those scattered around the world), however numerous and large they may be, are nothing other that *the original apostolic Church herself*, from which they all originated. They are *all original, all apostolic*, because they all confirm their complete unity... *No other law governs them but the one tradition of the same mystery*."[335] This doctrine of Tertullian's not only excludes the primacy of any Church, since all the Churches without exception are equally apostolic and full Churches,[336] but it also implies the same concept of unity that we find in Irenaeus: the identity of each Church with the tradition of the same mystery forms *the only law* governing the relationship of mutual unity of the Churches all over the world in the one catholic and apostolic Church. In this, precisely, lies the importance of the institution of Councils,[337] at which the "Bishops who are at the ends of the earth" would come together, insofar as they could, and make sure that they were all "in the mind of Jesus Christ." In the case where full identity could not be established, unity would be in jeopardy, and might be broken up by the exclusion of certain Churches from "communion."[338] In this way, the catholicity of each Church was not diminished but confirmed, insofar as she too was "in the mind of Jesus Christ." Such a consciousness of *unity in identity* among the Churches in different places was understood as a *meeting of all the Churches in different places at the same center: "in the mind of Jesus Christ."* Hence if in conclusion the question is posed as to what is the center of unity among the Churches throughout the world, the entire consciousness of the Church of the first three centuries would reject the idea of any one Bishop individually forming such a center.[339] *The only center of such unity for the Church of that period was Jesus Christ.* The Catholic Church throughout the world knew no other center of her unity. The coincidence and identity of the local Churches with this center formed the expression of their unity in the one Church, expressed through communion in the one Eucharist, from which Churches not identified with this center were cut off.

But how was it made certain that the Churches were identical with each other in the same center, i.e. in the "mind of

Jesus Christ"? What criterion was used to establish that the local Churches were united in the one "Catholic Church throughout the world"? This leads us to examine the deeper meaning of the catholicity of the Church which appears in the sources of the first three centuries as having the following three dimensions.

First of all, the *chronological* or *historical* coincidence of the local Churches with the past, and in particular with the original apostolic Church, was regarded as indispensable. This element of *reference back through history* was so strong in the Church's consciousness during the first three centuries that the terms *one Church* and *ancient Church* are linked together and interpret each other.[340] For Hegesippus, this historical reference back to the original Church, and the identity of each Church with this original Church, was the strongest argument against heresies.[341] For Tertullian, each local Church is fully apostolic and catholic precisely because she is none other than "the primitive apostolic Church herself."[342] It is not without significance, then, that all the ancient Councils, including indeed the Ecumenical Councils, grounded their decisions in what the Scriptures and the Fathers had in the past expressed as the faith of the Church.

A second point seen as indispensable was the *spatial* or *geographical* verification of the identity of the Churches in the same faith and life "in the mind of Jesus Christ." This meant that in order to be "catholic" each Church had to be identified with the other Churches and live in full communion with them. The necessity for this verification led to the appearance and establishment of the institution of Councils. The ultimate import of which during the first three centuries is revealed in the light of Ignatius' phrase: "the Bishops who are at the ends of the earth are in the mind of Jesus Christ."[343] But this element of geographical or *spatial* catholicity was not in itself sufficient for the unity of the "Catholic Church throughout the world." Its importance was absolutely dependent on the existence of the first criterion, i.e. that of going back chronologically and historically to the primitive Church, and the verification through this of the identity of each

Church with the original apostolic Church. Thus, supposing that the *majority* of the Churches coincided with each other but did not coincide with the original apostolic Church, then the opinion of the "majority" would have no force.[344] This meant that the "Catholic Church throughout the world," united through the Councils, did not form a unity *by addition* in which "catholic" would coincide with "majority," but a *qualitative* and *organic* unity in which what was "catholic" was identified with what was "true" and "original" as this appeared in the first apostolic Church.

Yet both the geographical or latitudinal dimension of the "Catholic Church" and the chronological or retrospective referral and connection with her original state of being remained unable to verify the identity of the Churches in the "mind of Jesus Christ" without a third component of catholicity, the *charismatic* or *sacramental*. It should be noted that both the reference back to the historical memory of the Church and the meeting of the Churches around the world in the same place (*epi to auto*) took place *in the person of the Bishop*. Thus, the reference of the Churches to the past was effected by drawing up *lists of Bishops* from which it was evident that each Church went back without a break to the Apostles while the meeting of the local Churches *in the same place* was effected through *episcopal* Councils. This event was not coincidental, but should be connected with the notion, clearly expressed by Irenaeus, that the truth of the Church is unbreakably bound up with the charism of the Priesthood, and is therefore preserved by the Bishops "who with the succession of the episcopate have received the certain *charisma* of truth, according to the goodwill of the Father."[*qui cum episcopatus successione charisma veritatis certum secundum placitum patris acceperunt*][345] But in this way the catholicity of the Church was organically and unbreakably bound up, in the ultimate analysis, with the unity of the Eucharist given that the *"charisma"* of the Priesthood[346] was bestowed only within the Eucharist.

These observations lead us to the conclusion that according to the sources of the first three centuries, the unity of the local Churches in the one "Catholic Church throughout the world" understood as their identity with the one whole Christ, was expressed in history: a) as a vertical relationship of each Church with the one and whole Christ mystically present in the one Eucharist, to which the Bishop was connected as the visible head, possessing the "charism of truth"; b) as a historical reference back to the past and the full identity of each Church with the primitive apostolic Church; and c) as a latitudinal extension of each Church to the inclusion and communion of the Churches everywhere on earth, if and insofar as the first two conditions held good for them. This tripartite identification of the Churches with each other and with the whole Christ was the ultimate and essential arbiter of the "common union of the Churches" through which the one, holy, catholic and apostolic Church was preserved and expressed.[347]

Summarizing the conclusions of Part Two, we may make the following observations:

The identification of the Divine Eucharist with the Church of God which is in a particular place, which as we saw in Part One was firmly established in the consciousness of the early Church, entailed maintaining *one* eucharistic synaxis "under the leadership of the Bishop" in each Church. From historical research into the sources, we have established that Ignatius' exhortation to maintain *one* Eucharist under *one* Bishop at *one* altar corresponded to an historical state of affairs. It was thus established that there was in fact only one synaxis to perform the Eucharist and one Bishop in each Church. This fact was not altered by the existence of "household" churches because, as has been established, there was not more than one such Church in each city (so that the household Church was "the whole Church" according to Paul), nor by the spread of Christianity into the countryside given that at the beginning and up to the middle of the second century the Christians from the countryside came together into the Church of the nearest city, and later they formed

Churches of their own with their own Bishops, the chorepiscopi, who were initially full Bishops. This principle of one Bishop presiding over the one Eucharist in each Church held good for all geographical areas, and the doubts about it implied at certain points of Eusebius' *Ecclesiastical History* have been proved by our research here to be groundless.

Such a unity of the whole Church of God in a certain place in the "one Eucharist under the leadership of the Bishop" had a decisive effect on the formation of the Catholic Church during the crucial period of the first three centuries. Thus initially and at the very first appearance of the term "Catholic Church," unity in the Divine Eucharist and in the Bishop was that historical reality which expressed in the fullest way the meaning of the catholicity which was gradually entering the Church's consciousness. The Apostle Paul's "whole Church," identified with the one Church of each place united in the Divine Eucharist, became St Irenaeus' "Catholic Church" which, as we have established, had no other meaning than the *fullness* and *wholeness* and *identity* of the body of Christ as this was realized and revealed in the one Eucharist under the one Bishop in which the "multitude" was united. Later, when around the middle of the second century heresies and schisms formed themselves into organized groups "outside the Church" but tending to the cloak themselves in the external marks of the Church, the emphasis in the "Catholic Church" was placed on orthodoxy and on the pure preservation of the apostolic preaching without this meaning that unity in the Divine Eucharist and in the Bishop ceased to be the main factor differentiating the Catholic Church from the heresies and schisms. The Eucharist was "in agreement" with orthodoxy and orthodoxy in agreement with the Eucharist (Irenaeus), while the Bishop was shown to be the successor of the Apostles both in the Eucharist and in orthodoxy (Hippolytus), preserving through the "charism of truth" (Irenaeus) which he had received at his ordination, performed exclusively during the Eucharist (Hippolytus), the identity of the faith and also the fullness of the Church (Cyprian).

Thus each Church, united in her Bishop who had been thus appointed, was a full Church identified with the *whole body of Christ*,[348] whence also the term "Catholic Church" was used during the first three centuries primarily and chiefly, as we have seen, of each such Church, and indeed in such a way that it could be declared that "there should be one Bishop in the Catholic Church."

This catholicity of each episcopal Church does not make her ecclesiologically and historically independent of the other Churches around the world. The consciousness which early appeared concerning the "Catholic Church throughout the world" (*Mart. Polyc.*) meant that although there were *Churches* around the world nevertheless there was in essence but *one Church*. This one Church throughout the world was not a sum total of parts, for, as we have seen, each Church in particular was the whole Church, and this for reasons connected not with the geographical extent of the Church but with her nature which is revealed especially in the one body of the one Eucharist. This one Church throughout the world was manifested in history as a unity not of parts but of *full circles* obliged to be *essentially identified with one another*. This *unity in identity* was manifested in time through identity with what the Lord and the Apostles taught (apostolic succession of bishops) and in space through identity with what the other Churches around the world lived and taught (institution of councils) while the absence of this identity automatically meant the creation of a schism.

The ultimate form of expression of such a Church throughout the world was unity in the Divine Eucharist and in the Bishop. "Communion" was the ultimate link in the "common union" (Eusebius), while each Eucharist was offered for the one, holy, catholic and apostolic Church from one end of the earth to the other, each Bishop being able to "concede" the Eucharist to the Bishop of another Church (Anicetus of Rome to Polycarp) and each believer able to partake in the Eucharist of another Church with the introduction and permission of his own Bishop. In this way, the unity of the faithful around the world was nothing other than a unity *through the*

Bishop and the Church to which each belonged. The living cell of church unity was the one Eucharist under the leadership of the Bishop and the "Catholic Church" expressed therein. It was only through the life of this cell that each Christian lived and all Christians together in all corners of the world who make up the one Catholic Church. Through this consciousness of unity, the Church of the first three centuries recognized *the Lord Jesus Christ as the one center of the unity of the Catholic Church throughout the world.* It was with Him that the "Bishops who are at the ends of the earth" had to be identified, and Him that each Bishop mystically and truly personified, in a full and catholic manner, as he presided over the Divine Eucharist through which the Church of God was revealed in each place.

NOTES TO PART TWO

[1] Ignatius, *Philad.* 4.

[2] See above, p. 66f.

[3] Ignatius, *Smyrn.* 8:1.

[4] Ignatius, *Magn.* 11:1. Cf. also *Tral.* 8:1, "Not because I know of anything of the sort among you; but since you are dear to me I put you on your guard, knowing the wiles of the devil."

[5] The term *apodiylismos* (Lat. *abstractio*) does not mean division into groups, but *disintegration* or divisions of an individualistic nature, as in 1 Corinthians ("I am of Paul," etc.) Cf. also the "passers by," or *isolated* people, in Ignatius *Eph.* 9:1 and *Rom.* 9:3.

[6] Ignatius, *Philad.* 3:1. This should have been taken into account by W. Bauer (*Rechtgläubigkeit und Ketzerei im ältesten Christentum*, 1964[2], p. 67) who wrongly regards what Ignatius says about unity as a mere wish on the part of the apostolic Father and talks about an "Ignatian faction" (*Ignatiusgruppe*) in order to support his theories about the preexistence and prevalence of heresy in the early Church which are otherwise proved groundless.

[7] See above, p. 50f.

[8] Thus e.g L. Cerfaux, *La Théologie de l'Église*, p. 145: "As the Christians did not always gather as a full assembly but formed separate groups within the same city which gathered less officially in private houses, we intend to speak of domestic churches." The

same view is also expressed by P. Batiffol, op. cit. p. 88; H. Leclercq, in *D.A.C.L.* IV/2, 1921, col. 2280; J. Jungmann, *The Early Liturgy*, p. 13; E.A. Judge, op. cit. p. 37 and P. Trembelas, "Worship in Apostolic Times" (in Greek) (*loc. cit.*). V. Stephanidis (op. cit. p. 34) goes so far as to assert that the household Churches were so numerous within the local Churches that they became centers of heretical teaching and that was why they were finally done away with. From what sources Stephanidis derived this information, we do not know. But these are representative examples of the widespread view that there were many household Churches within a local Church.

This idea formed the basis for the view of Protestant historiography that the Church grew gradually into catholicity; on this view, before 1 Clement, there was a variety of gatherings which is still preserved in the *Didache* while through 1 Clement and Ignatius we arrive at one assembly under the Bishop in place of several assemblies with corresponding implications for the elevation of the Bishop. See e.g. P. Carrington, *The Early Christian Church*, I, 1957, p. 476. For earlier scholars see G. Konidaris, "New Research Towards Solving the Problems of the Sources of Early Christianity," in *E.E.Th.S.* (1957-58), 1959, p. 232. The question which is raised and addressed for the first time here, namely whether there was more than one "household church" in each city, is consequently of tremendous importance for the formation of the Catholic Church.

⁹ This is another indication of the clear distinction between the notions of the "Christian family" and the Church, discussed above.

¹⁰ Aquila and Priscilla were Christians before they moved to Corinth. Cf. Harnack, "Probabilia über die Adresse und den Verfasser des Hebräerbriefs" in *Z.N.T.W.* 1 (1900), 16 f. Their move to Corinth was probably due to Claudius' edict expelling the Jews from Rome. Cf. F.F. Bruce, "Christianity under Claudius," in *Bulletin of the John Rylands Library* 44 (1962), 310. The story of these two people, as far as it can be reconstructed on the basis of Acts, Romans and 1 Corinthians, reveals their importance for the Pauline Churches. Both were linked with a Church "in their household" both in Ephesus (1 Cor. 16:20) and in Rome (Rom. 16:4). This may suggest that the "Church in the household" was usually linked with prominent people.

¹¹ See L. Cerfaux, *La Theologie*, p. 145, who accepts this, even though it is essentially incompatible with his view that the "household church" was a semi-official Church within the local Church.

¹² See above, p. 48f.

¹³ ibid.

[14] The significance of the expression "the whole church" (*hole he ekklesia*) for the origin of the term "catholic church" will be discussed below.

[15] This does not preclude the possibility that the Christians moved from one house to another as they would often have had to on account of the persecutions. What is important is the fact that in whatever house the Eucharist was celebrated, it included all the faithful of the city and was in consequence *one* Eucharist expressing the *one* Church sojourning in that place.

[16] This classic passage was probably the original form of the phrase "Church in the household," or *vice versa*.

[17] This is how it is interpreted by e.g. E.A. Judge, op. cit. p. 37. Cf F.J. Foakes Jackson - K. Lake (ed.), *The Beginnings of Christianity*, IV, p. 29.

[18] The reference to papyri (P. Ryl. 11, 76,10) in F.J. Foakes Jackson - K. Lake (ed.), op. cit. IV, p. 29, note 46, in support of such a meaning is unacceptable in the case of this passage because the verb with which the phrase *"kat' oikon"* is connected here does not signify motion. It is perhaps natural to understand *"kat' oikon"* as meaning "from house to house" if the verb in the sentence implies motion (e.g. in the phrase "it was distributed *kat' oikon"*). But this interpretation is impossible with a verb that conotes a state, such as "to break bread."

[19] "Saul laid waste the church, entering house after house (*kata tous oikous eisporeuomenos*)."

[20] "I did not shrink from declaring to you anything that was profitable, and teaching you in public and from house to house (*kat' oikous*)."

[21] 1 Cor. 11:16.

[22] 2 Cor. 11:28.

[23] See e.g. its influence on the formation of the Church's polity in G. Konidaris, *On the Supposed Difference*, p. 56.

[24] Ignatius, who writes epistles in the Pauline manner, preserves the by now established term "church," and indeed in a purely Pauline sense, as we shall see below; but he uses the term "house" with no connection to the Church (*Smyrn.* 13, *Polyc.* 8:2). This is the first indication in the sources that the phrase "Church in the household" has been abandoned. This is due to the fact that by Ignatius' time the term "church" had already prevailed as the expression of a reality which had formerly been expressed by several different terms.

[25] This probably took place around the end of the third century.

Cf. Noele Maurice - Denis Boulet, "Titres Urbains et Communauté," in *La Maison-Dieu*, No. 36, 1953, p. 14ff. In Alexandria, too, it seems that around the end of the third century the first Christian church building was established in honour of St Theonas. See Ch. Papadopoulos, *History of the Church of Alexandria* (in Greek), 1935, p.488.

[26] 1 Clem. 41:2: "It is not in every place, brethren, that the daily sacrifices are offered, or the prayers, or the sin-offerings, or the trespass-offerings, but in Jerusalem only. And even there they are not offered in every place, but only at the altar before the temple, once the offering has been carefully examined by the high priest and the ministers already mentioned. Those, therefore, who do anything contrary to the duty imposed by his will, are punished with death."

[27] Ignatius, *Philad*. 4. Cf. Ignatius, *Eph.* 20:2, and p. 91 above.

[28] "I live above one Martinus, at the Timotinian Baths; and during this time (I am now in Rome for the second time) I am unaware of any meeting of the Christians other than his" (*Martyrdom*, Ch. II; P.G. 6:1568).

[29] Justin, 1 *Apol.* 67. Cf. also 65.

[30] The Rome of the second half of the second century was a meeting place of many nationalities and of Christians from different parts of the empire. See G. La Piana, "Foreign Groups in Rome during the First Centuries of the Empire," in *The Harvard Theological Review* (1927), 183.

[31] E.g. in the matter of accepting the term "episkopos." See G. Konidaris, op.cit. pp. 55-56.

[32] It should be seen as highly significant that the Bishop initially went under the title "presiding presbyter" (*proestos presbyteros*) (see G. Konidaris, "Warum die Urkirche von Antiochia den "proestota presbyteron" der Ortsgemeinde als "ho Episkopos" bezeichnete," in *Münchener Theologische Zeitschrift*, 1961, pp. 269-84). This means that the institution of the Bishop was *par excellence* liturgical, and the whole of his authority stemmed from his position in the Eucharist. Because as Justin attests (1 *Apol.* 65 and 67), the term *proestos* ("president") was used to indicate the one who offered the Eucharist. Harnack (*Mission und Ausbreitung des Christentums in den drei ersten Jahrhunderten*, II[4], pp. 836, 841f.) talks about many places of worship and indeed parishes very early on, but on this point the following observations should be made: a) Harnack's statistic which raises the number of believers in Rome to about 30,000 is based on Eusebius and relates to the middle of the third century,

when, as we shall see later, the increase in the number of believers did indeed lead to the appearance of parishes; b) as to the information given by Justin in his reply to the Prefect, it should not be forgotten that he is trying to conceal the location of the eucharistic assembly, obviously so that the faithful would not be arrested; whereas, when he is writing his *Apology* and is not obliged to specify the location of the assembly, he does not hesitate to state clearly that *all* the faithful in Rome came together in one place for the celebration of the Eucharist; c) as to the division of Rome into 25 parishes between the times of Dionysius (259-68) and Marcellus (308/9), our only source is the *Liber Pontificalis*, which even Harnack himself does not consider reliable. Anyway, leaving that aside, these *tituli* do not necessarily signify eucharistic assemblies. Cf. also Part III below.

[33] A. Harnack, *Mission* , II, p. 278; R. Knopf, *Nachapostolischer Zeitalter*, 1905, p. 61 and K.S. Latourette, *A History of the Expansion of Christianity*, I, 1953, p. 110.

[34] Pliny the Younger, *Ep.* X, 97 and 98. Despite this, we consider that already in Paul's Epistles there is a suggestion that there were Christians in the countryside. The phrase "with all the saints who are in the whole of Achaea" (2 Cor. 1:1), placed in contradistinction to the Christians in the city of Corinth, probably indicates the existence of Christians outside the cities as well. Cf. above, p. 50f.

[35] Justin, 1 *Apol.* 67.

[36] J. Toutain, "Pagani, Pagus," in *Diction. des Antiquités Grecques et Romaines*, VI, p. 273ff; A. Grenier, "Vicus, vicani," ibid. V, p. 854ff.

[37] A. Grenier, *Manuel d'Archeologie gallo-romaine*, III, p. 696, where the inscription discovered in Solicia and dated 28 June 232 is published: "*Genio pagi Derveti peregrini qui posuer(unt) vico Soliciae...*"

[38] This theory was first developed by Imbart de la Tour in his work *Les Paroisses Rurales du IVᵉ au XIᵉ Siècle*, 1900 (this book was not available to us, but the gist of it can be found in *La Revue Historique*, vols. LX, LXI, LXVII and LXVIII). At least as regards the West, this had been the prevailing theory for a long time. W. Seston successfully set out to refute it in his article, "Note sur les Origines Religieuses des Paroisses Rurales," in *Revue d'Hist. et Philos. relig.* 15 (1935), 243-54.

[39] We base this supposition on the general character of Justin's *Apology*, written as it is in the name of all Christians generally, and on the fact that he knew other Churches besides that of Rome.

[40] This view is supported by the noteworthy fact that Dionysius of Corinth, who is writing at this time, knows of Churches only

"in cities." See Eusebius, *Eccl. Hist.* IV.23.10: "For from the beginning this has been your practice, to do good to all the brethren in various ways, and to send supplies to many churches in all the cities."

[41] *Das Institut der Chorbischöfe im Orient; historisch-kanonisch Studie* (Veröffentlichungen aus dem Kirchenhistorischen Seminar, II, 1), 1903.

[42] See above p. 94.

[43] Justin, 1 *Apol.* 65 and 67.

[44] There is, therefore, no basis for the view of earlier scholars such as Bergere (*Études Historiques sur les Chorévêques*, 1905), according to which the West did not know of chorepiscopi before the eighth century. The title certainly did not appear from the beginning, but the institution itself, as we shall see, existed earlier.

[45] See Hefele-Leclercq, *Histoire des Conciles*, II/2, col. 1210.

[46] ibid.

[47] Theodoret of Cyr, *Compendium of Heretical Fables* III.5, P.G. 83.408A.

[48] Eusebius, *Eccl. Hist.*, VII.30.10. Cf. Ch. Papadopoulos, *On Chorepiscopi and Titular Bishops* (in Greek), 1935, p. 6ff.

[49] V. Stephanidis (*Church History* p. 87) also refers to the passage in Eusebius' *Eccl. Hist.*, VII.24.6. But does that have to do with Bishops, or with presbyters according to the system of the Church of Alexandria?

[50] The Councils of Sardica (Can. 6) and Laodicea (Can. 57) forbade the installation of chorepiscopi henceforth. See V. Stephanidis, op. cit. p. 87. The information in Clement of Alexandria (*Who is the Rich Man Who shall be Saved*? 42), that when John was in Ephesus "He was invited to go out also into the adjacent lands of the Gentiles, in some places to install Bishops and in others to set in order whole Churches," probably refers to dioceses and rural Churches around Ephesus, which were ancient in origin.

[51] In the past, it was the view that the chorepiscopi were presbyters with semi-episcopal jurisdiction; that they were initially full Bishops has been maintained more recently, principally by F. Gillmann (op. cit.). Cf. Leclercq, *D.A.C.L.* III/1, 1435f. and Ch. Papadopoulos, *On Chorepiscopi*, p. 8.

[52] The Greek text is taken from the edition of Prof. H. Alivizatos, *The Sacred Canons* (in Greek; ed. *Apostoliki Diakonia*), 1949², p. 161ff.

[53] See Leclercq's detailed analysis of the texts in *D.A.C.L.* III/1, 1425f. From examination of the manuscripts, it emerges that Prof. Alivizatos' text, used here, is the most probable.

[54] Chiefly over the meaning of *"alla mên mêde presbuterous poleos"* and *"en etaira paroikia,"* on which see ibid. 1428f.

[55] So the Canon is interpreted by the Byzantine canonists Balsamon and Aristinos (P.G. 137.1160), as also by more recent foreign scholars, including R.B. Seckham, *The Text of the Canons of Ancyra* (Studia Ecclesiastica, III) 1891, p. 192. The text of the Canon is as follows: "Chorepiscopi are not allowed to ordain presbyters or deacons, not even presbyters of the city (*alla mên mêde presbuterous poleos*), without written permission from the Bishop, in another community (*en etaira paroikia*).

[56] It should be seen as indicative of this importance that the Canon of Neocaesarea, which is more or less contemporary with that of Ancyra, lays stress less on minimizing the importance of the chorepiscopi than on equating them with Bishops in the supreme ministry of the Divine Eucharist calling them "concelebrants" with the Bishops.

[57] A similar clear sign of the gradual decrease in the importance of the chorepiscopi appears in the 8th Canon of the Council of Antioch which deprives them of the right to issue "letters pacifical."

[58] V. Stephanidis (op. cit. p. 68) asks whether perhaps the concern here is with the name of Bishop being brought into disrepute because of quarrels between chorepiscopi and Bishops of the towns. But careful examination of the Canon makes it clear that the "degradation" is due to the smallness of the village: "but if there is a town that is growing so much in numbers of people that it is considered worthy of a bishopric, let it have [a Bishop]." H. Alivizatos, op. cit.p. 187.

[59] "It is not permitted simply to install a Bishop in a village or small town for which just one presbyter would suffice. For it is not necessary for Bishops to be installed there, in order that the name and authority of a Bishop may not be degraded" (ibid.).

[60] Among this generation was St Basil the Great, who contributed to the decrease in the importance of the chorepiscopi (*Letter to a Chorepiscopus*, in Alivizatos, op. cit. p. 390f.

[61] Alivizatos, op. cit. p. 207f.

[62] The disappearance of the chorepiscopi is confirmed by the fact that, contrary to the prevailing view, the number of Bishops fell rather than rising as time went on. For the years immediately following the fourth century, it is worthwhile investigating this fall in the number of Bishops on the basis of sources such as the Acts of the Councils, Minutes etc., as well as the works of Gerland-Gelzer and G. Konidaris.

[63] In earlier times, no one considered that the small number of Christians was degrading to the name and authority of a Bishop as the Council of Laodicea later thought. It is indicative of how things had changed in the meantime that when, for instance, Gregory the Wonderworker became Bishop of Neocaesarea in Pontus his flock initially numbered 17 Christians! (according to Gregory of Nyssa, *Life of St Gregory the Wonderworker*, P.G. 46.953).

[64] "That Bishops should not be appointed in the villages and country areas, but visitors (*periodeutai*) instead" (H. Alivizatos, op cit. p.207).

[65] The ordination of a chorepiscopus "at large" and not for a particular Church, which Ch. Papadopoulos talks about (*On Chorepiscopi*, p. 9), is in no way borne out by the sources. A Bishop without a specific Church is not to be found in the first centuries. As a basic ecclesiological principle, this applied to the chorepiscopus too.

[66] Eusebius, *Eccl. Hist.* IV.23.6.

[67] Thus for example K. Müller, *Beiträge zur Geschichte der Verfassung der alten Kirche* (in the series Abhandlungen d. Preuss. Akad. d. Wiss., phil.-hist., kl., No. 3), 1922, p. 7.

[68] See A. Harnack, *Mission*, II[4], p. 574.

[69] Eusebius, *Eccl. Hist.* IV.23.5.

[70] See *inter alia* Eusebius, *Eccl. Hist.* IV.23.

[71] *Eccl. Hist.* IV.23.7. Cf. G. Konidaris, *Ecclesiastical History of Greece* (in Greek), I, p. 407ff.

[72] E.g. in L. Duchesne, *Fastes Episcopaux de l'Ancienne Gaul*, 1907[2], pp. 40-43.

[73] E.g. in P. Nautin, *Lettres et Écrivains Chrétiens des IIe et IIIe siècles*, 1961, p. 93.

[74] See W.M. Ramsey, *Cities and Bishoprics of Phrygia*, I-II, 1897.

[75] See L. Duchesne, *Fastes Episcopaux*, p. 148.

[76] *Eccl. Hist.* V.4.1.

[77] Op. cit. p. 46f.

[78] For this distinction see G. Konidaris, *On the Supposed Difference*.

[79] *Eccl. Hist.* V.4.2.

[80] Despite the conclusions of W. Telfer, op. cit. p. 96.

[81] *Eccl. Hist.* VI.8.7 and 11.3.

[82] So the *Chronic. ad annum 212* (ed. Helm, p. 213): "Alexander was ordained the thirty-fifth Bishop of Jerusalem while Narcissus was still alive, and governed the Church alongside him" (*cum eo pariter*).

[83] Thus, G. Bardy in his edition of Eusebius' *Ecclesiastical History* in the series *Sources Chrétiennes*, No. 41, 1955, p. 156, note 13.

[84] *Eccl. Hist.* VI.11.3.

[85] E.g. *Eccl. Hist.* VI.34: *tois en paraptomasin exetazomenois* (those *found to be* in transgression).

[86] Eusebius is obviously making a similar mistake, on the basis of who knows what unclear sources, in the case of Anatolius Bishop of Caesarea in Palestine, of whom he writes: "Theotectus, bishop of Caesarea in Palestine, first ordained him as Bishop, intending to make him his successor in his own *paroikia* after his death, and for a short time both of them presided over the same Church. (*Eccl. Hist.* VII.32.21).

[87] See e.g Ch. Papadopoulos, *History of the Church of Alexandria* (in Greek), p. 484 and G. Konidaris, *G.C.H.*, pp. 142 and 243. Likewise E. Schwartz, *Die Kirchengeschichte des Eusebius*, III, 1909, p. ccxxi; W. Bauer, op. cit. p. 68 and W. Telfer, op. cit. p. 106.

[88] *Eccl. Hist.* IV.23.1. Cf. also III.4.11: "Besides these, that Areopagite, named Dionysius... is mentioned by another Dionysius, an ancient writer and pastor of the *paroikia* of the Corinthians, as the first Bishop of the Church in Athens."

[89] *Eccl. Hist.* IV.23.7.

[90] ibid. V.5.8. Cf. V.4.1.

[91] ibid. VI.43.21 and VII.3.

[92] ibid. VII.28.1: "Of these, the most eminent were Firmilianus, Bishop of Caesarea in Cappadocia, the brothers Gregory and Athenodorus, *pastors of the paroikies in Pontus*, and in addition Helenus of the paroikia in Tarsus and Nicomas of that in Iconium; and moreover, Hymenaeus of the Church in Jerusalem." Cf. ibid. V.24.14-15, where the same meaning should be given to the term *paroikia*. On this, see also below.

[93] Ibid. IV.1. Cf. III.14; IV.5.5; VI.8.3.

[94] Cf. characteristically ibid. VII.30.17, where the terms "catholic church" and *"paroikia"* are equated: "Therefore we have been compelled to excommunicate him, since he sets himself against God and refuses to obey, and to appoint in his place another *Bishop* for the *catholic church*; by divine Providence, as we believe, [we appoint] Domnus, son of the blessed Demetrianus, who formerly presided in a distinguished manner over the same *paroikia*..."

[95] Ibid. II.16: "And they say that this Mark was the first to be sent to Egypt, and that he proclaimed the Gospel which he had composed, and first established *churches* at Alexandria."

[96] Ibid. VIII.13.7.

[97] See Dionysius of Alexandria *apud* Eusebius, *Eccl. Hist.* VII.11.12, where "Egypt" signifes the countryside as opposed to Alexandria which is called "the city."

[98] "In the fourth year of Domitian, Annianus, the first [Bishop] of the *paroikia* in Alexandria, died after completing 22 years [in office], and was succeeded by the second [Bishop], Albius" (ibid. III.14). See likewise IV.1 and IV.5.5. In connection with Demetrius himself, too, the term *paroikia* is often used in the singular. Thus, "When Demetrius, who presided over the *paroikia* there [in Alexandria], found out about this later..." (ibid. VI.8.3). Likewise ibid. VI.19.15: "to Demetrius *the Bishop of the paroikia* [of Alexandria]."

[99] See above, p. 94ff.

[100] This view is supported by research on the liturgical texts from Egypt, which, as Prof. P. Trembelas shows (*Mikron Evchologion*, I, 1950, p. 216), remain inexplicable if what were later held to be "presbyters" of Alexandria during the first three centuries are not regarded as chorepiscopi. The way these pieces of evidence dovetail is noteworthy for the thesis of this work.

[101] See Eusebius, *Eccl. Hist.* X.4.68.

[102] First Ecumenical Council, Canon 8 (ed. Alvizatos, p. 28f.)

[103] *Smyrn.* 8.

[104] See above, Introduction.

[105] Augustine did this in his desire to combat the provincialism of the Donatists. Cf. P. Batiffol, *Le Catholicisme de Saint Augustin*, 1929[5], p. 212.

[106] Immediately after the third century, Cyril of Jerusalem gives the first synthetic definition of the catholicity of the Church, in which the concept of universality forms merely a part of the meaning of the term "Catholic Church": "She is called catholic because she extends throughout all the world, from one end of the earth to the other; and because she teaches universally (*katholikôs*) and completely all the doctrines that should come to men's knowledge... and because she brings into subjection to godliness the whole race of mankind... and because she universally treats and heals the whole species of sins... and possesses in herself every form of virtue which is named..." (*Catechetical Orations* 18.23, PG 33:1044). From the fourth century on, the term requires particular study. Cf. A. Göpfert, *Die Katholizität. Eine dogmengeschichtliche Studie*, 1876. In recent times, Roman Catholic theology in particular, for ecclesiological reasons and mainly in order to give ecclesiological import to the Bishop of Rome as universal Bishop, has identified catholicity totally with the worldwide character or universality of

the Church. Notable exceptions are (from the viewpoint of historical research on the term) J. Moehler, who strongly rejects the
identification of "catholic" with the "world-wide" or "universal"
Church, at least in respect of the sources from the first three centuries (*op. cit.*, French translation pp. 246-249); and from the viewpoint
of systematic theology, E. Mersch, *La Théologie du Corps Mystique*,
II, 1946², p. 234ff. and H. de Lubac, *Catholicisme. Les Aspects Sociaux
du Dogme*, 1947², p. 26. Y. M.-J. Congar (*Sainte Église. Études et
Approches Ecclésiologiques*, 1963, p. 158ff.) connects catholicity with
the idea of the "fullness of Christ" in which multiplicity is combined with unity. In modern Orthodox theology, the meaning of
the term "Catholic Church" has yet to be examined from an historical point of view, while from the viewpoint of systematic
theology Cyril of Jerusalem's synthetic definition largely prevails.
Thus, in I. Karmiris' *Synopsis* (pp. 89ff.) the following tripartite definition is given: "She is catholic firstly as being spread out and
including followers all over the world and throughout time, without any restrictions of place or time... Secondly... in the sense of
being orthodox - as opposed to the various heretical and schismatic churches... Thirdly, catholicity denotes the unity and
wholeness and identity of the Church as the body of Christ... From
the above it becomes clear that catholicity is not merely a quantitative mark of the Church, but also at the same time a qualitative
one...." For a similarly composite definition, encompassing the local, chronological, exterior and interior senses of *kath' olou*, see P.
Trembelas' *Dogmatics*, II, p. 356ff. Also to be found, however, is an
identification of catholicity chiefly and primarily with the geographical extension of the Church to the ends of the earth. So for
example in Ch. Androutsos, *Dogmatics of the Orthodox Eastern
Church*, 1907, p. 279. Cf. also K. Mouratidis, *The Essence and Polity*,
p. 178ff. Other Orthodox theologians, however, consider this identification admissible only on the assumption that the worldwide
character of the Church would be regarded as a consequence and
secondary element of catholicity, the essence of which should on
no account be understood in a quantitative or geographical sense,
as is presupposed by its identification with the worldwide and
universal character of the Church. Thus G. Florovsky observes in
"Le Corps du Christ" (*loc. cit.*, pp.24-27): "In the earliest dcouments,
the term *katholike ekklesia* was never used in a quantitative sense, to
denote the geographical spread of the Church... The universal geographical extent of the Church is but a manifestation or an
interpretation of this inner integrity, of the spiritual plenitude of

the Church... 'Catholic' as 'universal' has been taken into the current theological vocabulary, first of the West and later of the East as well... In fact, this was a terrible diminution of the grand idea of catholicity, an unhappy mutilation of the primitive conception. The main accent has been transferred to something that is merely secondary and derivative, and what is truly essential has been ignored... Catholicity in its essence is in no way a geographical or spatial concept... It is quite possible that at a given period heretics or indeed atheists might be more numerous than the faithful and indeed spread everywhere, *'ubique,'* and the Catholic Church might be reduced, empirically speaking, to a 'negligible quantity,' driven into the desert or into 'caves and holes in the ground...' 'Catholic' is not a collective name. The Church is not catholic only inasmuch as she gathers all the local communities..." Here, of course, we are investigating exclusively the sources from the first three centuries, in the light of which the question will be posed regarding the meaning of the term "Catholic Church" as it developed in the consciousness of the Church during that period.

[107] Aristotle, *Rhetoric* 1, 2, 15.

[108] Aristotle, *On Interpretation* 7, 1

[109] Aristotle, *Metaphysics* 2, 6, 7ff: *"katholou einai ai arkhai"* - "the principles are universals." Cf. *Nicomachian Ethics* 2, 7, 1: *"oi katholou logoi"* - "general statements."

[110] Aristotle, *Metaphysics* 4, 26, 2 [ET W.D. Ross, *The Works of Aristotle*, Oxford 1982]. Notable is the identification we observe here of catholicity with "wholeness" and "oneness."

[111] Aristotle, *On Interpretation* 7, 17.

[112] Polybius 6, 5, 3: "general (*katholike*) exposition" in contrast to "detailed discussion" (*kata meros logos*). Similarly 1,57,4; 8,4,11; 3,37,6: "These countries regarded from a general point of view" (*katholikoteron*).

[113] *On Composition of Words* 12: "For it is not in the nature of the thing to admit of general (*katholiken*) and technical comprehension."

[114] *Life of Pompey*, where "general (*katholou*) inquiry" is used in the sense in which Aristotle uses "general proof" (*Prior Analytics* I,1).

[115] Philo, *Life of Moses* II, 32 (ed. Cohn, Vol. I, p. 212).

[116] H. Wolfson, Philo, II, 1947, p. 181.

[117] Cf. G. Konidaris, *On the Supposed Difference* p. 45ff.

[118] See above p. 87.

[119] *Patres Apostolici* I, 1901, p. 283.

[120] *The Apostolic Fathers - Ignatius and Polycarp*, I, 1889, p. 310. Cf. E.C. Blackman, *Marcion and his Influence*, 1948, p. 15.

[121] *op. cit.* p. 166ff.

[122] *La Théologie de l'Église de s. Clement de Rome à s. Irénée*, 1945, p. 64ff.

[123] The view that catholicolicity=universality seems to have prevailed in Roman Catholic theology. See e.g. H. Moureau, "Catholicité," in *D.T.C.* II/2 (1939), col. 1999, and H. Leclercq, "Catholique," in *D.A.C.L.* II/2 (1910), col. 2624. This view is of course an inevitable consequence of Roman Catholic ecclesiology which takes each local Church to be a *segment* of the worldwide Church. Hence the efforts of Roman Catholic theology to interpret ancient catholicity too in this sense, as does e.g. P. Galtier, who writes in reference to Polycarp's time (and in total contempt of the highly significant passage from the *Martyrdom of Polycarp*, 16, 2) that: "each of the local Churches is like a section of the great universal catholic Church" ("Ad his qui sunt undique," in *Revue d'Histoire ecclésiastique* 44 (1949), 425.

[124] This was the conclusion drawn by H. Genouillac, *L'Église chrétienne au temps de s. Ignace d'Antioche*, 1907, p. 108. A different view was expressed by Kattenbusch (*Das apostolische Symbol*, II, pp. 920-927), according to which *katholike* in the passage of Ignatius under discussion means *una sola*; but this seems not to have found support.

[125] See above p. 13.

[126] "The multitude" (*to plethos*) is a technical term for the local Church. See F. Gerke, *Die Stellung des I. Clemensbriefes innerhalb der Entwicklung der altchristlichen Gemeinde-Verfassung und des Kirchenrechts*, 1931, p. 132. Elsewhere "the multitude" seems to mean the laypeople as opposed to the clergy and particularly the Bishop. See, in *Magn.* 6:1, *Tral.* 1:2 and 8:2.

[127] Cf. Ignatius, Eph. 2:2, 4:1; Magn. 7:1, 13:2; Tral. 2:1, 13:2; Philad. inscr., 2:1, 7:1-2 (concerning the character of priesthood by divine law. Cf. also 1:1: "Which Bishop, I know, obtained the ministry... not of himself, nor by men..."); Polyc. 4:1, 5:2, where marriage is explicitly added to those rites which have to be performed by the Bishop.

[128] He was fully aware that he was imitating Paul in this matter, as evidenced by the passage in the Epistle to the Trallians (inscr.): "which also I greet in its fullness, in apostolic character."

[129] An exception is the phrase "the Church in Syria" or "the Church of Syria"; but these should not be understood as "the Church of the province of Syria" but as the Church of Syria *par excellence*, i.e. Antioch, or as a straightforward reference by Ignatius

to the place where he is staying, as Lightfoot thinks (op. cit. p. 201). For the view that the phrase "Bishop of Syria" (Rom. 2:2) implies a sort of metropolitan authority, see G. Konidaris, *On the Supposed Difference* p. 47, and V. Corwin, *Saint Ignatius and Christianity in Antioch*, 1960, p. 44ff.

[130] Cf. Trallians and Romans, preamble. Cf. also P. Chrestou, *True Life according to the Teaching of Ignatius the God-bearer* [in Greek], 1951, p. 36.

[131] "Most worthy of God and most holy," etc.

[132] Ignatius, Eph. 5:1: "I reckon you [the Ephesians] happy as being joined to him [the Bishop] as the Church is to Jesus Christ and as Jesus Christ is to the Father."

[133] Ignatius, Eph. 5:2-3.

[134] Cf. p. 48 above.

[135] Cf. especially Ignatius, Eph. 20:2: the Eucharist is the "medicine of immortality."

[136] Eph. 13:1. To Polycarp 4:2. Cf. P. Chrestou, op. cit. p. 38.

[137] Cf. J. Romanides, *The Ecclesiology of St Ignatius of Antioch*, 1956, p. 10ff., and more generally C.C. Richardson, "The Church in Ignatius of Antioch," in *Journal of Religion* 17 (1937), pp. 428-443.

[138] Smyrn. 7:1: the Docetists abstain from the Eucharist "in order to avoid confessing that the Eucharist is the flesh of our Savior Jesus Christ which suffered for our sins, and which the Father in His goodness raised up."

[139] Magn. 1:2; Eph. 10:3.

[140] Tral. 2:3. For the identification of Church and altar see also Philad. 4; Magn. 7:2; Ephes. 5:2 and Tral. 7:2.

[141] See p. 45f. and 56f.

[142] Eph. 4:2.

[143] Smyrn. 1:2.

[144] Smyrn. 7:1.

[145] Eph. 4:2 and Tral. 11:2.

[146] Tral. 7:2.

[147] Tral. 1:1: "so that I see the whole multitude of you in him (Polybius)."

[148] Eph. 1:3. Cf. also Magn. 6:1, where the presbyterium with the deacons are added to the Bishop. This does not indicate any diminution in the significance of the Bishop, who, as it appears from the other passages, is the only person able to represent the Church - characteristically, Ignatius never says this of the presbyterium or the deacons, while he says it several times about the Bishop alone.

[149] Magn. 3:1-2.

[150] Magn. 3:2.

[151] To Polycarp, preface.

[152] Rom. 9:1. The interchange of the names "God" and "Christ" is usual in Ignatius and does not create an issue here.

[153] Smyrn. 9:1: "You should honor both God and the Bishop; one who does anything without the knowledge of the Bishop is worshipping the devil."

[154] To Polycarp 6:1.

[155] Philad. 3:2.

[156] See above p. 89, n. 70.

[157] Philad., preamble.

[158] Tral. 3:1.

[159] Baptism, the *agape*, the Eucharist, marriage etc. Cf. Magn. 4:1: "It is fitting not just to be called Christians, but actually to be such; just as some give a man the title of Bishop, but do everything without him. It seems to me that such people are not in good conscience, because they are not gathered together in an assured manner (*bebaios*) according to the commandment."

[160] Philad. 1:1.

[161] Philad. 7:1-2.

[162] Eph. 3:2: "I have therefore taken it upon myself first to exhort you to concur with the will (*gnomê*) of God. For Jesus Christ... is the will (*gnomê*) of the Father, as the Bishops too... are according to the will (or "in the mind - *en gnomê*) of Jesus Christ." [Translator's note: since the term *gnomê* has the sense of will, purpose and mind, there is no one English word which can translate it idiomatically in all cases. Thus when the last part of the above passage is quoted hereafter as "the bishops... are *in the mind* of Jesus Christ," it should be borne in mind that the phrase carries connotations of being "according to the will and purpose."]

[163] K. Bonis, op. cit. p. 21.

[164] Philad. 4.

[165] See above, p. 109f.

[166] As it is for example by E. von der Voltz, *Ignatius von Antiochen als Christ und Theologe*, 1894, p. 62f. In Plato and Philo (see Philo, Peri katask. 16-19), the relation of the notional prototype to the material and concrete antitype presupposes that the latter has real existence only insofar as it is a mirror of the former. According to Ignatius, however, the local Church constitutes a reality of herself from both the historical and the conceptual point of view. Thus, the Aristotelian sense of *katholou* is closer than Platonic philoso-

phy to the content of the term "Catholic Church."

[167] 1 Cor. 14:23; Rom. 16:23; cf. above, p. 96.

[168] I Clem. 46:7, echoing Paul (Eph. 4:4-6).

[169] Eph. 1:22, 1:10; Col. 1:19.

[170] See V. Ioannidis, "The Unity of the Church" p. 176f.

[171] Cf. Rom. 5. V. Ioannidis also connects the two (op. cit. pp. 175-7).

[172] Cf. also the term "Son of Man," on which see above, p. 55f.

[173] Col. 1:16.

[174] Eph. 1:22-23.

[175] Eph. 4:4.

[176] Col. 3:15.

[177] 1 Clem., preamble.

[178] 1 Clem. 2:2.

[179] Thus the Coptic text has *agion meris*, ("portion of the holy ones/of the holy things"), the Latin has "holy portion" and the Constantinopolitan codex has *agia mere*, ("holy places"). All these, and especially the phrase in the Coptic text, are probably references to the Eucharist.

[180] 37 and 46:7: "Why are there discords and outbursts of anger and dissention among you?... Why do we rend and tear apart and rebel against our own body, and reach such a point of madness that we forget that we are members one of another?"

[181] The reason is that use of the term "Bishop" came in late in the West; the institution of Bishops was, however, indicated by the collective term "the presbyters." See G. Konidaris, *On the Supposed Difference*, p. 35.

[182] Elsewhere he speaks of Enoch and Noah as "ministering" (*leitourgountes*) (9:3-4), as also of the angels (34:5), or of the Old Testament prophets as ministers (*leitourgoi*) of the grace of God (8:1).

[183] 1 Clem. 44:2-4.

[184] J. Daniélou (*Théologie du Judeo-Christianisme*, p. 409f.) places the institution (?) of the "eminent men" mentioned in 1 Clement between the Apostles and the Bishops, as successors of the *synedrion* of the Twelve with the primary task of establishing permanent ministers in various places. This theory is certainly questionable because subject of the "eminent men" in 1 Clement is very complex and there is no justification for elevating them into a permanent institution of the postapostolic era.

[185] 1 Clement 40:3 and 42:1-2. Cf. G. Konidaris, *On the Alleged Difference* p. 31.

[186] 14:1, 21:5 and 57:1.

[187] 40:5 and 41:7: the clergy and the laity form "orders," each of which has its own spheres of responsibility which it may not go beyond.

[188] The problem for the *Didache* consists in the gradual but almost complete disappearance of the charismatics. See *Didache* 13:4: "If you have no prophet...."

[189] 3 John 9.

[190] *Didache* 12:1-13:7.

[191] *Didache* 15:1. The similarity with *1 Clement* is shown also in the use of the term "tested (*dedokimasmenoi*) men" for those who are to be ordained (*1 Clement* 44). As to the preference for the term "Bishops and deacons" and its meaning, see G. Konidaris, *On the Supposed Difference* p.39f. According to Konidaris, the preference for the term "Bishops and deacons" is due on the one hand to the geographical area to which the *Didache* originates, namely the West (cf. Phil. 1:1), and on the other to its scriptural character (1 Clement, Paul) which suits the character of the *Didache* as a "metacatechetical handbook."

[192] The expression should be taken in an inclusive sense indicating the charismatics as a whole and consequently also the Apostles.

[193] *Didache* 9:4 and 10:5. For the connection of the "Bishops and deacons" with the Eucharist in the *Didache* cf. also A. Theodorou, *History of Dogma* I/1 (1963), p. 260.

[194] Polycarp's martyrdom has been dated to 22/23 February 156 through research done by E. Schwartz, *Abhandlungen der köninglichen Gesellschaft der Wissenschaften zu Göttingen*, VIII (1905), p. 125f.

[195] Lightfoot's view that the word "catholic" should be replaced with "holy" has no serious arguments in its favor since it rests on a single manuscript in Moscow which has probably altered the original text. On this see Funk, *Patres Apostolici* I (1901), p. 334 and Leclercq in *D.A.C.L.* I/2, col. 2626.

[196] *Mart. Polyc. inscr.*: "the Church of God which sojourns (*paroikei*) in Smyrna." A comparative examination of the sources up to the *Martyrdom of Polycarp* produces the following eloquent picture of how the terms "Church of God" and/or "Catholic Church" are used for the local Church:

Paul "the Church of God which is in Corinth" or "the whole Church"

1 Clement "the Church of God which sojourns at Rome."

Ignatius "the Church of God which is in Phil-adelphia."

Polycarp "the Church of God which sojourns at Philippi."

Mart.Polyc. "the Church of God which sojourns at Smyrna" or "the Catholic Church in Smyrna."

[197] *Mart. Polyc. inscr.*: "to all the *paroikiai* of the holy and catholic Church in every place."

[198] This was the meaning of *paroiko* (translated above "sojourn") at that time. See the relevant article in Kittel, *T.W.N.T.*

[199] This also serves to refute the views of G. Bardy (*La Théologie de l'Église* I, p. 56) who overlooks the catholicity of each local Church in his attempt to advance the Roman Catholic ecclesiology which presupposes the universal Church and the universal Bishop.

[200] Thus for example *inter alios* Leclercq in *D.A.C.L.* II/2, col. 2626 and F. Heiler, *Urkirche und Ostkirche*, p.3f.

[201] The fact that this passage clearly implies the unity of the Churches all over the world is another matter, and we shall deal with this later. Here we are looking at the meaning of the term "Catholic Church," which, as this text clearly shows, had not yet become identified with the "universal Church."

[202] *De Prescr. Haer.* 26:4 (P.L. 2:38): "*diversam et contrariam (regulam fidei) illi quam catholice (=catholicae) in medium proferebant.*" [They brought in (a rule of faith) different from and contrary to that put forward by the catholic (Churches)] "*Ecclesiae*" should be understood after the plural "*catholicae*" according to the interpretation of Labriolle-Refoulé in *Tertullien: Traité de la Prescription contre les Hérétiques* (Sources Chrétiennes 46), 1957, p. 123 n. 4.

[203] The contrary view of C. Butler ("St Cyprian on the Church," *Downside Review* 71 (1953), pp. 263-66) has not found support. It was disputed both by P.-Th. Camelot ("St Cyprian at la primauté," in *Istina* 1957, p. 423) and P.M. Benevot (*St Cyprian. The Lapsed- The Unity of the Catholic Church* (Ancient Christian Writers No. 25), 1957, pp. 74-75). This view had earlier been disputed by another Roman Catholic historian, P. Batiffol (op. cit. pp. 437-9), who observed that "the treatise *De unitate ecclesiae*... does not include a system of a universal Church, in other words of catholicism." How the fact that the term "*catholicae ecclesiae*" appears in the title of Cyprian's work can be reconciled with Batiffol's unfounded assumption that catholicity is identical with universality is impossible to understand.

[204] The existing maniscripts create problems as to the genuine-

ness of the word "catholic" in the title of the work. Some of them omit the term, which is why H. Koch (*Cyprianische Untersuchungen,* 1926, pp. 102-107) placed this work before the schism of Novatus when it is believed that Cyprian did not use the term "Catholic Church." But as C.H. Turner observes in his review of the above work of Koch's (in *English Historical Review,* 1928, p. 247), the term "Catholic Church" was already very widely used even in the West by the second century. To this, it should be added that only very few manuscripts lack the term "catholic" in the title of the work while the majority have it, as has been shown by H. Janssen, *Kultur und Sprache. Zur Geschichte der alten Kirche in Spiegel der Sprachentwicklung: von Tertullian his Cyprian* (*Latinitas christiana primaeva: Studia ad sermonem latinum pertinentia,* No. 8), 1938, p. 18 n.2. According to these mss., the term "catholic" belongs as a genuine part of Cyprian's work .

[205] As maintained by N. Afanassieff, "La Doctrine de la Primauté à la Lumière de l'Écclesiologie," in *Istina* 1957, pp. 401-420.

[206] Cyprian, Letter 49 (46).2.4: "*Nec ignoramus unum Sanctum Spiritum, unum episcopum in catholica esse debere.*" We find precisely the same phrase in Cornelius' letter to Fabian of Antioch (Eusebius, *Eccl. Hist.* VI.43.11): "For the avenger of the Gospel did not understand that there should be one Bishop in the Catholic Church." [Translator's note: numbering of Cyprian's Epistles is according to Hartel's edition (1871), with Migne's numbering in brackets. Where only one number is given, it refers to Hartel's numbering. The English translation in *Ante-Nicene Fathers* follows Migne's numbering, but see *ANF* vol. 5, p. 301, note 3.]

[207] This sense is impossible because nowhere in the sources for the first three centuries does there occur the idea of one Bishop for the whole world. The term "*episcopus episcoporum*" is used by Tertullian ironically. See below.

[208] See above, n. 206.

[209] See e.g. Cyprian's Letter 45 (42).1.

[210] Letter 55 (52) 1.2: "*Scripsisti etiam ut exemplum earundem litterarum* ad Cornelium *collegum nostrum transmitterem, ut deposita omni solicitudine jam sciret te secum,* hoc est cum catholica ecclesia, *communicare.*"

[211] Cyprian, *Ep.* 66 (69).8.3: "*episcopum in ecclesia esse et ecclesiam in episcopo.*"

[212] By Prof. Bonis, op. cit. p. 40.

[213] The same goes for both 1 Clement and the *Didache,* where, as we have seen, the Bishop, implied within the term "presbyters" or

"Bishops and deacons," is connected emphatically with the offering of the eucharistic Gifts and not with preaching. Even Justin (*c.* 150 AD), who refers plainly to the liturgical preaching of the Bishop (1 Apol. 76), sees no need to stress his teaching authority as is done from the *Martyrdom of Polycarp* onwards.

²¹⁴ *Martyrdom of Polycarp* 16:2.

²¹⁵ Eusebius, *Eccl. Hist.* IV.22.3,5. We have underlined "in every succession" and "in every city" because of their importance for the catholicity of each local Church: apostolic succession appears as "successions" in the plural exactly as catholicity presents itself as "Catholic Churches." Each local Church possesses both the whole succession of all the Apostles and catholicity, i.e. the fullness of the Church. This consciousness is expressed at the same period in connection with the Paschal controversies by Polycrates of Ephesus who writes to Victor of Rome that the Roman Church cannot impose her local traditions upon the other local Churches because the other Churches too have a self-sufficiency in tradition as being connected with "great luminaries" (Eusebius, *Church History* V.24.2-8). In the same spirit, Irenaeus also writes to Victor, observing in conclusion that "the disagreement over the fast demonstrates our agreement in faith" (Ibid. 12-13).

²¹⁶ He personally knows of three generations including the first successors of the Apostles. Cf. Konidaris, *Historian, Church...* (in Greek), p. 6f.

²¹⁷ See e.g. *Adv. Haer.* III.3.3 (PG 7:849ff.)

²¹⁸ *Adv. Haer.* IV.23.8 (PG 7:1047f.)

²¹⁹ *Adv. Haer.* IV.26.2. On the nature of the episcopal office according to Irenaeus see also H. Alivizatos, "The Significance of the Episcopal Office According to Irenaeus" (in Greek), in *Nea Sion*, 10 (1910), 336ff.

²²⁰ Eusebius, *Eccl. Hist.* V.20.4f. See G. Dix, "Ministry," *loc. cit.* p. 202.

²²¹ See C. Schneider, *Geistesgeschichte des Christentums* I, 1945, p. 287.

²²² Quoted in Epiphanius, *Adv. Haer.* 33.6.7 (PG 41:568). Cf. B. Reynders, "Paradosis: Le progrès de l'idée de Tradition jusqu'à saint Irénée," in *Rech. de Théol. anc. et médiév.* 5 (1933), 172f. If the "teacher" referred to in Justin's Second Apology (2) is the author of this letter, then the core at least of this letter can be dated back to 155 AD. Cf. G. Dix, "Ministry" p. 202f.

²²³ Cf. Tertullian, *Adv. Valent.* 4, where we learn that Valentinus was an unsuccessful candidate for Bishop of the Church of Rome.

[224] See Clement of Alexandria, *Strom.* II.106.4, and Hippolytus, *Philos.* 7.20.1. Cf. H.F. von Campenhausen, *Kirchliches Amt*, p. 172f.

[225] The creation of the New Testament canon passed through the same development. When the Church of Rome defined the four Gospels and the Pauline Epistles as the "canon of truth," this was nothing other than an "anti-canon" set against the canon formed by Marcion to prove the "apostolicity" of his doctrines. Cf. G. Dix, "Ministry," p. 202f.

[226] E.g. *Adv. Haer.I.6.2 and III.3.4, as also I.16.3.*

[227] *op. cit. IV.33.8* (PG 7:1077).

[228] "The Gospel is the pillar of the Church." *op. cit.* III.10.8 (PG 7:835).

[229] E.g. *op.cit.* I.10.1-2.

[230] *op. cit.* III.12.5. Cf. I.10.3: "The whole existing Church having one and the same faith."

[231] *Adv. Haer.* III.12.5.

[232] *Adv. Haer.* III.3.3 (PG 7:850).

[233] *De Prescr. haer.* 30.2 (PL 2:42): "*constat illos* [Marcion et al.] *et catholicae primo doctrinam credisse apud ecclesiam Romanensem*" ["It is known that (Marcion et al.) at first believed the doctrine of the Catholic (Church), in the Church of Rome."] *Adv. Marc.* IV.4 (PL 2:365): "*Marcion pecuniam in primo calore fidei catholicae ecclesiae contulit*" ["In the initial ardour of his faith, Marcion brought money to the Catholic Church."]

[234] "*In honorem tamen ecclesiae catholicae in ordinationem ecclesiasticae disciplinae sanctificate sunt...*" "*In catholicam ecclesiam recipi non potest.*" H. Lietzmann, *Das Muratorische Fragment und die Monarchianischen Prologe zu den Evangelien*, 1933.

[235] "*una tamen per omnem orbem terrae ecclesia diffusa esse.*"

[236] Cf. F. Heiler, *op. cit.* p. 4. We cannot, however, see what basis there can be for the view that Clement makes a distinction between "local heresies und schisms" and a "universal worldwide Church (Weltkirche)." The contrast between locality and universality does not exist in the passage of Clement which Heiler adduces nor in other texts of this period. The distinction is simply between heresy and orthodoxy.

[237] *Strom.* VII.17 (ed. Staehlin, III p. 75.1.8. PG 8:548A): "Their human assemblies were later than the Catholic Church."

[238] Ibid.: "chopping up the tradition and clandestinely digging through the wall of the Church."

[239] *Strom. VII.17 (PG 8:552A).*

[240] Ibid., (PG 8:552B).

[241] *Adv. Haer.* IV.18.5 (PG 7:1028).

[242] Cf. A.W. Ziegler, "Das Brot von unseren Felder. Ein Beitrag zur Eucharistielehre des hl. Irenäus," in *Pro mundi vita, Festschrift zum eucharistischen Weltkongress* 1960. Herausgegeben von der theologischen Facultät der Ludwig-Maximilian Universität, 1960, pp. 21-43.

[243] See *Adv. Haer.* V.2.3 (PG 7:1126-1127). Cf. also P. Gaechter, "Unsere Einheit mit Christus nach dem hl. Irenäus," in *Zeitschrift für katholische Theologie* 58 (1934), 516.

[244] Cf. above, p. 17.

[245] See the sources in W. Elert, *op. cit.,* where it is shown that for the early Church, particularly the Eastern Church, right faith was an essential precondition for participation in the Church's Divine Eucharist.

[246] The problem of heresy *per se* does not concern us here given that it is investigated at length in a study to follow on the Church's unity in faith during the first three centuries. For the present, see H.E.W. Turner, *The Pattern of Christian Truth. A Study in the Relations between Orthodoxy and Heresy in the Early Church,* 1954; S.L. Greenslade, *Schism in the Early Church,* (no date), and also *eiusdem* "Der Begriff der Häresie in der alten Kirche," in *Schrift und Tradition,* ed. K.E. Skydsgaard und L. Vischer (WCC) 1963, pp. 24-44.

[247] In the New Testament the term has this meaning so that Paul can write "there must be factions (*haireseis*) among you..." (1 Cor. 11:19); but it was not long before it became a technical term indicating a belief which is false and dangerous to the Church (Ti. 3:10).

[248] Hence, the heretics were regarded by the church writers of the second century as offspring of the philosophers. See H.E.W. Turner, *op. cit.* p. 7f.

[249] See G. La Piana, "The Roman Church at the End of the Second Century" in *Harvard Theological Review 18 (1925), and G. Bardy, La Question des Langues dans l'Église Ancienne,* 1948, p. 93.

[250] Eusebius, *Eccl. Hist.* V.28.10.

[251] *Philos.* 9.12.21 (PG 15:3386. Ed. Wendland, p. 249. I. 20-21): "They were ejected from the Church by us, and attached themselves to them [the followers of Callistus] and swelled the numbers of his school."

[252] He regards it is a scandal that "they, past all shame, try to call themselves a Catholic Church." *Philos.* 9.12.25 (PG 15:3387; Wendland p. 250. I. 21-23).

[253] *Against Celsus* 6.27 (PG 11:1333A). Cf. *Homily on Isaiah 7.3* (PG 13:291): "*haeretici sunt... sed nos ecclesiastici sumus.*"

[254] *On the Gospel of Luke* 16 (PG 13:1841B): *"Ego quia opto esse ecclesiasticus et non ab heresiarcha aliquo sed a Christi vocabulo nuncupari... cupio esse et dici Christianus."* - "Because I want to be a churchman and be named after Christ and not after some heresiarch... I want both to be and to be called a Christian."

[255] *On Levit.* 14 (PG 12:553-554).

[256] "Inquiring whether they are believers, whether they are churchmen, whether they are not sullied by heresy." From the *Didascalia of the Apostles*, as transmitted by the *Apostolic Constitutions* 11.58 (ed. Funk, p. 167).

[257] J. Scherer, *Entretien d'Origène avec Héraclide et les Évêques ses Collègues sur le Père, le Fils et l'Âme*, 1949. Also in *Sources Chrétiennes* No. 67, 1960, to which references are given here.

[258] According to P. Nautin, *op. cit.* p. 231, reading *prosferousa* (the feminine participle agreeing with "the offering of the Eucharist") instead of *prosforou* agreeing with "[dia] Iisou Christou."

[259] See below, Part III.

[260] See the prayer of ordination for a Bishop (ed. Dix, pp. 4-6), where the Bishop receives through it (a) the very "guiding spirit" which, according to the Christological sense of Ps. 51/50:14, strengthened the Lord in carrying out His messianic work, and (b) "the power which Thou gavest to the Apostles."

[261] Ibid. Other powers of the Bishop are added to these in the prayer: "And in the highpriestly spirit to have power to remit sins according to Thy commandment, to ordain according to Thy command, and to loose every bond according to the power which Thou gavest to the apostles."

[262] See Jn. 7:43; 9:16; and 10:19, where "schism" means not a permanent division but a temporary disagreement. Specifically on Paul, see J. Dupont, "Le Schisme d'après Saint Paul," in *1054-1954: L'Église et les Églises*, I, 1954, p. 117f.

[263] See 1 Cor. 1:10, where the subject is a disagreement between individuals rather than groups (cf. J. Munck, *Paulus und die Heilsgeschichte*, 1954), and also 11:18, where Paul is talking about selfish divisions involving, not groups, but "each one" (11:21) at the Lord's Supper. Similarly 12:25, where the "schism" likewise refers to the individualism of certain the members of the Church of Corinth. Besides, the explanation of the term "schism" by "quarrelling" (*eris*) in 1 Cor. 1:11 confirms this meaning given that "quarrelling" here means nothing more than a disagreement of a personal character as is accepted by commentators (see *inter alios* P. Backmann, "Der erste Brief auf die Korinther," in Kommentar

zum N.T., 7, 1910², p. 567; J. Weiss, *Der erste Korintherbrief* (Mayer 5), 1910⁹, p. 15).

²⁶⁴ See S.L. Greenslade, *op. cit.* p. 18f.

²⁶⁵ *Epist.* 59 (55).20: *"florentissimo illic* [in Rome] *clero tecum praesidenti et sanctissimae atque amplissimae plebi..."* ["...to the most distinguished clergy there (in Rome) who preside with you, and the most holy and large congregation..."]. The strict distinction between clergy and laity in the local Church is not Cyprian's invention, for, as we have already seen, in 96 AD (1 Clement) the Church had a clear consciousness of such a distinction. The terms *plebs* and *ordo* belong to Tertullian (*Monog.* 11 and 22; *Exhort. castit.* 7). Cf. also Cyprian's *Epist.* 59(55).18 and 40(35).1.

²⁶⁶ See *Epist.* 80(82).1, where the orders of Christian citizens dealt with by the decree of Valerian (257 AD) (*senatores, egregii, viri, equites romani*) do not constitute orders in the Church.

²⁶⁷ An epistle of Cornelius of Rome to Fabius of Antioch (251 AD) informs us that at that time the Church of Rome had 46 presbyters, 7 deacons, 7 subdeacons, 42 acolytes, 52 exorcists and readers and "innumerable" laity. For the Church in Carthage, we do not have precise figures, but we have evidence of the existence of a Bishop, presbyters, deacons, subdeacons, acolytes, exorcists and readers (*Epist.* 29(24); 34(28).4; 45(42).4; 49(46).3 etc.).

²⁶⁸ *Epist.* 12(37),1: *"Officium vestra diligentia repraesentet"* ["Let your diligence be the representative of my office"] Cf. also *Epist.* 5(4).1.

²⁶⁹ He writes characteristically of the presbyters that their obedience to the Bishop is such that only when they rebel, as did Novatus in Carthage and Novatian in Rome, do they acquire independence and a history of their own: *"quando aliqui de presbyteris, euangelii nec loci sui memores, sed neque... nunc sibi praepositum episcopum cogitantes, quod numqam omnino sub antecessoribus factum est, cum contumelia et contemptu praepositi, totum sibi vindicent"* ["since some presbyters, mindful neither of the Gospel nor of their own place, and not even... considering the bishop now set over them, claim for themselves complete [authority] in a contemptuous affront to the bishop - something that was never in any way done under our predecessors"], *Epist.* 16(9).1.

²⁷⁰ *Epist. 14(5).1.*

²⁷¹ *Epist.* 57(54).3. Cf. also 49(46).1.

²⁷² *Epist.* 34 (28). 3-4.

²⁷³ The difference between *consilium* and *consensus* has already been pointed out by R. Sohm (*Kirchenrecht* p. 234): "The assembly

of the community simply says yes."

[274] Epist. 55 (52). 8: "*Et factus est episcopus a plurimis collegis nostris qui tunc in urbe Roma aderant.*" ["He was made bishop by many of our colleagues who were present in Rome at that time."]

[275] The Bishop was not understood as the "representative" of his Church during the first centuries. In his person, as we see in Ignatius, the Church was not "represented" - by way of delegation - but *expressed* and *presented* in her entirety. Cf. the correct observations of Archim. S. Harkianakis (*op. cit.* p. 46) on the distinction between the terms *antiprosopevsis* (representation) and *parastasis* (presentation).

[276] "*Ecclesia super episcopos constituatur.*" *Epist.* 33 (27).

[277] "*Episcopum in ecclesia esse, et si qui cum episcopo non sit in ecclesia non esse*" - *Epist.* 66 (69). 8; a clear echo of Ignatius, *Smyrn.* 8.

[278] *De Unitate* 17.

[279] See A. Phytrakis, *Reactions Against the Veneration of Saints in the Ancient Church and their Causes,* 1956, pp. 4 and 38. Cf. eiusdem, *Relics and Tombs of the Martyrs in the First Three Centuries,* 1955. p. 9f.

[280] *Dogmengeschichte* vol. 1 (fourth edition), p. 417. According to Harnack's view, the prevailing belief before the schism of Novatus was that the Church was not episcopocentric but a *consortium* of bishop, clergy and laity.

[281] The highly significant passage is this: "*Dominus noster, cujus praecepta metuere et servare debemus, episcopi honorem et ecclesiae suae rationem disponens in evangelio loquitur et dicit Petro: Ego tibi dico quia tu es Petrus, et super istam petram aedificabo ecclesiam meam, et portae inferorum non vicent eam, et tibi dabo claves regni caelorum, et quae ligaveris super terram erunt ligata et in caelis, et quaecumque solveris super terram erunt soluta et in caelis. Inde per temporum et successionum vices episcoporum ordinatio et ecclesiae ratio decurrit ut ecclesia super episcopos constituatur et omnis actus ecclesiae per eosdem praepositos gubernetur.*"

["Our Lord, whose precepts we should fear and observe, setting out the honor of the bishop and the order of His Church, speaks in the Gospel and says to Peter: 'I say to thee that thou art Peter, and on this rock I will build my Church, and the gates of Hell shall not prevail against it, and I will give unto thee the keys of the Kingdom of Heaven, and what thou shalt bind on earth shall be bound also in heaven, and whatever thou shalt loose on earth shall be loosed also in heaven.' Hence through changing times and successions the ordination of bishops and the order of the Church flow on, so that the Church is founded upon the bishops and every action of the Church is directed by those same bishops who are set over her."] *Epist. 33 (27). 1. Cf. also* Epist. 66 (69). 8. It should be noted that this passage implies that *every Bishop* (and not only the Bishop of Rome) is a successor of Peter given that the above saying of the Lord refers to "the honor of the bishop and the order of His Church."

[282] *Epist.* 44 (41). 1.

[283] *Epist.* 45 (42). 1: *"ut ad catholicae ecclesiae unitatem scissi corporis membra conponerent"* - ["to bring together the members of the divided body into the unity of the Catholic Church."]

[284] *"contra institutionis catholicae unitatem alium episcopum fieri consensisse; id est, quod nec fas est nec licet fieri, ecclesiam alteram institui." Epist.* 46 (44). 1.

[285] *De Unit.,* 5.

[286] *de Unit.,* 6: *"Qui alibi praeter ecclesiam colligit Christi ecclesiam spargit."*

[287] *Epist.* 66 (69). 8: *"Si qui cum episcopo non sit, in ecclesia non esse...."*

[288] The term *cathedra* connotes the symbol of authoritative teaching. Irenaeus, *Evang. Dem.* 2.

[289] In more detail, the argument in *De unitate* is as follows: In the person of Peter, the Lord "founded one *cathedra*" (*"unam cathedram constituit"*), and, therefore, "primacy is given to Peter" (*"primatus Petro datur"*). But each local Church through her Bishop is founded upon Peter and his *cathedra.* Thus "anyone who does not hold to this unity, merely believes that he is holding to the faith" (*"hanc... unitatem qui non tenet, tenere se fidem credit."*) Cf. below.

[290] *Epist.* 69 (76). 1. The same view had already been expressed about 30 years previously by Councils in Africa (220 AD, Council of Carthage, as indicated in *Epist.* 73, 3 and 71, 4), Asia Minor (*Epist.* 75, 9f., Council of Iconium around 235 AD mentioned by Firmilian in a letter to Cyprian), Antioch and N. Syria.

[291] *Epist.* 69 (76). 7.

[292] *De unit.* 8 or *Epist.* 69 (76). 8.

[293] *Epist.* 69 (66). 10.

[294] *Epist.* 69 (66). 11: *"cuncti haeretici et schismatici non dant Spiritum sanctum."*

[295] *Epist.* 69 (76). 5-6.

[296] The oneness of the priesthood is inseparably joined to the onesness of the Eucharist and cannot be understood in any other way. See *Epist.* 43 (40). 5: *"Aliud altare constitui aut sacerdotium novum fieri praeter unum altare et unum sacerdotium non potest."* ["No other

altar can be instituted, no other priesthood can be established apart from the one single altar, the one single priesthood."] Cf. *De Unit.* 17 and 14 (PL 4:513 and 510).

[297] *Epist.* 70, 3.

[298] The same agreement among the African Churches was expressed in 256 at a Council of 87 bishops (see *Sententiae episcoporum* in Hartel's edition of the works of Cyprian, vol. I p. 435f.) The Council of Carthage in 251 had already declared by its canon all that has been said above about the meaning of "Catholic Church" in Cyprian. The "Catholic Church" according to this canon is contrasted not only with heresies, but also with schismatic groups, and is defined not simply by right belief but as the sphere of every operation of grace, such as Baptism (see H. Alivizatos (ed.), *The Holy Canons*, p. 220f.). On the importance of this Canon for the unity of the Church, cf. also G. Konidaris, G.C.H., p. 235.

[299] *Epist.* 75.4.

[300] Hence, the harsh language it uses in several places against the primacy of Rome (Ibid.)

[301] He who is outside the Catholic Church is *"alienus a spiritali et deifica sanctitate"* (Ibid., 8) which suggests that the Catholic Church is the only Spirit-bearing and sanctifying communion.

[302] Eusebius (*Eccl. Hist.* VII.5.3-5) testifies to Dionysius of Alexandria's disagreement with Stephen of Rome.

[303] *Epist.* 75, 6. It is not, however, certain that Firmilian is here referring specifically to the ecclesiology under discussion.

[304] Eusebius, *Eccl. Hist.* VII.5.5. The ecclesiological isolation of Rome was so marked that it may have been the reason why Stephen did not, it seems, carry out his announced intention of breaking communion between Rome and the dissenting Churches, and why his successor Xystus II hastened to restore unity by making concessions.

[305] Right before the African Council of September 256. J. Quasten (*Patrology* II, p. 368) takes the years between 256 and Cyprian's death as the time of its composition.

[306] *De Rebaptismate*, ed. W. Hartel as an appendix to the works of Cyprian.

[307] A basic presupposition in the ecclesiology of *De Rebaptismate* is the distinction between the baptism of water and that of the Spirit. As a curious consequence of this distinction, the idea appears in this text that the Church is in exclusive possession of the Holy Spirit (whence she can baptize in the Spirit), but not of the Lord (with whom the baptism of water is clearly linked here).

[308] The idea that outside the Church there is no salvation was first formulated by Origen (*Hom. on Joshua son of Nun* 3.5, PG 12:841B).

[309] Fr. Georges Florovsky poses this problem sharply and analyzes the difficulties it presents from the viewpoint of ecclesiology in his article "The Doctrine of the Church and the Ecumenical Movement," in *The Ecumenical Review* 2 (1950), 152-161.

[310] Cyril of Jerusalem (*Catech.* 18.23, PG 33:1044) was the first to introduce the idea of universality into the definition of catholicity (see above, p. 126, n.4). But it should be noticed that he does not yet regard this universality as synonymous with catholicity but as one element which can describe it among others. Only Augustine, for reasons that are well-known (see above p. 126, n.3), identified the catholicity of the Church completely with her universality.

[311] On this see the detailed analysis of L. Philippidis, *History of the New Testament Period* (in Greek), pp. 33f. and 240-257, which sets out the factors contributing to unity in the Hellenistic world, namely: unity in administration, law, the state cult, means of international exchange and manners; a very broad network of road and sea communications; and a sense of the unity and worldwide character of the state.

[312] Cf. Ibid., p. 257.

[313] 1 Pet. 1:1: "... to the elect, the exiles of the dispersion...." Likewise at 5:9: "Knowing that the same experience of suffering is required of *your brotherhood throughout the world.*"

[314] *Didache* 9.4.

[315] *To Diogn.* 6.1f.: "To put it simply, what the soul is in a body, so are the Christians in the world. The soul is scattered throughout all the members of the body, and [so are] the Christians throughout all the cities of the world... and Christians... hold the world together."

[316] Ibid. 12.1 and 8. The text is obscure. Nautin (*Lettres et Écrivains,* p. 169), after some delicate textual work, reconstructs it as follows: "You will always reap from God what is desirable, what the serpent does not touch, nor does error defile; nor Eve is corrupted, but believed to be virgin [*alla parthenos pistevetai*], and to be salvific proves, and apostles receive understanding, and clergy are gathered together, and the Passover of the Lord comes forth and is betrothed to the world, and in teaching the saints the Word is glad, through whom the Father is glorified: to whom be glory to the ages. Amen." As Nautin understands it (*op. cit.* p. 170): "the new paradise is the Church, and the Church for him is composed firstly

of the orders which preside at the eucharistic assembly."

[317] Cf. H. Alivizatos, *The Cause of the Disputes over Easter in the Second Century* (in Greek), 1911, pp. 14, 16 and 103: the root cause was the catholicization of the Church and not simply the question of fasting (or of the duration of the fast, as B. Lohse has tried to prove (*Das Passafest der Quartadecimaner*, 1953, p. 113).

[318] Cf. G. Konidaris, *The Formation...*, p. 38f.

[319] Cf. P. de Labriolle, *La Crise Montaniste*, p. 39. Doubts are expressed by P. Batiffol, *op. cit.* p.265; I. Lebreton, "Le Développement des Institutions à la fin du IIe s. et au Debut du IIIe s.', in *Recherches des Sciences Religieuses*, 1934; and G. Bardy, *La Théologie*, I, p. 203. Labriolle's view (cf. also G. Konidaris, *The Formation*, p. 38) is however supported by the evidence of Tertullian, *De Jejunio* 13.

[320] An anti-Montanist, quoted in Eusebius, *Eccl. Hist.* V,16.10. Cf. Ibid. 28.6 and 9: "having been excluded from communion."

[321] Eusebius, *Eccl. Hist.* V.24.9.

[322] See the evidence for this in W. Elert, *op. cit.*

[323] Eusebius, *Eccl. Hist.* V.24.14-17.

[324] Syriac *Didascalia* 12 (ed. Connolly, p. 122).

[325] See P. Trembelas, "Contributions to the History of Christian Worship," in *E.E.Th.S.* (1958/60), 1963, p. 38f. On the same subject of the historical evidence for "supralocal" unity, see also C. Vogel, "Unité de l'Église et Pluralité des Formes Historiques...," in *L'Episcopat et l'Église universelle* (Unam Sanctam 39), 1962, p. 601f.

[326] Ignatius, *Eph.* 3.2.

[327] Cf. G. Konidaris, *The Formation*, p.27; here we have the "prelude" to the Ecumenical Council.

[328] *Le Corps Mystique*, II, p. 30.

[329] See in E.W. Benson, *op. cit.* pp. 197-199, and A.D. d'Alès, *La Théologie de Saint Cyprien*, 1922, p.121f.

[330] *De Unit.*, 6.

[331] *Epist.* 66 (69). 5: The Lord's words to the Apostles (Lk 10:16) were addressed to all the Bishops. It should be noted how Cyprian refers to the Apostle Peter as the foundation of the Church's unity: "God is one, and Christ is one, and the Church is one, and one is the throne (*cathedra*) which the Lord's word founded upon Peter" ("*Deus unus est et Christus unus et una ecclesia et cathedra una super Petrum Domini voce fundata*") (*Epist.* 43 (40). 5). The nature of this one Church founded upon Peter is made clear by a careful study of the passage immediately following: "no other altar can be instituted, no other priesthood can be established apart from the one single altar, the one single priesthood" ("*Aliud altare constitui aut*

aliud sacerdotium novum fieri praeter unum altare et unum sacerdotium non potest") (Ibid.). From this it is quite clear that Cyprian has in mind here the proliferation of altars within one and the same local Church because of schisms (besides, it is clear from the whole text of the letter that this is what it is talking about); and consequently the ecclesial unity founded on the one throne of Peter is to be found in the episcopal Church which does not admit a second altar. In consequence, each bishop sits on the one throne of Peter. Cf. also *De Unit.*, 4. In view of this, one is justified in asking whether there is any ground, at least as far as the sources of the first three centuries go, for the view (see also in Archim. S. Charkianakis, *op. cit.*, p. 44f.) that the hierarchy "in its entirety" constitutes the successor of the Apostles in such a way that the college or "choir" of the Twelve is shared out in the succession to the particular Bishops. Such a collective unity of the episcopate, a unity by addition which easily permits the maintenance of a special office for the Pope as unifying is his person the college of the Apostles which is parcelled out among the various Bishops, is the underlying basis for the theory which has recently appeared among Roman Catholic theologians concerning the "collegiality" of the Bishops. On this see *inter alia* the collections *Le Concile et les Conciles*, ed. B. Botte et al., 1960; and *L'Épiscopat de l'Église Universelle*, ed. Y. Congar and B. Dupuy, 1962, esp. pp. 17-28, 227-328, 481-535, and also J. Colson, *L'Épiscopat Catholique: Collégialité et Primauté dans les Trois Premiers Siècles de l'Église*, 1963; J. Hamer, *op. cit.* p. 237f.; P. Stockmeier, "Bischofsamt und Kircheneinheit bei den Apostolischen Vätern," in *Trier Theologische Zeitschrift* 63 (1964), 321/35; W. de Ries, "Die Kollegiale Struktur der Kirche in den ersten Jahrhunderten," in *Una Sancta* 19 (1964), 296-317, and P. Rusch, "Bischof. Die Kollegiale Struktur des Bischofsamtes," in *Zeitschrift für Kathol. Theologie* 89 (1964), 257-85. On this theory from the viewpoint of the conclusions of our research, see general remarks below (General Conclusions).

[332] See J. Zeiller, "La conception de l'Église aux Quatre Premiers Siècles," in *Revue d'Histoire Ecclésiastique* 29 (1933), 582.

[333] *Adv. Haer.* I.10.2: "For the languages around the world are different, but the force of the tradition is one and the same. The Churches established in Germany do not believe differently or hand down anything different, nor do those among the Iberians, nor those among the Celts, nor those in the East, nor in Egypt nor in Libya, nor those established in the central regions of the world. But as the sun, God's creature, is one and the same all over the world, so also the proclamation of the truth shines everywhere

and illumines all who wish it to come to knowledge of truth. Neither will the very powerful speech of those who preside over the Churches say anything different from this (for no one is above the teacher), nor will one who is feeble in speech diminish the tradition. For since the faith is *one and the same*, one who can say much about it has not increased it, nor has one who can say little diminished it." Cf. A. Benoit, *Saint Irénée: Introduction à l'Étude de sa Théologie*, 1960, p. 215f. It should be noted that while Irenaeus is able to talk here about many "Churches" he does not talk about many "faiths." The "Churches" can be in the plural; it is sufficient that they are identical in the one faith. This relates to the remarks of J. Daniélou, *"Mia Ecclesia,"* p. 135f.

[334] See *Adv. Haer.* V.20.1: "Those who preside over the Church, to whom the whole world is entrusted, watchfully guard the apostolic tradition, testifying to us that they all preserve *one and the same faith... the same spiritual gifts... they live according to the same laws...*" The repetition of "the same" is indicative of their unity *in identity.*

[335] *De Praescr.* 20. 5-7; cf. ibid. 21. 4-7.

[336] It is worth noting the way in which Tertullian refers to the Church of Rome, placing it on the same level as any other apostolic Church: "Are you in Achaea? You have Corinth. You are not far from Macedonia? You have Philippi, you have Thessalonike. If you can get to the shores of Asia, you have Ephesus. If you are in Italy, you have Rome..." In all these Churches, without exception, you will find "the very thrones of the apostles still preeminent in their places, where their authentic writings are read" etc. (Ibid. 36. 2.

[337] We cannot here concern ourselves in detail with the question of the nature of the conciliar system when it first appeared in history. A work dedicated specifically to this is in preparation.

[338] Eusebius, *Eccl. Hist.* V.16.10.

[339] It is noteworthy that Tertullian uses the title *"episcopus episcoporum"* ironically (*De Pudic.* 1.6. Cf. *De Monog.* 17) in reference to the Bishop of Rome (or of Carthage, according to E.W. Benson, *op. cit.* pp. 30-31, H. von Campenhausen, *Kirchliches Amt*, pp. 251 and 259, and W. Telfer, *The Forgiveness of Sins*, 1960, pp. 62 and 67).

[340] This is to be observed particularly in the works of Irenaeus and Clement of Alexandria. See passages in J. Daniélou, *"Mia Ecclesia,"* p. 139.

[341] See above, p. 128f.

[342] *De Praescr.* 20.5-7 and 21.4-7.

[343] Ignatius, *Eph.* 3.2. See above, n. 216.

[344] The principle of majority decision, formulated for the first time in the 6th Canon of the First Ecumenical Council, related to questions of order. Could it be applied also to substantive issues such as those of faith on which numbers never seem to have been a criterion for decisions? Many Councils, even ones which were ecumenical as to their composition, such as that of Ephesus in 449, were unable to impose their decisions upon the consciousness of the Church; while others which were smaller in numbers and lacked geographical ecumenicity, such as the Second Ecumenical Council, expressed the "Catholic Church" faithfully. The criterion for truth in the Church has never been *quantity* or *number*, and often in history the true, "catholic" Church has been overshadowed by the numerical weight of heretics and schismatics.

[345] Irenaeus, *Adv. Haer.* IV.26.2: *"qui cum episcopatus successione charisma veritatis certum secundum placitum patris acceperunt."*

[346] That the term *"charisma"* in this passage of Irenaeus should be understood as meaning the Priesthood, which is always bound up with the Eucharist, see G. Dix, "Ministry," pp. 209-210. Cf. also A. Ehrhardt, *op. cit.* pp. 107-24. Contrary views are expressed by scholars such as K. Müller, *"Das Charisma Veritatis und der Episcopat bei Irenaeus"* in *Z.N.T.W.* 23 (1924), 216-22; D. van den Eynde, *Les Normes de l'Enseignement Chrétien*, 1933, p. 187 and E. Molland, "Irenaeus of Lugdunum and the Apostolic Succession," in *Journal of Ecclesiastical History* 1 (1950), 25f. Although these views are favored by the silence of the texts of Irenaeus, they conflict with the very ancient use of the term *"charisma"* in connection with ordination even from New Testament times (1 Tim. 4:14 and 2 Tim. 1:6).

[347] "The common union of the Churches," an expression highly characteristic of the theses in this work, is used by Eusebius (*Eccl. Hist.* V.24.9) of the second century Councils, and reveals the deeper meaning of the institution of Councils when it first appeared. The truly supreme importance of this institution lies in the fact that through it the Churches in various places are shown to be in essence *one Church* only in the whole world without ceasing to be in themselves full "Churches."

[348] Cf. the remarks of Metropolitan Dionysius of Servies and Kozani in *Oikodomi, Ecclesiastical and Literary Bulletin* 2 (1959) (in Greek), 126: Each single Church united with her Bishop, in which the mystery of the Divine Eucharist is celebrated, "is not simply a part of the whole within the one, holy, catholic and apostolic Church; but inasmuch as she communes in the whole in the unity

of the Holy Spirit, she is herself one, holy, catholic and apostolic Church, i.e. the 'fullness' and the 'body of Christ.'" Again, Prof. N. Nissiotis rightly observes ("*Worship*...," p. 198) that through the Divine Eucharist "a local community does not pray alone, but as part of the universal, Catholic Church in the world, and as a part which *contains the whole truth in its fullness by offering the one Eucharist*." Cf. also J. Meyendorff, "Sacrements et Hiérarchie dans l'Église," in *Dieu Vivant* 26 (1954), pp. 81-91, and P. Evdokimov, *L'Orthodoxie*, 1959, p. 130. This fullness of each local Church at least in the sources from the first three centuries is now recognized, albeit without being linked with the Divine Eucharist, by certain Roman Catholics such as B. Botte, "La Collegialité dans le Nouveau Testament et chez les Pères Apostoliques," in *La Concile et les Conciles. Contribution à l'Histoire de la View Conciliaire de l'Église*, 1960, p. 14f., where he observes that "the local Church appeared hierarchically organized, with the bishop who is her leader, the presbyterium which assists him and the deacons who are his ministers. But she also appeared as autonomous. Above the bishop there was nothing, and he was, humanly speaking, completely independent." Similarly, J. Hamer (*op. cit.* p. 38f.) remarks on the basis of the sources of the early Church that "it is not in adding together the local communities that the whole community which constitutes the Church is born; but *each* community, however small, represents the whole Church."

PART III

DEVELOPMENTS

The Development of the One Eucharist "Under the Leadership of the Bishop" into Many Eucharistic Assemblies Led by Priests. The Emergence of the Parish and Its Relationship to the Unity of the Episcopal Diocese

Chapter One

The Emergence of the Parish

From our research up to this point, we have established that the principle underlined by Irenaeus concerning *one* Eucharist and *one* Bishop in each Church corresponded to an historical reality. Thus, the original eucharistic unity was manifested as strictly *episcopocentric* with corresponding implications for the formation of the Catholic Church about which we have spoken already in the previous chapter. But how long did this initial state of affairs last in the Church? Certainly not indefinitely. As the situation in the Church today testifies, the assembly of the "whole Church" in only one Eucharist "under the leadership of the Bishop" no longer exists. This is due to the appearance and establishment of the institution of *parishes*. The appearance of the parish marked the definitive break-up of the original unified, episcopocentric Eucharist into *many presbyterocentric* Eucharists.

But how was the way prepared for the parish, and when did it appear in history? To this question, so fundamental to the history of church unity,[1] the answer has yet to be given. In the existing handbooks of church history and worship, the origins of the parish appear highly obscure. The late V. Stephanidis gives as the first evidence concerning parishes the foundation of twenty-five parishes in Rome by Marcellus of Rome in the year 300.[2] Certainly, however, it was not Marcellus who introduced the institution of parishes. Of the period before Marcellus, Stephanidis confines himself to saying that "as the Christian community grew, more church assemblies (parishes) were formed with their own presbyters and deacons, who were dependent on one and the same

197

Bishop."[3] But this general observation throws no light on the obscure historical origins of the parish.[4] Thus the whole problem of the origin of the parish, which is of direct and essential concern to the object of our study, remains open.

In order to examine this problem, we shall concentrate on the following two questions:

a) How is the transition from the original unified, episcopocentric Eucharist to the many presbyterocentric parishes portrayed in the sources? In this way the whole problem will be posed not as we present it but as the sources present it; and

b) What historical factors prepared the way for the appearance of the parish, and what are the first indications in the sources concerning the appearance of parishes? This will lead to a determination, albeit approximate, of the time at which parishes first appeared.

1. The problem of the emergence of the parish as it appears from comparative study of the sources.

The transition from *"one* Eucharist under the leadership of the Bishop" to *several* parishes under presbyters is vividly depicted in the sources of the first four centuries. This is demonstrated chiefly by the *change* noted in the sources *regarding the position and responsibility of the Bishop and the Presbyters within the Divine Eucharist.* In order for this change to be understood, it is necessary to examine the position of the Bishop and the Presbyters in the Divine Eucharist first according to the most ancient of the existing sources, and then according to those later.

a) The position of the Bishop and the Presbyters in the Divine Eucharist according to the sources up to the middle of the third century.

We have already seen that the *"whole* Church," in the Apostle Paul's phrase, *"being"* or *"sojourning"* in a particular place, would "come together in the same place" mainly on the Lord's day to "break bread"[5] in *one* single synaxis "under the leadership of the Bishop."[6] At the center of this synaxis of the whole "church" or the "church of God" and behind the "one altar" stood the throne of the "one Bishop" who was seated "in the place of God" and was regarded as the living "icon of Christ"[7] in which was expressed the unity of the "multitude" of the "Catholic Church" of God sojourning in that place.[8] In a circle around this throne were seated "the Presbyters" or "the presbyterium" on their *synthronon*,[9] while "the deacons" stood by the Bishop assisting him and thus connected *with him*[10] in the celebration of the Eucharist. In front of all these and opposite them stood the "people of God,"[11] that order in the Church established by the "one baptism," so that through their indispensable presence and participation in the Eucharist the full and perfect unity of the Church of Christ might become an historical reality.[12]

In the synaxis thus described along general lines, there were "orders" and *spheres of responsibility strictly distinguished from one another.*[13] These spheres of responsibility, which no member of the Church was permitted to overstep,[14] were necessarily accompanied by a corresponding "charism"[15] which was bestowed by the Holy Spirit "who distributes charismata" at a particular moment always connected with the Eucharist.[16] For the clergy who led the Eucharist, this moment was ordination; for the laity who responded and gave their affirmation, the moment was baptism and chrismation which formed the "ordination" for entry into the order of laity.

Of these spheres of responsibility, the supreme and highest belonged to the Bishop. He was called to offer the Eucharist to God in the name of the Church, thus offering up before the heavenly Throne *the whole body* of Christ, the One in whom "the many," "the whole Church," united, come to be "of God," given back to the Creator to whom they belonged thanks to their redemption from Satan by Christ who took them upon in Himself.[17] In the same way, the Bishop formed the center through which the "whole Church" had to pass as one body at the supreme moment of her unity. Thus the Bishop's position and responsibility in the Eucharist, leading naturally to his position and responsibility in the life and activity of the Church generally,[18] *was unique.* No one else had such a responsibility in the Eucharist.

The uniqueness and exclusiveness of the position and responsibility of the Bishop in the Divine Eucharist is indicated by all the existing liturgical and canonical texts of the first three centuries. Apart from what St Ignatius and St Justin write on the subject,[19] this fact is attested by two texts from the beginning of the third century which probably reflect an earlier situation and represent two different geographical areas, Rome and Syria. These are the *Apostolic Tradition* of Hippolytus and the Syriac *Didascalia Apostolorum*.

The *Apostolic Tradition*, the liturgical kernel of which probably goes back to a much earlier time than that of Hippolytus,[20] and the authenticity of which is today coming to be accepted by all,[21] is a most valuable text for the history of the ecclesial ministries. While this text includes the prayers for the ordination of almost all the ministers then existing, *in only one ordination prayer does it include a reference to offering the Gifts of the Eucharist; this is that of the Bishop.* According to this prayer, the Bishop was ordained generally to "shepherd the flock" of the Church under him, and more specifically to *"offer to Thee* [God] *the gifts of Thy holy Church,*[22] i.e. to offer the Eucharist.[23] No one else received this responsibility at his ordination according to this very ancient text.

In case this text might be regarded as reflecting only the church life of the West, coming as a confirmation and survival of the liturgy of Justin, who ascribes the right to offer the Eucharist only to the "president" of the eucharistic synaxis,[24] we see that the Syriac *Didascalia Apostolorum*, a text contemporary with the *Apostolic Tradition* of Hippolytus, bears witness to the same state of affairs in the East too, specifically in Syria where a similar view had earlier been expressed by Ignatius. This text is a translation of a lost Greek original made in Syria immediately after the composition of the Greek, i.e. at the beginning of the third century,[25] and provides a full description of the eucharistic synaxis in which the Bishop dominates, the Presbyters being consigned almost to oblivion.[26] According to this text, the Eucharist is offered *only through the Bishop* who for this reason occupies *the place of God* in the Church.[27]

As a direct consequence of this unique position of the Bishop in the offering of the Divine Eucharist there was the remarkable fact that *only the Bishop* was originally called by the title *hiereus* or *sacerdos*. This title, like its synonym *archiereus*, was originally used of Jesus Christ in the sense of His offering of Himself to the Father on behalf of mankind.[28] But precisely because this offering was perpetuated through the Divine Eucharist, in which, as we have seen, it was its "president," the Bishop who made the offering; it was not long before this title was transferred to the person of the Bishop. We see this in the *Apostolic Tradition* of Hippolytus in which the Bishop is called *"archiereus,"*[29] and we find it clearly in Cyprian. According to the latter, the Bishop is *inter alia* the *sacerdos* of the Church.[30] This property belongs so exclusively to the Bishop that, according to the same Father, in his absence there is no *sacerdos* in the Church.[31]

But while this was the position and responsibility of the Bishop in the Divine Eucharist, what was the liturgical function of the Presbyters according to the texts of this period? This question which from a more general viewpoint concerns the relationship between the Presbyter's sphere of responsibility and that of the Bishop, is one of the most fundamental questions, to which the answer has not been given fully at least by Orthodox theology.[32] This problem, which is organically bound up with the origin of the parish given that the leadership of the parish was entrusted to the Presbyter, concerns us here only as it relates specifically to the Divine Eucharist[33] and to a particular period in history.[34]

In order to determine the exact position of the Presbyters in the Church during the years in question, it is essential to distinguish between the Presbyters *as a group*, as the "presbyterium" according to the terminology of the sources, and the Presbyters *as individuals*, and look at each of these cases separately. Firstly, it should be stressed that as the "Presbyterium," i.e. collectively, the Presbyters are found from the beginning in a very close relationship with the Bishop. This extends to the point of partaking in the same title so that they are often referred to together with the Bishop as "Presbyters" or "co-Presbyters."[35] This fact was not unrelated to the way the Presbyters were positioned at the Divine Eucharist. As has already been shown, at each eucharistic gathering, the "Presbyterium" surrounded the Bishop as his "council" or *synedrion*, occupying the thrones around him, according to the evidence implied, as we have seen, in the Apocalypse of John,[36] and clearly confirmed in texts even of the fourth century.[37] This presence of the Presbyterium in the Divine Eucharist was directly related to the offering of the Gifts. First Clement (ch. 44) already speaks of the "Presbyters who offer the gifts of the episcopê," obviously together with the Bishop, who is implied in the term "Presbyters" at this early period.[38] Besides, Ignatius expresses the same connection of the Presbyters with the Bishop through the highly significant phrase "the Bishop *with* the Presbyterium and the deacons" which occurs in a text referring to the Eucharist.[39] And even the *Apostolic Tradition* of Hippolytus, which, as we have seen, ascribes to the Bishop the function of offering the gifts by right of his ordination enjoins a certain sort of active participation by the Presbyters at the sacred moment of the blessing and offering of the Eucharist performed by the Bishop when it writes: "let the deacons bring the offering to him (= the Bishop), and let him, laying his hand on the offering *together with the whole Presbyterium*, say in thanksgiving..."[40] This obscure passage, the significance of which for the recognition or otherwise of the Presbyters' right to concelebrate and join in the blessing with the Bishop has generated much discussion,[41] implies the participation of the Presbyters either in reciting the eucharistic prayer or in laying their hands on the gifts. Whichever it may be, this participation should not be understood as having the same significance as the action of the Bishop. When the same writer of this text enjoins a similar action on the part of the Presbyters at the ordination of a Presbyter, whereby they are called to place their hands on the ordinand together with the Bishop, he hastens to explain that this does not signify ordination "because the Presbyter has authority *for one thing only, to receive*; but he does not have authority to give ordination. Hence he does not ordain anyone into the clergy, but through the laying on of his hands at the ordination of a Presbyter he simply *places a seal (sphragizei)* while the Bishop *ordains.*"[42] In consequence, this has to do with an act of *assent and approval* of what is done by the Bishop. It does not have to do with the Bishop's blessing which is decisive for the changing and offering, a blessing which belonged exclusively to the Bishop by virtue of a special charism he acquired, as we have seen, at his ordination. This position taken by the *Apostolic Tradition* regarding the Bishop's responsibility for offering the Divine Eucharist is not essentially in conflict with the understanding of 1 Clement concerning "the Presbyters who offer the gifts of the episcopê." The fact that 1 Clement calls the Eucharist "the gifts of the episcopê" at a time when the terms "Presbyters" and "Bishops" were synonymous[43] shows that the Eucharist belongs to that institution which would shortly give its name to a permanent designation for the "presiding Presbyter" who offered the Eucharist. Similarly, the offering of the Eucharist would remain the task of "the episcopê" *par excellence,* while the Presbyters, since they were seated with the Bishop at the synaxis *as a college,* would be the closest of any order in the Church to the episcopal ministry of offering,[44] *but without yet having, therefore, received the right to offer the Gifts at the individual ordination of each man to the Presbyterate.* This precisely leads us to an examination of the function of the Presbyters understood *individually* according to the sources of the first three centuries.

The prayer for the ordination of a Presbyter given by the *Apostolic Tradition,* in contrast with that for the ordination of a Bishop, knows nothing of the Presbyter's right to offer the Eucharist. Instead of such a function, the candidate being ordained to the rank of Presbyter receives the charism: (a) for governing the people of God with a pure heart, as continuing the work of the presbyters of the Old Testament chosen by Moses,[45] and (b) for teaching and admonishing the people.[46] Indeed, the Presbyters initially appear as administrative counsellors to the Bishop forming "the Bishop's council (*synedrion*)."[47] This is how the Presbyters are described in the Syriac *Didascalia*, which perceives them as an advisory body whose purpose was to settle, together with the Bishop, differences arising between members of the Church so that those who repented and were reconciled could then receive forgiveness from the Bishop and thereafter participate in the Eucharist.[48]

As for the teaching ministry of the Presbyters, there is evidence that early on they were identified with the teachers. When the ministers of the Church are ennumerated in the *Shepherd of Hermas*, in the place of the presbyters it has the term "teachers,"[49] which clearly replaces the term "Presbyters."[50] Similar evidence is afforded by Tertullian,[51] Origen,[52] and Cyprian,[53] and also by the practice of the Church during the time under discussion. Thus it is known that Origen, Clement etc. who were Presbyters[54] taught the people in Alexandria at assemblies on Wednesdays and Fridays.[55] Similar assemblies are provided for in Rome by the *Apostolic Tradition*, and again they were the responsibility of the Presbyters and deacons.[56] These assemblies took place for teaching and prayer (on the pattern of the synagogue) *but never to celebrate the Eucharist*.[57] Thus, the Presbyters function as teachers mainly outside the Eucharist preparing the catechumens and admonishing the faithful through Scripture reading and prayer while the *eucharistic sermon* remained principally the task of the Bishop as Justin and Hippolytus testify.

From all this it is evident that the existing texts of the first three centuries know no authority of the Presbyter to lead his own eucharistic synaxis individually given that he participated in it as part of a college as the "Presbyterium." Thus the leadership and offering of the Eucharist formed the principle work of the Bishop who alone received such a right at his ordination being appointed the *sacerdos* of God in the Church. But how different things appear in the fourth century sources! This amazing change in the existing texts will be demonstrated by comparing the sources already examined with corresponding sources from the fourth century. (See table at page 280).

b) The place of the Bishop and the Presbyters in the Divine Eucharist according to the fourth century sources.

The most notable change in the texts, indicative of the development which had occurred in the meantime as to the Presbyter's relation to the Divine Eucharist, is to be observed in those texts of the fourth century which are *reworkings* or *translations* of the texts of the first three centuries which we have already looked at. Comparison of these texts will be presented later in the form of a diagram so as to make the differences clear once we have looked in detail at the information in these texts.

1. As we know,[58] the Epistles of Ignatius appeared around the end of the fourth century under a new, pseudepigraphal form with the original text altered and six spurious letters added to the seven genuine ones. If the changes introduced in this spurious edition are studied carefully, they reveal that in the interim the Presbyters had come to be identified with the "priests" and are called by this term which Ignatius knows nothing of in reference to Presbyters.[59] If we take into account the fact that nowhere in the sources of the first three centuries is the term "priest" used to denote the Presbyter,[60] something that can be seen especially from the end of the fourth century on,[61] it is clear that *something changed* during the fourth century regarding the position of the Presbyter in the Divine Eucharist. Indeed, we discover similar changes in another text contemporary with that of the spurious letters of Ignatius. Thus:

2. It is remarkable what changes the *Apostolic Tradition* of Hippolytus itself underwent during the fourth century. As we know,[62] this text was the source of a large number of liturgical and canonical collections in the East. A close look at these versions as they relate to the ordination of the Presbyter reveals the developments which had clearly taken place during the fourth century. Thus the eighth book of the so-called *"Apostolic Constitutions"* and what is called the "Epitome" of it (or "Constitutions of Hippolytus"), put together in Syria around 380 as reworkings of the *Apostolic Tradition* of Hippolytus, *change* the original prayer for the or-

dination of a Presbyter taken from the *Apostolic Tradition by adding the phrase*: "and that he may perform the spotless *sacred rites (heirourgiai)* on behalf of Thy people...," which most likely implies the offering of the Eucharist.[63] Hence, the use of the term "priest" to mean both Bishop and Presbyter occurs clearly for the first time in the text in question: "both the bishops and the presbyter priests."[64]

Equally remarkable changes are made in the *Apostolic Tradition* by the other version of it, the so-called "Canons of Hippolytus," written in about the year 500 in Syria. According to this text, when a priest is ordained everything is done as at the ordination of a Bishop except for the enthronement, and the prayer for the ordination of a Bishop is read with the exception of the name of bishop. To this is added the revealing explanation that the Presbyter is on a par with the Bishop in everything apart from the throne and the authority to ordain.[65] This understanding of the relationship of the Presbyter to the Bishop is of especial importance for the history of the ecclesial ministries, since, as we shall see shortly, it appears widespread from the end of the fourth century onwards.

The fact that these versions introduce changes which had not yet become general, and consequently represent a crucial point in time for the developments that were taking place, is shown by the existence of other versions of the *Apostolic Tradition* which appeared at the same period but in more conservative circles, and keep more closely to the original text of the *Tradition*. Thus, the Ethiopian translation of the *Tradition* characteristically includes a special prayer for the ordination of a Presbyter which differs from that for the ordination of a Bishop *only in the section referring to the functions peculiar to each of these degrees.* Specifically, in the prayer for the ordination of a Presbyter, the prayer for the ordination of a Bishop is repeated *without the section referring to the offering of the Eucharist* in place of which it has the phrase: "to share in succouring (*synantilamvanesthai*) in purity of heart and to govern Thy people,"[66] faithfully preserving the content of the *Apostolic Tradition* of Hippolytus. A similar remnant of the ancient view of Presbyters is another version of the *Ap-*

ostolic Tradition known by the name of "The Testament of our Lord Jesus Christ" and belonging to the beginning of the fifth century. This text too, faithful to its source, teaches that the Bishop is ordained "diligently and with all fear to offer to Thee the gifts of Thy holy Church," whereas the Presbyter is ordained "to share in succouring and to govern Thy people."[67] It should be noted that "recent investigations have shown that (this text) reproduces Hippolytus more reliably than anyone else."[68] These cases in the Coptic version and the "Testament," contrasting as they do with those in the eighth book of the Apostolic Constitutions and the Canons of Hippolytus, bear witness that even in the fourth century the promotion of the Presbyter individually to become the "priest" who leads the Eucharist had not spread everywhere. In certain circles, however – and indeed the widest and most significant of them, as shown by the example of the very widely distributed *Constitutions* – this promotion had taken place without having become fully established by the end of the fourth century.

3. Similar conclusions follow from the fate of the other very ancient and basic text, the (Syriac) *Didascalia of the Apostles*. Around the end of the fourth century, this text appears under the form of the first six books of the "Constitutions" which we have already discussed. At about the same period, there also appears the surviving Ethiopian version of the *Didascalia* which seems to draw on a lost Greek original.[69] Comparison of these versions with the original core of the *Didascalia* reveals that whenever there is something in these versions about the presbyter offering up the Divine Eucharist, it is an *addition* to the original third century text.[70]

4. All the above changes to the original texts at the points referring to the Presbyter's relation to the Eucharist coincide chronologically with the appearance of the view that the Bishop differs from the Presbyter *only* in the right to ordain. Thus, Jerome asks, "in what do the Bishops differ from the Presbyters except in the power to ordain?"[71] while St John Chrysostom stresses: "only in ordination do [Bishops] surpass Presbyters, and in this alone do they seem to have

superiority over them."[72] Similar examples abound during the time of these Fathers.[73]

It is evident that in the time of these Fathers the practice, which in history always precedes the theory, had already rendered the view of presbyters in the *Apostolic Tradition* of Hippolytus so outdated that not even a memory of it was preserved in regard to the relation between Presbyter and Eucharist. The Presbyters had already become leaders of their own eucharistic assemblies and "priests,"[74] striving indeed in some cases – unsuccessfully – to take the next step towards equality with Bishops, i.e. the right to ordain as was attempted several times during the fourth century.[75] The parish was now an historical reality both in fact and in theory.

But what came between the original situation handed down by Ignatius, Justin, Hippolytus and the author of the *Didascalia* and that familiar to those who revised and translated them around the end of the fourth century? Here we have the problem of the parish as our comparative study of the sources presents it. The historian is called to fill in the gap opened before him by this comparison of texts.[76] This is one of the most impenetrable blanks in the whole course of history. For while the change from one to several eucharistic assemblies was one of the most important events in the Church's life, the way it came about was so silent that it left no trace of disturbance in the unfolding of history. What is the reason for this? We shall now examine the factors which prepared the way for the appearance and establishment of the parish.

2. The historical preparation and the first appearance of the parish.

In order for the Presbyter to be connected permanently and individually with a particular ecclesial community-parish in such a way as to be recognized as its "priest," meaning the one who offers the Divine Eucharist in its name, a long period of preparation was necessary covering almost the whole period of the first three centuries. This preparation, which led so silently to the break-up of the original *one* Eucharist through the parish, consisted in the appearance and presence of the following historical preconditions:

1. *The possibility of replacing the Bishop in his ministry of leading the Eucharist* had already been recognized by the beginning of the second century. This is attested by the writer who above any other stresses the Eucharist "under the leadership of the Bishop," St Ignatius, when he adds to his exhortation: "Let that be deemed an assured eucharist which is under the leadership of the Bishop" the phrase *"or one to whom he has entrusted it."*[77] From this, it is evident that there existed a recognized possibility of someone else taking the Bishop's place in the leadership of the Eucharist obviously when he himself was prevented from being present at it. Although Ignatius does not write or hint anything about this substitute for the Bishop, he would certainly have come from the Presbyterium.[78] This was natural since the Presbyterium was regarded as connected with the Bishop as closely as "strings to a lute"[79] and took an active part in the celebration of the Mystery.[80] It was precisely because of this possibility for the Presbyters to take the place of the "presiding Presbyter" in the leadership of the Eucharist when he was prevented from leading it that 1 Clement could write of "the Presbyters" in general as those "who offer the gifts of the episcopê."[81] We find this possibility for the Presbyter to take the Bishop's place in the task of offering the Eucharist being put into practice both in the middle of the third century and at the beginning of the fourth.[82]

This sort of substitution, however, was still a long way from the one Eucharist being broken up and the Presbyter becoming the one to offer the Eucharist on a permanent basis. For as we have seen, at least up to the time of Hippolytus, the Presbyter did not receive this right by virtue of his ordination.[83] We should in consequence regard this substitution as taking place *ad hoc* during this period and not as a ministry belong to the nature of the Presbyter. Besides, the possibility of such a substitution, as Ignatius testifies, does not fragment the "one Eucharist" on which he continues to insist in his letters.

But while the possibility of the Presbyter taking the

Bishop's place when the latter was absent from the Eucharist did not signal either the break up of the "one" Eucharist or the promotion of the Presbyter to become its permanent leader. It cannot have failed to assist greatly in the silent transition from one Eucharist to many parishes. For this possibility, put into practice repeatedly and over a long period of time, must have contributed much to the lack of reaction when, with the appearance and establishment of the parish, the permanent leadership of the eucharistic assembly was assigned to the Presbyter.

2. It is also likely that some contribution was made to the historical preparation for the parish by the existence of assemblies for prayer and teaching "without the celebration of the Mysteries." This custom already appears in the *Apostolic Tradition* of Hippolytus, as we have seen, as a permanent and regular institution.[84] These assemblies, the leadership of which was assigned to the Presbyters with the help of the Deacons[85] and which usually took place on Wednesdays and Fridays, were the chief field for the ecclesial activity of the Presbyters, who, besides, received at their ordination the charism of educating the people.[86] When these assemblies became a permanent feature during the first three centuries, that created *a sort of presbyterocentric unity*. Even though giving this unit a eucharistic character was, as we have seen, studiously avoided, is not impossible that this unit was used *as a basis* for the formation of the parish, being given a eucharistic character when the number of Christians increased greatly. This forms a seemingly plausible hypothesis which, however, should not be accepted without reservations. For, as we have seen,[87] these assemblies for Scripture reading and prayer under the leadership of Presbyters and without the Eucharist continued even in the fifth century by which time the parish was already well established.

3. But is it possible that what served as the first form of the parish were the groups of Christians of various ethnic and cultural backgrounds which existed in Rome in large numbers from the middle of the second century? The existence of such groups was first maintained by G. La Piana[88]

and seems beyond dispute. But the attempt of that writer and others[89] to conclude from this that each of these groups formed a eucharistic assembly under Presbyters is not well founded. First of all, this theory runs counter to the information provided by Justin that the Christians in Rome, not only from the city but also from the surrounding villages, came together in *one* eucharistic assembly under the leadership of the "president" (Bishop).[90] Curiously, this important piece of information from Justin is not taken into account by La Piana even though it carries historical weight. La Piana bases his view mainly on one passage of Irenaeus referring to the paschal controversy. In this passage, Irenaeus refers to the practice of the Bishops Anicetus, Pius, Hygeinus, Telesphorus and Xystus of Rome to send the Eucharist to those who did not observe the same manner of celebrating Easter.[91] But nothing in this text implies that the Eucharist was "sent" to groups of Christians in Rome, or indeed under the leadership of Presbyters.[92] The view that the Bishops of Rome in the second century "sent the Eucharist to the Presbyters from Asia, just as they did for all the other *groups* in the community,"[93] cannot be supported from this passage. The sending of the Eucharist referred to in this passage may mean (a) the practice of the *Fermentum* which will be discussed below; but more probably either (b) the sending of the Eucharist to individuals who had not taken part in the episcopal synaxis in accordance with Justin's information on the subject,[94] or (c) the "concession" by the Bishop of Rome of his place as offering Bishop to the Bishops from Asia Minor who were visiting Rome as Eusebius informs us;[95] or even (d) the practice of "exchanging the Eucharist among the Bishops at the feast of Easter under the name of blessings."[96] Anyway, no definitive conclusion about the existence of parishes in Rome during the second century can be based on this passage of Irenaeus. The most likely meaning of which is probably that the Eucharist was "sent" "by the deacons" "to those who were not present," in accordance with what Justin tells us, even though these people came from Asia Minor and did not observe the same manner of celebrating Easter as the

Romans. Thus, the second century must be ruled out as a probable time for the parish to have appeared.

4. If we go now to the beginning of the third century to look for historical factors in the preparation for and appearance of the parish, the situation we shall encounter is as follows. The very valuable text of the *Apostolic Tradition* of Hippolytus which belongs to this period and testifies to one episcopocentric Eucharist on Sunday includes the following noteworthy detail: it enjoins that the Bishop should give the divine Eucharist to all the people with his own hands *if possible*.[97] What significance can this conditional clause have for history? J. Colson sees in it the existence of parishes in Rome during Hippolytus' time.[98] This conclusion, however, is entirely arbitrary. For the above text does not imply that if the Bishop could not give the Eucharist to everyone, then there should be separate eucharistic assemblies (parishes). Precisely what it does mean is immediately made clear by the text: if the Bishop is unable to distribute the Divine Eucharist to everyone on his own, then he should be helped by the Presbyters.[99] Consequently, this has to do with the distribution of the Divine Eucharist in the same assembly and not with its celebration in separate assemblies (parishes). Although this conditional clause in the text ("if possible") in no way implies the existence of parishes in Rome, it is, however, indicative of the increase in the number of Christians to the point where *it had perhaps begun to be difficult for all the faithful to gather for one Eucharist.* Do we perhaps have here precisely the key to understanding the historical preconditions for the parish?

The historical conditions of the period when the *Apostolic Tradition* was written favor this hypothesis. At precisely that time, the Church was experiencing one of her most prolonged periods of peace and freedom owing to the policies of the emperors between the death of Septimius Severus in 211 and Decius' ascent to the throne in 249. As a result of this peace, the Christians increased significantly in number not only in the country areas but mainly within the large cities such as Rome.[100] This fact began to make it difficult for all the members of the local Church to gather at one Divine Eucharist. From this we are justified in supposing that in writing the *Apostolic Tradition* and using more ancient liturgical texts as its core and basis, Hippolytus, with the conservatism characteristic both of him and of Rome, wanted not to alter the original liturgical core which provided for distribution of the Eucharist by the Bishop alone, and yet to adapt it to the conditions created in the meanwhile by the increase in the numbers of Christians. This is why he added "if possible." This hypothesis of ours is not groundless when it is taken into account that Hippolytus seems to have adapted the *Apostolic Tradition* to the situation of his time in other points mainly matters of doctrine.[101] All this shows (a) that in the first half of the third century, the increase in the number of Christians within the cities started to create problems for the eucharistic assemblies, and (b) that the solution of these problems, in Rome at least, was approached with great conservatism as regards maintaining the ancient tradition according to which the whole of the local Church was united around one Eucharist under one Bishop who alone was ordained to lead it. Did this approach to the problem, conservative though it was, lead gradually to the Eucharist becoming the permanent responsibility of Presbyters in parishes? We know nothing of this for certain from the sources of the first half of the third century.

5. Right in the middle of the third century, however, new historical conditions arise to make the problem of maintaining *one* eucharistic assembly for the whole city still more difficult and pressing. This is why the texts of this period show an increase in the Presbyters' sphere of liturgical responsibility in the Eucharist; the significance of which needs to be investigated.

The new historical conditions consisted in a change in the policy of the Roman emperors which began under Decius and was intensified by Valerian. The policy of tolerance towards the Christians implemented by the Syrian imperial dynasty was now judged harmful and dangerous to the state at a time when its security was seriously threatened especially from the East. To address this new situation, the emperors Decius and Valerian attached particular importance to the internal state of the empire, and tried to restore the strict obedience which had prevailed in earlier times.[102] Hence, the legislation of Decius which required every citizen to make a public act of confession of his dedication to the official state religion and imposed the severest penalties on any who refused to comply. Despite the fact that many imperial officials showed remarkable elasticity in implementing this legislation by exhausting every means of extracting a voluntary confession and often ignoring the legislation completely, the new situation had very serious consequences for the Christians. It is, however, characteristic of this period that it was mainly the Bishops of the Churches who suffered the consequences of the new legislation.[103] As a result, many Churches were long deprived of their liturgical leadership, whether because of the death of their Bishop at the hands of the executioner, or because of his exile or flight, or even because of his apostasy. Thus, the Church of Carthage had not seen her Bishop Cyprian for fifteen whole months. For the same reason and at the same period, the Church of Alexandria was for a long time deprived of the presence of her Bishop Dionysius. Similarly, the diocese of Rome remained vacant for about two years after the martyrdom of Pope Xystus II.[104] The problem consequently arose in acute form: who would lead the Divine Eucharist in the absence of the Bishop?

A solution to this problem could not be sought apart from strengthening the liturgical function proper to the Presbyters. Thus, it is to be observed at this period that episcopal duties are quite broadly and explicitly assigned to Presbyters. When Cyprian was away from his Church, he entrusted his duties to the Presbyters and Deacons.[105] Among these duties was included the celebration of the Divine Eucharist.[106] It seems that the Presbyters and Deacons of Rome likewise concentrated in their hands the whole leadership of the Church of Rome after the death of Fabian (250).[107] As for Egypt, we learn from a letter of Dionysius of Alexandria that the regular eucharistic assemblies in Alexandria went on during the time when Dionysius was absent.[108] These cases from Africa, Rome and Alexandria suffice to show the extension of the Presbyters' functions for practical reasons. As was natural, this led to the connection of the Presbyters in practice with the function of offering the Gifts; and in combination with the rapid rise in the number of Christians in the first half of the third century, as already noted, it contributed to making *the middle of the third century the time when the parish first appeared in practice.*

6. Thus in two texts indicative of conditions in the middle of the third century, we have been able to find *the first indications* of the existence of a form of parishes. These texts, and the elements in them which give an indication concerning parishes, are as follows:

(a) In one of Cyprian's letters to the clergy of Carthage, mention is made of a Presbyter of Didda(?), Gaius by name, who was excluded from ecclesial communion *with his deacon* because he had communicated with the lapsed and offered their Eucharist.[109] Who was this Presbyter and what degree of independence did he have from the Bishop so as to be called the Presbyter *of a particular community*, and to *have his own deacon*? We do not know. It is however evident that the Presbyter in question had a more permanent connection than usual with a particular community which, it appears, was at a distance from Carthage and unable to unite with the city's eucharistic assembly; and there was a deacon attached to him who assisted him in the celebration of the Divine Eucharist. Thus, we notice straight away two elements which were both irreconcilable in theory with the notion of Presbyters prevailing in the third century, and had not in practice appeared anywhere earlier: (a) *a Presbyter connected individually with a certain community*, and (b) *a deacon attached to a Presbyter.*[110]

(b) In a text going back to the second half of the third century or beginning of the fourth,[111] known as the *Acta disputationis S. Achelai cum Manete haeresiarcha*,[112] it is mentioned that the heresiarch Manes visited a village outside the city of Carcharai (?) in Mesopotamia which was called Diodorus, and its priest was likewise called Diodorus.[113] Of course, this text does not tell us what exactly were the functions of this Presbyter. It is characteristic, however, that he is called "presbyter of that place" ("*presbyter loci illius*"), and this is indicative of the surprising connection between the name of a Presbyter and that of his own community. The fact that the original Syriac text and the Greek derived from it[114] are not preserved can in no way affect the fact that the name of this Presbyter is connected with a certain community.

Such a connection is clear evidence that from the middle of the third century, as a result of the practice over a long period, Presbyters had already begun to be regarded as having their own communities. We should place in this context the phenomenon *which appeared at the same period of Presbyters being linked with country communities* which did not have their own Bishops (chorepiscopi), but depended on the Bishop of the city. Dionysius of Alexandria witnesses to this when he writes: "When he was in Arsenoe... he gathered together *the Presbyters and teachers of the brethren in the villages...*,"[115] which implies a permanent connection of the Presbyters with the communities in the countryside. What was the function of these Presbyters there, we do not know. But the very fact that they were permanently connected with communities of their own is a clear indication of the earliest form of the parish especially when it is connected with the other peices of information from the same period which we have already discussed.

From all this, we conclude that the first indications concerning the appearance of the parish should be placed around the middle of the third century. The parish appeared at that time *as a result of necessity*. The rapid rise in the number of Christians in the cities and perhaps also in the rural interior, and the lengthy absence of the Bishops from their Churches which followed obliged the Church to entrust the leadership of the Eucharist to the Presbyters on a more permanent than usual basis and to break up the one Eucharist under the leadership of the Bishop into several assemblies centered on Presbyters. So at this period, for the first time, Presbyters appeared attached individually and permanently to communities of their own. This was the original form of the parish. Between this point and the full and unreserved recognition of the Presbyters' right to offer the Eucharist which we observe in the fourth century, a few intervening generations cover the time, necessary in any historical development, between the establishment of a reality *in practice* and its establishment *in theory*. The changes in the liturgical texts which we have already discussed at length come as the theoretical validation of the parish once it was established in practice. In this way, we are able to fill in the gap between the original form of these texts and their reworking or translation that being the problem of the origin of the parish as it is posed by the sources.

This development was *not revolutionary* but natural.[116] The close connection from the beginning between the "Presbyterium" and the Bishop who offered the Eucharist, and the possibility of a substitute taking the Bishop's place at the Eucharist, had prepared the Church's consciousness to accept the new situation. But this smoothness in transition from the one state of affairs to the other could not diminish the significance of the fact that the original *one* Eucharist under the Bishop, through and in which each Church was manifested in history as the whole, catholic and unified body of Christ, no longer existed. Do we not then encounter such a problem in the consciousness of the Church at this period? How did the Church's consciousness construe the emergence of the parish in relation to the unity of the Church in the Eucharist and the Bishop? This is the problem to which we must now turn our attention.

Chapter Two

The Appearance of the Parish and the Unity of the Church in "One Eucharist, Under the Leadership of the Bishop"

The appearance and establishment of many parishes within each Church raises the basic question for historical research: what happened to the Church's original consciousness that the one Eucharist "under the leadership of the Bishop" incarnates and expresses the unity of the Church of God which is in a certain place, now that because of the many parishes the members of this Church had ceased to come together into *one* Eucharist? This question introduces the fundamental problem of the relation of parish unity to the unity of the episcopal diocese as the early Church understood it. To what extent did the appearance of the parish create *a sort of self-contained eucharistic unity* within the unity of the diocese?

This question is exceedingly difficult to answer. The existing sources contain scarcely any systematic or theoretical clues to the solution of this problem. We shall, therefore, be obliged to draw the evidence essential for throwing light on our problem mainly from the practice and life of the early Church. Through appropriate interpretation of this evidence, we shall attempt to examine how the parochial eucharistic assembly related to the episcopal eucharistic assembly. To this end, we shall look at this relationship (a) during the transitional period, from the first appearance of the parish in the middle of the third century up to its consolidation in the fourth century, and (b) at the time when the institution of parishes was fully consolidated, and thereafter.

1)The relation of the eucharistic unity of the parish to episcopal eucharistic unity during the transitional period when parishes were first appearing.

During the crucial transitional period from the first appearance of the parish in practice around the middle of the third century to the definitive recognition of it in theory in the fourth century, when in many places the Presbyter began to receive *through his ordination* the right to offer the Eucharist, the few indications which exist reveal on careful examination that in order for Presbyters to assume any of the Bishop's liturgical responsibilities, it required: i) an express mandate from the Bishop, and ii) clearly defined limits to the powers conveyed to them. These two preconditions were not fulfilled once and for all through ordination, but were required in each particular case.

Ignatius already testifies to these preconditions when he writes regarding substitution for a Bishop in his ministry in the Eucharist, "or one to whom *he* (i.e. the Bishop) has entrusted it."[117] The whole sense of the passage in which this phrase occurs makes it clear that the emphasis is placed by Ignatius on the word "he," so as to ensure the episcopocentric character of the eucharistic synaxis, which is what interests Ignatius in this passage. It is precisely in this spirit of Ignatius' that episcopal functions begin to be assigned widely and now more permanently to Presbyters when the parish first appears around the middle of the third century. This is made clear by the letters of Cyprian and Dionysius of Alexandria, who, as we have seen, are connected with the first indications of parishes.

Thus concerning the forgiveness of the lapsed, which only the Bishop could give as of right, Cyprian entrusts this to the Presbyters because of his long absence, but only in cases of people on their death-bed.[118] As for other cases, the Presbyters were obliged to await the return of their Bishop.[119] This position of Cyprian's is, besides, consistent with his basic ecclesiological principle according to which the Church is governed by the Bishop according to divine law.[120] The other clergy are his indispensable advisors,[121] as the Laity too give their assent on serious matters.[122] But any action by the Presbyters without the express instruction of the Bishop was unacceptable according to Cyprian.[123] The same applies with the aforementioned example of episcopal responsibilities being delegated in Alexandria during the absence of its Bishop, Dionysius.[124] The performance by Presbyters of episcopal duties, which included assembling the faithful to celebrate the Eucharist, was possible only "when I had given the instruction," as Dionysius writes.[125] Hence the eucharistic synaxis that takes place without him is in essence nothing other than the Eucharist *which is under his leadership*, which *he had joined in convoking* and at which he was spiritually present.[126]

These examples make it plain that at its first hesitant appearance in history, the parish was not a self-contained eucharistic unity but a mere extension of the episcopal Eucharist designed to cope with dire practical needs. But did it form a self-contained eucharistic unity from the mid-fourth century onwards, once the parish was fully established and the Presbyter began to be ordained in order, *inter alia*, to "offer the sacrifice"?

2)The relationship of the eucharistic unity of the parish to episcopal eucharistic unity once the institution of parishes was established.

The appearance and establishment of the parishes as discrete eucharistic assemblies within the bosom of the episcopal diocese provoked no apparent reaction, but it did create within the Church's consciousness the problem of maintaining *one* Eucharist under the leadership of the Bishop despite the existence of the parishes. The attempt by the early Church to provide a solution to this problem is depicted dramatically in the practice known as the *Fermentum*.[127] This practice consisted in sending with the acolytes a portion of the Eucharist which had been celebrated by the Bishop to those who had been unable to participate in it, and above all to those assemblies whose Eucharist was celebrated by Presbyters (parishes). In the latter case, the Presbyter had to mix this portion of the episcopal Eucharist in with the Eucharist which he himself celebrated.[128] This custom appears to have been widespread in the West,[129] but was undoubtedly known more widely, as G. Dix shows.[130] But although this fact has generally been recognized by scholars, its significance for the history of the unity of the Church was much greater than that usually ascribed to it. The *fermentum* presents in a dramatic way the Church's hesitations about abandoning the principle of celebrating *one* Eucharist as an expression of her unity. For how else can we make sense of the fact that amidst fears and persecutions and adverse weather conditions, two Acolytes – an office established precisely for this purpose[131] – traversed the roads and often went even beyond the boundaries of the city in order to take the parish assemblies a portion of the Eucharist that was under the leadership of the Bishop? Was the Presbyter's Eucharist not sufficient? Clearly the *fermentum* was for the early Church something more than a mere symbol of unity: it was the expression of a dire and fundamental necessity. The full justification for it lies only in the Church's conviction that a Eucharist independent of that one Eucharist which is under the Bishop was unthinkable, and that in consequence, the parish Eucharist celebrated by Presbyters *needed the Bishop's presence within it in some way*. From an historical viewpoint, then, the *fermentum* represents a period at which ancient elements of the consciousness concerning the unity of the Church in the Eucharist and the Bishop still survived in the Church. Its disappearance, therefore, coincided in the East with the end of the fourth century,[132] that is to say, the time when, as we have seen, the parish was becoming stabilized in theory as well as practice; but in conservative Rome it disappeared much later – perhaps after the ninth century[133] – having been preserved under various highly remarkable liturgical forms.[134]

But if the *fermentum* disappeared, the principle which it expressed so graphically was preserved under the form of many elements in liturgy. This principle, which formed the basis for the relation of the one Eucharist under the Bishop to the several parish Eucharists under Presbyters, consisted, as we have seen, in the need in some way to ensure the living presence of the Bishop in the parish Eucharist so that *in reality there was not more than the one Eucharist in the same Church* just as it was originally. To go into all the details of these elements would of course require a special study into the history of eucharistic worship after the fourth century. Such a study goes beyond the chronological limits of the present work; but because of the importance of these elements for throwing light on situations in the years studied here in relation to the unity of the Church in the one Eucharist, we shall not pass by without setting out some of these elements, albeit in general terms, in the following points.

1. It should not be seen as mere chance that even after the appearance of the parish and when the right to celebrate the Eucharist was already assigned to Presbyters through their ordination *all the surviving texts of Liturgies go under the names of Bishops and not of Presbyters.*[135] Doubtless such Liturgies would have appeared under the names of Presbyters, if in the early Church the Presbyter had become through the parish the leader of a full and self-contained eucharistic assembly, i.e. in every way equal to the Bishop as regards the Eucharist. By contrast, most of the works concerned with the teaching and catechetical instruction of the people are preserved under the names of Presbyters[136] while the Eucharist remained in this way too essentially an episcopal ministry.

2. It is remarkable that even today *the commemoration of the Bishop's name,* and that indeed at the supreme moment of the Anaphora, has remained an absolutely indispensable element in the Presbyter's liturgy. This commemoration seems to go back to earliest times.[137] The fact that the Presbyter is obliged to commemorate the name not of just any Bishop but of *the Bishop of the place in which the Eucharist is being celebrated* indicates the significance of the action which obviously has the purpose of making the parish Eucharist under the Presbyter an *organic and inseparable component of the one Eucharist under the Bishop* through which the Church of God sojourning in that place is united into one body. If the Presbyter were celebrating the Eucharist independently of the episcopal Eucharist and by right of his ordination, would

it not be more natural for him to commemorate the name of
the Bishop who had ordained him, or the Bishop of the
Church he came from?

3. Similar conclusions may *perhaps* be drawn from the
necessity of celebrating the Eucharist on an antimension bear-
ing the signature of the Bishop. What of course came to be
regarded as the fundamental significance of the antimension
was the presence of the sacred Relics on the Altar especially
in cases where a chapel had not previously been consecrated.[138] It seems, however, that in parallel with this purpose
the antimension also served as a living expression of the necessity for the Bishop's permission as a prior condition for
every non-episcopal Eucharist. This hypothesis is justified
by the following sources which are usually overlooked. Already in the writings of Dionysius the Areopagite, it is
implied that there is a relation between the antimension and
the Presbyter's dependence on his Bishop. Just as the priest
cannot perform chrismation, we read there, without the
chrism which only the Bishop can bless, so neither can he
"perform the mysteries of the divine communion unless the
symbols of communion have been placed on the most divine altar."[139] That this has to do with some sort of
antimension and not simply with the consecration being
performed once and for all by the Bishop, is implied by the
fact that these "symbols" are placed on an altar which is already consecrated ("most divine"). The connection made by
the author of these writings between this practice and the
analogous practice of the chrism blessed by the Bishop alone
being used for chrismation suffices to prove that exactly the
same relation of dependence on the Bishop exists in the case
of the Eucharist headed by a Presbyter. But even if it were
accepted that, as is usually thought, the antimension appeared and became widespread mainly after the iconoclast
controversy.[140] The idea that it signifies the the Presbyter's
dependence on the Bishop in the celebration of the Eucharist is not absent from the few sources which inform us about
its use in the early Church. The 31st Canon of the Council in
Trullo (691/2) laid down that no Presbyter was permitted to

celebrate the Eucharist in a chapel without the permission of the local Bishop.[141] Balsamon, one of the earliest sources to give us clear information about antimensia, relates this canon to the antimension in his interpretation of it, and writes: "For this reason, it seems, antimensia were devised, and come from the local Bishops... not only in place of the dedication, opening and consecration [of the chapel], but also *to show that the rite performed in the chapel takes place with episcopal consent.*"[142] It should be noted that at that period the Bishop never celebrated in a chapel, i.e. a private church which did not have an episcopal throne.[143] Thus, the necessity for an antimension, being connected with chapels, relates not to the Bishop's Eucharist but to that of the Presbyters. Hence another source concerning the antimension, the anonymous metropolitan of Vella (early thirteenth century), writes that antimensia are given *to Presbyters* "and they cannot celebrate them."[144] Thus, the antimension appears in the sources as a sort of successor to the *fermentum* connected with the principle of the dependence of the parish Eucharist on the Bishop – a principle which the *fermentum*, as we have seen, expressed so dramatically in earlier times.

4. To all this should be added the notable hesitancy with which the early Church proceeded with the break up of the one Eucharist under the Bishop once this was imposed by practical necessity. A careful reading of Egeria's *Travels*, to which we have already referred repeatedly, reveals that even in the fourth century in the populous Church of Jerusalem, where throngs of believers converged from all corners of the Christian world, *only one* Divine Eucharist was celebrated regardless of the great number of faithful. This was the Eucharist at which the Bishop of Jerusalem presided, and which was celebrated in the characteristically-named *"ecclesia major;"*[145] in other words the cathedral, while at feasts, the faithful gathered at the other churches for the celebration of the Eucharist, but again not in groups but all together *under the leadership of the Bishop,* and the "great church" would stand idle on those days.[146] Here we have a remarkable attempt to save the original one Eucharist under the Bishop from suc-

cumbing to the pressure of the necessity for parishes. This discouragement of the proliferation of eucharistic assemblies which was so far forgotten in the West in the Middle Ages[147] – and later among the Orthodox too, clearly as a result of Western influence – must be the basis underlying the prohibition in the Canons against more than one Eucharist being celebrated on the same day, by the same priest, at the same altar. This prohibition is ancient,[148] and as it is characteristically formulated in the sixth century in the West (Synod of Auxerre), it contains the points that one cannot celebrate two Liturgies on the same day at the same altar, and that *if the Bishop has celebrated the Liturgy* at one altar, *no one else is allowed to celebrate on that day.*[149] We could not have a clearer expression of the purpose underlying this prohibitory regulation: it has to do with the necessity for the one Eucharist "which is under the leadership of the Bishop" to remain the center of unity *par excellence* for the "whole Church," as it was in earliest times.

Through all these elements in the liturgical life of the early Church, the relationship she recognized between the parish Eucharist and the episcopal Eucharist is clearly brought out. Far from being a self-contained and self-sufficient eucharistic unity, the parish made its appearance as an *extension* within the area of the diocese of the one Eucharist "which is under the leadership of the Bishop." Hence the Eucharist celebrated by Presbyters had a continuing need not only for episcopal permission, but also for the living presence of the Bishop in such a way that in reality there was but the *one single altar* (*monogenes thysiasterion*)[150] in the whole diocese. In this way the parish ended up being nothing other than the *spatial distribution of the Presbyters' synthronon, while the one and only center of eucharistic unity was still the episcopal throne, from which every parish Eucharist drew its substance.*[151]

To sum up the conclusions of the Part III, we may make the following points.

Insuperable practical needs, such as the rapid rise in the

number of Christians during the first half of the third century and the prolonged absence of Bishops from their Churches during the persecutions in the middle of that century, led to the appearance in history of parishes, as separate, presbytero-centric Eucharist assemblies within the episcopal Church. This event brought with it corresponding developments in the functions of Bishops and Presbyters. As a comparative study of the liturgical and canonical texts of the first four centuries has shown, whereas originally only the Bishop was ordained to offer "the gifts of the episcopê," in the fourth century this ministry of the Bishop was added into the original prayers for the ordination of Presbyters in such a way that the right to ordain was the only difference remaining between these two ministers. This development marked the consolidation of the parish. But before this development could be firmly established in the Church's consciousness, the way had to be prepared by the appearance of the parish *in practice* (and not yet in theory) which on the evidence adduced from the sources we have dated to the middle of the third century.

As was natural, however, this development could not remain without ecclesiological implications. The original preservation of *one* Eucharist "which was under the leadership of the Bishop" in each Church was the living expression of the unity of the Church of God sojourning in that place in one complete body, the whole body of Christ. Breaking up this one Eucharist into several would consequently be equivalent to schism of the gravest sort. Hence, the problem of the relation existing between the presbyterocentric parish Eucharist and the one episcopocentric Eucharist was not wholly absent from the consciousness of the early Church. Through the practice of the *fermentum* and many other means whereby the proliferation of eucharistic assemblies was discouraged and an attempt was made to keep the presbyterocentric Eucharist in a relationship of organic and essential dependence on the one episcopal throne, a solution was found to the problem: the parish did not form a self-sufficient and self-contained eucharistic unity, but an extension in space of the one self-same episcopocentric Eucharist. The Presbyter thus, celebrated the Eucharist in the name of the Bishop who remained the only true head of this mystical body of the Church of God. The thrones of the *synthronon* were dispersed, but they did not form discrete centers of eucharistic unity. They were simply *radii* of the same circle constantly dependent on the one center which was occupied by the Bishop. Thus, each local Church continued even after the appearance of the parishes to be, as described in the second part of our study, *one full circle*, one body, the very body of Christ manifested in history in one Eucharist.

NOTES TO PART THREE

[1] Cf. above, p. 44f.

[2] V. Stephanidis, *op. cit.* p. 87. We do not know where he took this information from since he cites no reference. (Perhaps he takes it from Harnack, *Mission*, II⁴, pp. 836, 841f., where a similar view is expressed.) As a result, we have been obliged to search for probable sources for this information and have finally located them to the *Liber Pontificalis*. The unreliability of this source is shown by the confusion and contradictions into which it falls. Thus, according to this same *Liber*, a) parishes appeared at Rome under Evarestus (beginning of the second century) (*"Hic titulos in urbe Roma dividit presbyteris"* ["he divided the parishes among presbyters in the city of Rome"] – ed. Duchesne, I, p. 55); b) Marcellus (308/9) *"titulos in (urbe) Roma constituit quasi diocesis propter baptismum et penitentiam et sepulcuras martyrum"* ["set up parishes like dioceses in [the city of] Rome to provide baptism and penance and burial for the martyrs"] (Ibid. p. 75); c) Urban I (223-230) *"ministeria sacrata argentea constituit et patenas argenteas posuit"* ["instituted sacred vessels of silver and gave as an offering patens of silver"] Ibid. p. 63); and d) Cletus (76-88) *"ex praecepto beati Petri presbyteros ordinavit in urbe Roma"* – ["at the direction of the blessed Peter, ordained presbyters in the city of Rome"] (Ibid. p. 53). [Translation adapted from *The Book of the Popes*, I, ET L.R. Loomis, New York 1916.] It is thus admittedly hard to know which to choose!

[3] *op. cit.* p. 87. Cf. also G. Konidaris, *G.C.H.*, p. 243f.

[4] The whole problem of the origin of the parish appears very confused in the work of the late professor and indeed presents con-

traditions. Thus, starting from the assumption that the rank and importance of the Bishop were enhanced as a result of the Church's struggle "against dissenters within... and enemies without, it follows that with time *the number and significance of Bishops increased*. Christian communities in cities which had not hitherto had Bishops saw to acquiring them" (p. 86). But while this assumes that the Bishops were originally few and presided over large communities only, while smaller communities did not have Bishops, further he writes that "initially... the Bishop presided over a Christian community which formed a church assembly (parish)...," and that with the increase in the number of Christians the one parish (of the Bishop) was extended into several parishes under the same Bishop (p. 87). But if the Bishop did indeed "initially preside over one Christian community – parish," how can it be said that there were Christian communities which initially did not have Bishops? Whom did those parishes come under? Another Bishop? But in that case, how is it true that each Bishop initially presided over one church assembly only, if there were other communities which did not have Bishops of their own but came under another Bishop? The confusion and contradiction stem from the erroneous assumption that initially there were some communities without Bishops which in turn presupposes the unfounded view that the importance of the episcopal rank increased with time on account of heresies and persecutions. This view has been imposed by recent historiography, especially Protestant historiography. If one rids oneself of these assumptions and connects the unity of the church assembly with the Eucharist and the Bishop, as we do here, it then becomes quite clear that from the beginning an ecclesial (= eucharistic) assembly was unthinkable without a Bishop, and that regardless of heresies and persecutions the significance of the Bishop was so fundamental that at its inception each Christian community would have its own Bishop. Contrary to the prevailing view that the number of Bishops increased with time, the evidence of history is that proportionate to the constantly increasing number of Christians, the number of Bishops actually *fell* over time, thus inevitably entailing the ever greater extension of the Bishop's administrative jurisdiction (fewer Bishops = larger dioceses = increase in administrative rights and responsibilities). Cf. above p. 110, n. 61.

   [5] See above, Part I, Ch. 1.

   [6] See above, Part II, Ch. 1.

   [7] See above, Part I, Ch. 2, especially p. 66f. On this cf. also the study of O. Perler, "L'Évêque Représentant du Christ...," in

L'Épiscopat et l'Église Universelle, pp. 31-36.

[8] See above, Part II, Ch. 2.

[9] See above, p. 66f.

[10] The original connection of the deacons directly and exclusively with the Bishop is clearly attested by texts such as *Apostolic Tradition* 9.2, the Syriac *Didascalia* etc. This is due to the fact that, as we have seen, the Bishop continued to be the leader of the Eucharist to which the ministry of the deacons was principally connected. Cf. above p. 82, n. 139.

[11] See above, p. 67.

[12] See above, p. 79, n. 111.

[13] See above, p. 62.

[14] See 1 Clement 40:3 – 41:4.

[15] See above, p. 61f.

[16] See above, pp. 61f. and 193, n. 346.

[17] See above, p. 54f.

[18] See above, Part II, Ch. 2.

[19] Ignatius *Smyrn.* 8.1 and Justin 1 *Apol.* 65 and 67. Cf. above p. 102, n. 32.

[20] See A. Harnack in *Theologische Literaturzeitung* (1920), 225.

[21] The first person to write about the authenticity of this work was E. Schwartz, *Über die pseudoapostolischen Kirchenordnungen* (Schriften der wissenschaftlichen Gesellschaft in Strassburg 6), 1910, who simply expressed the opinion that the Latin text of the so-called Egyptian Tradition represents the Apostolic Tradition of Hippolytus which was thought lost. This view of Schwartz' was first proved right through serious arguments by R. H. Connolly, *The So-called Egyptian Church Order and Derived Documents* (Texts and Studies, 8,4), 1916, and received still further support from H. Elfers, *Die Kirchenordnung Hippolyts von Rom*, 1938. The text circulated more widely through the anonymous work *Die Apostolische Überlieferung des hl. Hippolytus*, 1932, but the best critical edition hitherto remains that of G. Dix, *The Treatise on the Apostolic Tradition of Saint Hippolytus of Rome*, 1937, to which has been added those of B. Botte, *Hippolyte de Rome: La Tradition Apostolique* (*Sources Chrétiennes*, No. 11), 1946, and more recently *Eiusdem: La Tradition Apostolique de Saint Hippolyte* (Liturgiewissenschaftliche Quellen und Forschungen, Heft 39), 1963.

[22] *Apostolic Tradition* 3 (ed. B. Botte in *Liturgiewissen. Quellen*, p. 7): "*Da, cordis cognitor Pater, super hunc seruum tuum, quem elegisti ad episcopatu[m], pascere gregem sanctam tuam, et primatum sacerdotii tibi exhibere sine repraehensione, seruientem noctu et die, incessanter*

repropitiari vultum tuum et offere dona sancta[e] ecclesiae tuae, sp[irit]u[m] primatus sacerdotii habere potestatem dimittere peccata secundum mandatum tuum..."

"O Father who knowest the heart, bestow on this Thy servant whom Thou hast chosen to the episcopate to shepherd Thy holy flock and to fulfil the high-priestly office without reproach, serving night and day; unceasingly to make supplication before Thy face; and to offer the gifts of Thy holy Church, and in the spirit of the high-priesthood to have the power to remit sins according to Thy command..."

[23] To these, there are of course added in the prayer all the other powers of the Bishop such as that of remission of sins, baptism, chrismation etc., which likewise originally belonged exclusively to the Bishop, and do not occur in the prayer for the ordination of a Presbyter in this text either.

[24] *1 Apol.* 67: "And the president similarly offers up prayers and thanksgivings, according to his ability, and the people gives assent saying the Amen, and there is a distribution and partaking by each of the things for which thanks has been given..."

[25] See J. Quasten, *Patrology* II, 1953, p. 147f. Cf. P. Galtier, "La Date de la Didascalie des Apôtres," in *Revue d'Histoire Ecclésiastique* 42 (1947), 315-351.

[26] Cf. P. Trembelas, "Contributions to the History of Christian Worship," p. 88.

[27] Syriac *Didascalia* 9 (Tr. R.H. Connolly, *Didascalia Apostolorum: The Syriac Version Translated and Accompanied by the Verona Fragment*, 1929, p. 86f.): "This man (=the Bishop) is your chief and your leader and he is your mighty king. He rules in place of the Almighty; but let him be honored by you as God, for the Bishop sits for you in the place of God the Almighty." Again, Ibid. p. 94: "... the Bishops, who have loosed you from your sins, who by the water regenerated you, who filled you with the Holy Spirit, who reared you with the word as with milk, who bred you up with doctrine, who confirmed you with admonition, and made you partake of the Holy Eucharist of God, and made you partakers and joint heirs of the promise of God."

[28] See Heb. 2:17; 3:1; 4:14-15; 5:1, 6, 10; 6:20; 7:17, 26; 8:1; 10:21 etc., and 1 Clement.

[29] Apostolic Tradition 3.5 and 9.1.

[30] Cyprian *Epist.* 3 (65) to Bishop Rogatianus (Hartel, 729): *"Graviter et dolenter commoti summus... lectis litteris tuis, quibus de diacono tuo conquestus es quod immemor sacerdotalis loci tui et officii ac*

ministerii sui... sacerdotali potestate fecisses... cum... Chore, Datham et Abiron qui sacerdoti praepositi se adequare...ique consumpti sunt... ut probaretur sacerdotis Dei ab eo qui sacerdotes facit vindicari..."

"We were deeply and sorely distressed... on reading your letter, in which you complained about your deacon that [he had been] heedless of your priestly position and of his own office and ministry... You might do by your priestly power... Korah, Dathan and Abiram dared to make themselves equal with the priests set over them, and they were devoured... that it might be proved that God's priests are avenged by Him who makes priests..."

Cf. *Epist.* 66 (69); 55 (52); 58 (56) (Hartel pp. 731, 733, 629, 630, 672).

[31] *Epist.* 66 (69). 5 (Hartel, 730), where the situation when the Bishop is absent from the Church is described thus: *"ecce jam sex annis nec fraternitas habuerit episcopum, nec plebs praepositum, nec grex pastorem, nec ecclesia gubernatorem, nec Christus antistitem, nec Deus sacerdotem."*

"For six years now the brotherhood has not had a bishop, nor the people a chief, nor the flock a shepherd, nor the Church a helmsman, nor Christ a representative, nor God a priest."

[32] See I. Evtaxias, *Stipulations Concerning Priestly Authority in the Canon Law of the Orthodox Eastern Church*, I, 1872, p. 19: "determining the scope of the priestly authority of the Presbyter, especially in relation to that of the Bishop, is a very difficult question." Evtaxias then goes to the heart of the problem when he asks (p. 120): "In the exercise of his priestly authority, should the Presbyter be seen as the proxy or representative of the Bishop? If he is thus regarded, then what properly constitutes the rank of Presbyter, what is its distinguishing feature? If he cannot be regarded as the Bishop's representative but as exercising an authority which he possesses of himself, in what then does his own authority consist, and how does it differ from that of the Bishop?"

[33] On the content of the office of Presbyter more generally, see G. Dix, "Ministry," and J. Colson, *Les Fonctions Ecclésiales aux Deux Premiers Siècles*, 1956, where there is also an extensive bibliography; and on priesthood more generally in G. Bardy, "Le Sacerdoce Chrétien du 1er aux Ve s.," in *Prêtres d'Hier et d'Aujourd'hui* (*Unam Sanctam* 28), 1954.

[34] I. Evtaxias again acknowledges that there is a problem from an historical viewpoint and poses it sharply without of course attempting to solve it when he writes that the canon law prevailing today as regards the priestly authority of the Presbyter "did not

prevail from the beginning in the Church." (*op. cit.* p. 20).

[35] See G. Konidaris, *On the Supposed Difference*, p. 55. It should be added that the term "co-Presbyter" continues to be used even at the end of the second century to include the Bishop (see Apology of the Bishop of Hierapolis in Eusebius, *Eccl. Hist.* V.16.5) and in the third (see Eusebius, *Eccl. Hist.* VII.5.6. Cf. VII.11.3 and VII.20).

[36] See above, p. 67.

[37] Eusebius hints at this in his panegyric on the dedication of the Church in Tyre (*Eccl. Hist.* X.4.46), but it is more clearly described by Egeria in the chronicle of her visit to Jerusalem (ed. Pétré, *Etheriae peregrinatio*, 1948, p. 192): "*Ecce et commonetur episcopus et sedet susum nec non etiam et Presbyteri sedent locis suis.*" ["Then they send for the Bishop, who enters and sits in the chief seat. The Presbyters also come and sit in their places." ET J. Wilkinson, *Egeria's Travels*, London, 1971, § 24.4] The architecture of the ancient Christian churches also testifies to this *synthronon*. See G. Soteriou, *Christian and Byzantine Archaeology*, I, 1942, p. 185f.

[38] See above, n. 35.

[39] *Philad.* 4: "Have one Eucharist; for there is one flesh of our Lord Jesus Christ and one cup for the union of His blood; one altar, as also one Bishop together with the Presbyterium and the deacons." On the significance of *hama* ("together with") here, see G. Konidaris, *On the Supposed Difference*, p. 52. The interpretation of the sources as a whole, on which Prof. Konidaris rightly insists, requires looking at 1 Clement along with Ignatius so as to find out what each of these sources contributes. Thus the passages: 1 Clem. 42.5; 44; 54; 55, and from Ignatius *Philad.* 7.1, 4.1; *Magn.* 7.1-2; 6.2; 7.2; *Eph.* 3.2, 4.1; *Tral* 7.2 etc. coincide in recognizing the basic position of the Presbyters in the Eucharist in which they too, like the Bishop, "were seated" (*kathistanto,* the term is indicative of this position that they occupied). This makes it natural that with the appearance of parishes they should have been assigned a eucharistic function, as we shall see below.

[40] *Apostolic Tradition* 4.2 (Botte in *Liturgiewissen. Quellen*, p. 10): "*Illi (= to the Bishop) vero offerant diacones oblationes, quique imponens manus in eam cum omni praesbyterio dicat gratia[n]s agens: D(omi)n(u)s vobiscum.*"

[41] Between the Roman Catholic B. Botte (*Hippolyte, Tradition Apostolique*, p. 30), upholding the view that we have here a "true concelebration" implying the offering of the Eucharist by the Presbyters, and the Orthodox N. Afanassieff (*Trapeza Godpodnja*, 1952, p. 3), who maintains that the Presbyters here are not concelebrating

and joining in the offering of the Eucharist, but simply showing their assent to the offering performed by the Bishop.

[42] *Apostolic Tradition* 9 (Botte in *Sources Chrétiennes*, p. 40): "*Praesbyter enim solius habet potestatem ut accipiat, dare autem non habet potestatem. Quapropter clerum non ordinat; super praesbyteri vero ordinatione consignat* (= *sphragizei*, Coptic ed.) *episcopo ordinante.*"

[43] See above, n. 35.

[44] It should not be forgotten, besides, that the whole Church offered herself as the body of Christ through the Bishop; hence the prayer of the anaphora was said by the Bishop, but always in the first person plural. Just as this in no way removed the particular and exclusive character of the episcopal ministry, the same applies to the participation of the Presbyters noted above.

[45] The prayer for the ordination of a Presbyter in the *Apostolic Tradition* 8 (Botte, *Sources Chrétiennes*, p. 56-8) goes as follows: "*Deus et pater domini nostri Jesu Christi respice super servum tuum istum et inpartire spiritum gratiae et consilii praesbyteris ut adiubet et gubernet plebam tuam in corde mundo sicuti respexisti super populum electionis tuae et praecepisti Moisi ut elegeret praesbyteros quos replesti de spiritu tuo quod tu donasti famulo tuo. Et nunc, domine, praesta indeficienter conservari in nobis spiritum gratiae tuae et dignos effice ut credentes tibi ministremus in simplicitate cordis laudantes te per puerum tuum Christum Jesum per quem tibi gloria et virtus patri et filio cum Spiritu sancto in sancta ecclesia et nunc et in saecula saeculorum. Amen.*"

["O God and Father of our Lord Jesus Christ, look down upon this Thy servant and impart the spirit of grace and counsel of the presbyterate, that he may succour and govern Thy people with a pure heart, as Thou didst look upon Thy chosen people and didst command Moses to choose presbyters whom Thou didst fill with Thy Spirit which Thou gavest to Thy servant. Now also, O Lord, grant that the spirit of grace may be preserved in us continuously, and make us worthy that in faith we may minister to Thee in simplicity of heart, praising Thee through Thy Child (or "servant") Jesus Christ, through whom to Thee be glory and power, to the Father and the Son with the Holy Spirit in the holy Church, now and ever and unto ages of ages. Amen."]

[46] "Being filled with the word of teaching in meekness to educate Thy people" (in the Coptic edition). The Latin, which is the basic text, omits this phrase. This should however be attributed not to its absence from the original text but to its loss later, as G. Dix has established through comparative study of the manuscripts (*The Treatise on the Apostolic Tradition*, p. 13).

[47] Ignatius, *Magn.* 6.1 and *Tral.* 3.1.

[48] Syriac *Didascalia* 9 (Connolly, p. 80f.). Cf. P. Trembelas, "Contributions," p. 87f.

[49] *Shepherd of Hermas*, Vision iii.4: "apostles and bishops and teachers and deacons."

[50] This is supported by careful examination of the entire passage. After "apostles and bishops and teachers and deacons," we read "those who have exercised the office of bishop (*episcopesantes*) and taught and served as deacons (*diakonesantes*)." This implies that the writer had in mind the actual ranks of the three ministers, including the Presbyter. Similar conclusions clearly follow from a careful reading of the passages Simil. ix.25, 2; ix.26, 2, and ix.27, 2, where the functions of the three ranks are indicated as follows:

Simil. ix.25, 2 = "apostles and teachers, those who have preached and taught"

" ix.26, 2 = "deacons... those who have served as deacon"

" ix.27, 2 = "bishops, who have sheltered deprived peoples... ministers to the Lord."

[51] *De Praescr.* 3: "*Quid ergo? si episcopus, si diaconus, si vidua, si doctor, si etiam martyr lapsus a regula fuerit, ideo haereses veritatem videbuntur obtinere?*" ["What then? If a bishop, or a deacon, or a widow, or a teacher (*doctor*) or even a martyr should depart from the rule (of faith), will heresies therefore appear to have acquired truth?"]

[52] *Hom. on Ezek.* 2.2 (PG 13:682C).

[53] *Epist.* 29 (Hartel, p. 548): "*cum presbyteris doctoribus lectores diligenter probaremus, Optatum inter lectores doctorum audientium constituimus...*" ["We carefully tested readers with the teacher-presbyters, and appointed Optatus among the readers of the teachers of the hearers."]

[54] Eusebius, *Eccl. Hist.* VI.6 and 8, 4-6. Cf. also VI.19.12-14.

[55] See Ch. Papadopoulos, *History of the Church of Alexandria* (in Greek), p. 494.

[56] *Apostolic Tradition* 39 (Botte, in *Liturgiewiss. Quellen*, p. 86): "*Diaconi autem et presbyteri congregentur quotidie in locum quem episcopus praecipiet eis. Et diaconi quidem ne negligant congregari in tempore omni, nisi infirmitas impediat eos. Cum congregati sunt omnes, doceant illos qui sunt in ecclesia, et hoc modo cum oraverint, unusquisque eat ad opera quae competunt ei.*" ["But let the deacons and the presbyters congregate daily in the place where the bishop has instructed them to meet. And let the deacons not neglect to come together at all times unless prevented by infirmity. When everyone has con-

gregated, let them instruct those who are in the church, and when they have prayed in this way, let each go about his own business."]

⁵⁷ This is shown clearly in the passage quoted above. The non-eucharistic assembly under the leadership of the Presbyters continues even up to the fifth century as an "ancient custom," as the church historian Socrates attests (*Eccl. Hist.* V.22, PG 67:636): "Again in Alexandria, on the fourth day (Wednesday) and the day called the preparation Scriptures are read, and the teachers interpret them, and everything proper to the synaxis takes place apart from the celebration of the mysteries. This is an ancient custom in Alexandria. For it appears that Origen did most of his teaching in the church on these days."

⁵⁸ See D. Balanos, *Patrologia*, 1930, p. 46. Cf. J. Quasten, *Patrology*, I, p. 74.

⁵⁹ Thus in the longer form of the Epistle to the Philadelphians, and specifically in Ch. 4 which concerns the one Eucharist which is under the Bishop, there is added *inter alia*: "Let the rulers be obedient to Caesar; the soldiers, to the rulers; the deacons, to the presbyters, the high priests. The presbyters, the deacons and the rest of the clergy, with all the people and the soldiers and the rulers and Caesar, to the bishop." (VEPAD II, 308; W. Cureton, *Corpus Ignatianum*, London, 1849, pp. 93-5). Also notable is the alteration in Ch. 9 of the same Epistle. In the original, genuine text, we read: "The priests too are good, but the high priest is better," which is a reference to the Jewish priesthood. The author of the spurious version transfers this to the three degrees of priesthood with the purpose of identifying "priests" (*hiereis*) with the presbyters: "The priests and deacons are good, but the high priest is better..." (VEPAD II, 311; Cureton p. 99).

⁶⁰ See above, p. 201.

⁶¹ See e.g. the works of so-called Ambrosiaster, *Liber Questionum Veteris et Novi Testamenti* 101, 5 (Souter, p. 196), and *Comm. in I Tim.* 3.10 (PL 17:496), where the term *sacerdos* is already used for the Presbyters. Cf. T.G. Jalland, "The Doctrine of the Parity of Ministers," in Kirk (ed.), *Apostolic Ministry*, p. 320f., and below.

⁶² See J. Quasten, *Patrology* II, p. 183f. and D. Moraitis, *History of Christian Worship* (in Greek), p. 127.

⁶³ *Apostolic Constitutions* VIII.16.3-5 (ed. Funk, I, 522): "... do Thou Thyself now look upon this Thy servant who is put into the Presbyterium by the vote and determination of the whole clergy, and fill him with the spirit of grace and counsel to succour and govern Thy people in purity of heart... and... that being filled with

works of healing and the word of teaching, he may instruct the people in meekness and... perform the spotless sacred rites on behalf of Thy people..." Likewise in the *Epitome*, 6 (Funk, p. 79f.)

The "sacred rites" may of course refer not to the Eucharist but to other ministries. (Already in the Catholic Epistle of James 5:14, the "Presbyters" perform the anointing of the sick.) The function of offering, which belongs to the Bishop, is not clearly ascribed to the Presbyter by this text, while that of "blessing" is: "the Bishop blesses, he does not receive the blessing; he lays on hands, ordains, offers... The Presbyter blesses, he does not receive the blessing, he receives blessings from a Bishop and a fellow-Presbyter, and likewise gives it to a fellow-Presbyter; he lays on hands, he does not ordain, he does not deprive, but he does separate those who are under him if they are liable to such punishment." (*Apostolic Constitutions* VIII.28, 2-3. Funk I, p. 530.) What is the difference between "blessing" and "offering"? If the first does not refer to the Eucharist, then the Presbyter does not yet offer this. This is rendered doubtful, however, by the comparison of the Presbyter with the deacon a little further on: "for it is not lawful for the deacon to offer the sacrifice or to baptize or to perform either the little or the great blessing, nor may a Presbyter perform ordinations" (Ibid. 46.11). Why does it not say here that the Presbyter does not offer, but locates the difference in ordaining? Clearly, we have a situation which is not yet fully developed, in which it is a fact that the Presbyter has become the "offerer" of the Eucharist, but this reality has not yet become fully established in theory. The interest of this from an historical point of view scarcely needs to be stressed.

[64] *Apostolic Constitutions* VIII.8.1 (Funk, I, 466): "*oi te episkopoi kai oi presbyteroi heireis.*" Cf. also VIII.46.10: "we distributed to the Bishops the functions of the highpriesthood, and to the Presbyters those of the priesthood..."

[65] H. Achelis, *Die ältesten Quellen des orientalischen Kirchenrechts. Die Canones Hippolyti* (Texte und Untersuchungen 6, 4), 1891, p. 42f.

[66] See the text in P. Trembelas, *Mikron Evchologion*, p. 250.

[67] See text, Ibid., p. 248.

[68] J. Quasten, *Patrology*, II, p. 185.

[69] Ibid., p. 151.

[70] Thus in *Apostolic Constitutions* III.20.2, the work of the Presbyter is presented as different from that described in the *Didascalia* through the addition of "offering up" (= the sacrifice): "neither the Presbyter nor the deacon is to ordain clergy from among the laity,

but it is only for the Presbyter to teach, offer up, baptize and bless the people, and for the deacon to assist the Bishop and the Presbyters..." Cf. also II.27.3: "for they (the Bishops) are your high priests; your priests are the Presbyters, and your levites are those who are now deacons." The same can be observed in the Ethiopian *Didascalia*, where it is laid down that: "Presbyters and deacons do not ordain; the Presbyter teaches, baptizes, blesses the people, censes and offers up the sacrifice" (Ethiopian *Didascalia* 17 – tr. J.M. Harden, *The Ethiopic Didascalia Translated*, 1920, p. 98).

[71] *Epist.* CXLVI, 1 (PL 22:1194): *"Quid enim facit excerpta ordinatione Epicopus, quod Presbyter non facit?"*

[72] *On 1 Tim.* 11 (PG 62:553).

[73] Cf. above, n. 61.

[74] Canon 18 of the First Ecumenical Council already calls the Presbyters "offerers." Cf. also Canon 1 of Ancyra and Canons 9 and 13 of Neocaesarea (ed. H. Alivizatos, pp. 32, 167f., 157). Curiously, the Council of Arles (Canons 15/16) also calls the deacons "offerers": *"De diaconibus quos cognovimus multis locis offerre. Placuit minime fieri debere."* ["Of deacons, whom we know to be offering in many places. It has been resolved that this should not happen."]

[75] We see this in the case of Aerius, of whom Epiphanius tells us (*Adv. Haer.* 75.3.3, PG 42:505BC) that he "abandoned the poorhouse and led astray a large following of men and women... his speech was raving more than the human condition; and he said, 'What is a Bishop compared with a Presbyter? The one is in no way different from the other. For there is one order and one honor, and one rank. The Bishop lays on hands, but so does the Presbyter. The Bishop gives the ablution, and the Presbyter likewise. The Bishop performs the dispensation of worship, and the Presbyter likewise. The Bishop sits upon the throne, and the Presbyter also sits.' In this way he deceived many, and they held him as their leader." For similar examples from Alexandria at the same period, see Dix, *The Treatise on the Apostolic Tradition*, p. lxxx.

[76] The attached table makes this gap clear and indisputable.

[77] *Smyrn.* 8.1.

[78] Cf. P. Trembelas, *Dogmatics*, III, p. 166f. for supporting arguments.

[79] Ignatius, *Eph.* 4.1.

[80] See above, p. 202.

[81] See above, p. 202.

[82] See Eusebius, *Eccl. Hist.* VI.44.3-4; Cyprian, *Epist.* 5 and Egeria's *Travels*, Ch. 4 (Pétré, p. 112). Cf. also below.

[83] See above, p. 203f.

[84] See above, p. 204.

[85] *Ibid.*

[86] See above, p. 222f.

[87] See above, n. 57.

[88] "The Roman Church at the end of the Second Century," in *The Harvard Theological Review* (1925), 201-77.

[89] See e.g. G. Dix, *A Detection of Aumbries*, 1942, p. 17f. and J. Colson, *Les Fonctions*, p. 70.

[90] See above, p. 93.

[91] Irenaeus' letter to Victor (Eusebius, *Eccl. Hist.* V.24.15): "But the presbyters before you who did not observe it themselves sent the Eucharist to those from the *paroikies* who did observe it."

[92] The phrase "to those from the *paroikies*" cannot mean "parishes" because the term *paroikia* in Eusebius, as we have seen, has the sense of the diocese, i.e. the complete episcopal community. See above, p. 118.

[93] G. La Piana, Ibid. p. 218.

[94] Justin, *1 Apol.* 67.5: "there is a distribution to each and participation in the things for which thanks has been given, and it is sent to those who are not present by the deacons."

[95] As Nautin thinks, not without reason (*Lettres et Écrivains*, p. 81). In this case *epempon* ("sent") should be interpreted as *parepempon*(?) ("let pass"), according to Nautin.

[96] As Prof. D. Moraitis thinks, *History of Christian Worship* (in Greek), p. 189f.

[97] *Apostolic Tradition* 24.1 (ed. Dix, p. 43): "si potest."

[98] *Les Fonctions*, p. 330.

[99] *Apostolic Tradition* 24. 2 (ed. Dix, p. 44).

[100] On the basis of the information in Eusebius (*Eccl. Hist.* VI.43), Harnack (*Mission...*, II⁴, pp. 836f. and 851f.) puts the number of members of the Church of Rome around the middle of the third century at about 30,000. Certainly not all of them took part in the eucharistic assemblies every time.

[101] See examples in H. Elfers, *op. cit.* pp. 50-54 and R. H. Connolly, "The Eucharistic Prayer of Hippolytus," in *Journal of Theological Studies* 39 (1938), 350-369.

[102] M.H. Baynes, "The Great Persecution," in *Cambridge Ancient History* XII, p. 656f.

[103] Cf. Eusebius, *Eccl. Hist.* VI.28.1. This must have taken place no earlier than the year 235. For the relevant dates see M. Besnier, *L'Empire Romain de l'Avènement des Sévères au Concile de Nicée*, 1927, p. 107.

[104] See the characteristic description of this state of affairs in the fourth century *Catalogus Liberianus*, as restored by Duchesne, *Liber Pontificalis*, I, 1886, p. 7.

[105] *Epist.* 5 (4). 1: "*Quoniam mihi interesse nunc non permittit loci condicio, peto vos pro fide et religione vestra, fungamini illic et vestris partibus et meis, ut nihil vel ad disciplinam vel ad diligentiam desit.*" ["Since the condition of the place does not permit me to be with you now, I beg you for the sake of your faith and religion to perform there both your own duties and mine, that nothing may be lacking as to either discipline or diligence."] Cf. *Epist.* 14 (5). 2.

[106] *Epist.* 16 (9). 2: "*offertur nomine eorum (lapsorum) et... eucharistia illis datur, cum scriptum sit: Qui ederit panem aut biberit calicem Domini indigne, reus erit corporis et sanguinis Domini.*" ["The offering is made in their name (of the lapsed) and... the Eucharist is given them, although it is written: He who eats the bread and drinks the cup of the Lord unworthily, is guilty of the body and blood of the Lord."] Cf. *Epist.* 15 (10). 1 and 17 (11). 2.

[107] *Epist.* 8(1).

[108] *Letter Against Germ.* 6 (PG 10:1324): "But I also gathered together those in the city more zealously, as if I were with them; absent in body, as I have said, but present in spirit." The same Father likewise relates (see Eusebius, *Eccl. Hist.* VI.44.2) that during his long absence from Alexandria on account of the persecution a certain Presbyter sent the Eucharist with a child to an old man on his deathbed who had lapsed and repented. This incident does not refer clearly to the offering of the Eucharist by the Presbyter in the assembly, but more likely to sending a piece of the Eucharist from what was kept at home for private communion in accordance with ancient custom (see Tertullian, *De Orat.* 19 and *Ad uxor.* 11.5, PL 1:1183 and 2:1296). Nevertheless, it is yet another indication of the situation created by the long absence of the Bishop.

[109] *Epist.* 34(27). 1: "*Integre et cum disciplina fecistis, fratres carissimi, quod ex consilio collegarum meorum qui praesentes aderant, Gaio Didensi presbytero et diacono eius censuistis non communicandum, qui communicando cum lapsis et offerendo oblationes eorum in pravis erroribus suis frequenter deprehensi...*" ["You acted rightly and with discipline, dearest brothers, in that on the advice of my colleagues who were present, you decided not to communicate with Gaius of Didda and his deacon, who, by communicating with the lapsed and offering their oblations, have frequently been taken in their wicked erors..."]

[110] The deacons had from the beginning been attached to the

Bishop and not to the presbyters because their principal task was to serve in the offering of the Divine Eucharist as we have seen already (see above, p. 83, n. 51).

[111] It cannot be later because Cyril of Jerusalem know and uses it (*Cathech.* 6.20f.).

[112] This work is attributed to a certain Hegemonius, about whom we know nothing, and is preserved only in Latin. It was published first by L.A. Zacagni in 1698 and later by Migne (PG 10:1405-1528), M.J. Routh, *Reliquae Sacrae*, 1848, and in a critical edition by C.H. Beeson, *Hegemonius, Acta Achelai* (Die griechischen christlichen Schriftsteller, 16), 1906.

[113] PG 10:1492A: "In the course of his flight, Manes came to a certain village at a distance from the city which was called Diodorus. And there was a presbyter of that place who was himself called Diodorus (*erat autem presbyter loci illius nomine et ipse Diodorus*), a quiet and mild man, a man of faith and of very good repute..."

[114] According to Jerome, *De viris illust.* 72. J. Quasten (*Patrology* III, 358) takes the Greek to be the original.

[115] Eusebius, *Eccl. Hist.* VII.24.6. Firmilian of Caesarea in Cappadocia, similarly, refers in a letter to Cyprian to "rural Presbyters" ("*unum de Presbyteris rusticum*") in Cappadocia around the year 235. See Cyprian, *Epist.* 75, 10, 4.

[116] See above.

[117] *Smyrn. 8.1.* Cf. above, p. 208.

[118] *Epist.* 18 (12).1. Cf. *Epist.* 19 (13).2 and 20 (14).3.

[119] *Epist.* 15, 16 and 17 (Migne 10, 9 and 11).

[120] *Epist.* 33 (27).1. Cf. above, p. 139f.

[121] *Epist.* 38 (33).1.

[122] *Epist.* 14 (5).4.

[123] *Epist.* 15, 16 and 17 (Migne 10, 9 and 11). Cyprian reprimands with the utmost severity those presbyters and deacons who did not follow his instructions as to the reinstatement of the lapsed who had repented. Cf. also his view on Presbyters above, p. 174 n. 166.

[124] See above, p. 214.

[125] *Letter to Fabius of Antioch,* 11 (PG 10:1309). If the celebration and distribution of the Eucharist by presbyters had been regarded as a usual practice, taken for granted as being within their competence, it would not be so pointedly stressed by Dionysius that this took place on his instruction. Likewise, in Eusebius, *Eccl. Hist.* VI.44.3-5. The active participation of the Presbyters in the celebra-

tion of the Eucharist (see above, p. 219f.) does not seem to have made them literally "concelebrants" as shown by the fact that the term "concelebrant" was used around the middle of the third century to indicate rather the Bishops; thus for example by Dionysius of Alexandria to Basileides (PG 10:1272. That Basileides was a Bishop, see Eusebius, *Eccl. Hist.* VII.26.3). Similarly in the letter concerning Paul of Samosata (in Eusebius, *Eccl. Hist.* VII.30.2), the term "concelebrants" probably refers to the Bishops. The phrase "To Dionysius and Maximus and all those throughout the world who are our concelebrant Bishops and Presbyters and deacons and to all the Catholic Church under heaven" (*"Dionysio kai Maximo kai tois kata ten oikoumenen pasin sylleitourgois hemon episkopois kai presbyterois kai diakonois kai pase te hypo ten ouranon katholike ekklesia"*) admits of the following interpretations: i) "concelebrants" (*"sylleitourgois"*) is attached to the preceding names, Dionysius and Maximus, and to the term "Bishops" which follows, so as to indicate the Bishops who are of the same rank as those sending the letter; ii) "concelebrants" refers to all that follows, i.e. Bishops, presbyters and deacons, in which case the deacons too would be characterized as "concelebrants," which is unlikely at that period (see *Apostolic Tradition* 9.2. Cf. P. Trembelas, "Contributions," p. 46). The first possibility, therefore, seems more probable. The whole problem of the "concelebration" of Presbyters appears very difficult. On the basis of what has been written above (p. 220f.) in connection with the *Apostolic Tradition*, it becomes essential to make a distinction between two senses in which the "concelebration" of the Presbyters may be understood: on the one hand their assent and "seal" upon what the Bishop has done, and on the other a "concelebration" identical with the Bishop's action of offering. J. Hanssens (*"De concelebratione eucharistica,"* in *Periodica* 17 (1927), 143-21, (1932), 219), finds support for this distinction in the sources, distinguishing between *concelebratio caeremonialis* and *concelebratio sacramentalis*. While the latter may perhaps have been known earlier in the West, according to Hanssens it was never recognized in the East. This view of Hanssens' on the basis of the sources is reagrded as having great weight. Thus E. Herman in *D.D.C*, V, 505, after studying the literature on the subject, remarks that "the minute criticism of the sources undertaken by Fr Hanssens tends to prove that the East never knew of sacramental concelebration, either at ordinations or outside ordinations (that is to say, in the Eucharistic sacrifice) before the eighteenth century."

[126] See passages above, n. 108.

[127] Cf H. Fries, *op. cit.* p. 175.

[128] On the origin and history of the *Fermentum*, see J.A. Jungmann, "Fermentum," in *Colligere Fragmenta (Festschrift Alban Dold)*, 1952, pp. 185-190. On the etymology of the term in connection with Mt. 13:33, see P. Batiffol, *Leçons sur la Messe*, 1920[7], p. 34.

[129] The *decretum* in the *Liber Pontificalis* attributed to Pope Siricius in the fourth century instructs the presbyters to renew each week the *Fermentum* they received from their Bishop (ed. Duchesne, I, pp. 216 and 168). Shortly afterwards, at the beginning of the fifth century, Innocent I (*Ep. 25 ad Decentium*; PL 20:556) clearly informs us that every Sunday, the Pope sends the Presbyters of the parishes portions of the Eucharist consecrated by him at the episcopal Liturgy so that the Presbyters could mix them into the Chalice of the Eucharist celebrated by them.

[130] *A Detection of Aumbries*, pp. 16-20.

[131] See G. Dix, *The Shape of the Liturgy*, p. 105: the acolytes came into being as assistants to the deacons specifically in their task of conveying the Eucharist "to those who were not present," according to the testimony of Justin (*I Apol. 67.* Cf. also above). Hence the acolytes' *sacculum*, the linen bag in which they conveyed the *fermentum* to the parishes. See the details of their ordination in P. Jounel, "Les Ordinations," in *L'Église en Prière. Introduction à la Liturgie*, ed. A.G. Martimort, 1961, p. 502.

[132] G. Dix, *The Shape of the Liturgy*, p. 134. According to Dix, a possible vestige of the *fermentum* in the East was the practice found there, from the fourth century onwards, of placing a part of the holy bread in the Chalice after its fraction by the priest and before communion. Apart from the symbolic meaning usually given to this action, it remains otherwise inexplicable given that the priest partakes separately of the Body from the Paten and the Blood from the Chalice. Hence Dix's hypothesis, although not proved, appears highly probable.

[133] Ibid., pp. 21 and 134.

[134] Thus according to the most ancient *ordo* of the papal Liturgy, attributed to Pope Zachariah (eighth century), the pope sets down a portion of the Eucharist on the Altar without mixing it in the Chalice obviously so that it should remain there for use at subsequent Liturgies. This curious rubric is today explained as a survival of the *fermentum* by distinguished specialists such as P.L. Haberstroh, *Der Ritus der Brechung nach dem Missale Romanum*, 1937, p. 41 and B. Capelle, *Travaux liturgiques*, II, 1962, pp. 302-306. It is noteworthy that the most ancient version of the *ordo primus*, found

in a ninth-century manuscript (see M. Andrieu, *Ordines Romani*, II, pp. 101 and 59-60), connects this action with the necessity for the altar not to cease to have the Eucharist: *"Ita observant ut dum missarum solemnia peraguntur, altare sine sacrificio non sit."* ["They take care that while the rites of the mass are being performed, the altar should not be without the sacrament."] This version of the original *ordo* already betrays a certain modification given that it does not require the celebrant to mix the portion of the papal Eucharist with his own. This mixing was explicitly required in earlier orders, such as that attributed to St Amand (eighth century), which directs that, in the case where the Pope is not celebrating, the celebrant before Holy Communion and the "filling of the Cup" *"deportatur a subdiacono oblationario particula fermenti quod ab Apostolico consecratum est... mittit in calicem"* ["the oblationary subdeacon brings him particles of the *fermentum* which was consecrated by the Apostle (= the Pope) and he puts it into the Chalice."] (see text in PL 78:948C). According to the same *ordo*, on Holy Saturday every year, the ancient *fermentum* was observed just as in earlier times: *"Et transmittit unusquisque presbyter mansionarium de titulo suo ad ecclesiam Salvatoris, et expectant ibi usque dum frangitur sancta, habentes secum corporales. Et venit oblationarius subdiaconus et dat eis de sancta quod pontifex consecravit, et recipiunt ea in corporales, et revertitur unusquisque ad titulum suum et tradit sancta presbytero. Et de ipsa facit crucem super calicem et ponit in eo et dicit Dominus vobiscum. Et communicant omnes, sicut superius."*

["And each presbyter sends a doorkeeper from his parish to the church of the Saviour and they wait there until the fraction of the Holy Things, having corporals with them. And the oblationary subdeacon comes and gives them some of the Holy Things consecrated by the pontiff, and they receive it in their corporals, and each one goes back to his parish and gives the Holy Things to the presbyter. And he makes the sign of the Cross with it over the Chalice and puts it in the Chalice and says: 'The Lord be with you.' And all receive communion, as above."]

(See text in L. Duchesne, *Origines du Culte Chrétien*, 1889, p. 454).

[135] Thus we have for example Liturgies of Hippolytus as Bishop of Rome, James as Bishop of Jerusalem, Gregory of Nazianzus, Basil the Great, Cyril of Alexandria, John Chrysostom *et al.*

[136] One might reasonably ask, for example, why major church figures such as Clement, Origen *et al.*, who were presbyters, remained known in history as teachers but not as authors of Liturgies. This could perhaps be a chance occurrence if it did not hold good

for all the well-known Presbyters in early history.

[137] Chrysostom (*On the Obscurity of the Prophets* 2.5, PG 56:182) tells us that "all together we hear the deacon commanding this and saying, Let us pray for the Bishop, and for the aged, and for succor, and that he may rightly divide the word of truth... Those who are initiated know what is said. For this has never been permitted in the prayer of the catechumens." Besides, it is known that the names of the Bishops were written in the Diptychs, from which they were erased, as happened with Chrysostom, in case of deposition (cf. Cyril of Alexandria, *Letter to Atticus*, PG 77:352), and were read after the exclamation "Especially for our Most Holy Lady..." (The above information, as also seen in note 17, comes from the suggestions of Professor P. Trembelas, to whom the author is most grateful for this and for all his valuable assistance.) This ancient practice is also attested by the 13th Canon of the Protodeutero Council (861), when it punishes by deposition any presbyter or deacon who, while a charge is pending against his Bishop and before the synodical sentence, "dares to depart from his (= the Bishop's) communion, and does not mention his name in the sacred prayers of the liturgies according to what has been handed down to the Church..." (Alivizatos, *Sacred Canons*, p. 315).

[138] Hence some consider the antimension superfluous when there is a consecrated church. See e.g. K. Kallinikos, *The Church Building and the Rites Performed in it* (in Greek), 1921, p. 215f..

[139] *On the Church Hierarchy* 5.5 (PG 3:305).

[140] This view is at variance with the fact that antimensia made of stone or wood appear very early, and in Rome (see note 17 above) they occur clearly in connection with the presbyters' Eucharist. Cf. J. Jungmann, *Missarum Solemnia*, II, 1952, p. 244. These may indeed go back to the third century. See Leclercq in *D.A.C.L.*, art. "Autel."

[141] "We determine that clergy who celebrate the Liturgy or baptize in chapels which are in houses should do so with the consent of the local Bishop..." (Alivizatos, p. 89).

[142] PG 137:613-616.

[143] Ibid., 912.

[144] Synodal Replies of the Archbishops of Constantinople, in PG 119:812. On the connection of the antimension with the presbyter's Eucharist in the West too, cf. notes 17 and 22 above.

[145] The use of this term or its synonym *ecclesia senior* for the cathedral, the Bishop's seat where "the whole Church" would gather for the celebration of the Eucharist, in contrast to the sepa-

rate parish assemblies, is noteworthy because it is interchanged with the term *ecclesia catholica* in many cases, e.g in the ancient Georgian Lectionary (see text in M. Tarchnishvilli, *Le Grand Lectionnaire de l'Église de Jérusalem*, I, 1959). This comes as a remarkable confirmation of the theses set out here, especially in Part II Chapter 2, in connection with the term "Catholic Church." The close relation between the one Eucharist under the Bishop and the consciousness concerning a "Catholic Church" is attested in a very characteristic way by such a use of the term in the liturgical language of the fourth century. Perhaps, it was the use of the term "Catholic Church" to mean the cathedral, the episcopal seat in which "the whole Church" came together, that gave rise to the use of the term "*catholikon*" for the central church in a monastery. This is likewise of interest from the point of view of the history of the term "Catholic Church."

[146] According to Egeria's *Travels*, the Bishop took part in all the services and indeed the liturgies, whereas each of the churches in Jerusalem was used for the Eucharist only on certain days in the year, when the Bishop would celebrate there, so that in reality only the Eucharist under the Bishop was celebrated. On each of these churches in detail, see the edition of the *Travels* by H. Pétré, pp. 57-64f.

[147] Characteristically, it is unheard of in the early Church for individual liturgies to be performed privately by the priests, a practice introduced in the West during the Middle Ages as a manifest and historically noteworthy abandonment of the ecclesiological character of the Eucharist (see above, p. 23f.).

[148] In the early Church, only Rome allowed the Pope, exceptionally, to celebrate three liturgies at Christmas, Easter and Pentecost. See P. Trembelas, "One Celebrant and Several Liturgies on the Same Day" (in Greek), in *Orthodoxos Parousia* (1964), 269-75. It is, however, noteworthy that this was not permitted to take place at the same altar (Ibid.). Anyway, we find no similar exception to the rule in the East. Hence, Professor P. Trembelas suggests (Ibid., p. 271f.) that as a solution to modern problems, when a priest is obliged to celebrate more than one liturgy on the same day the Liturgy of the Presanctified can be celebrated. This is in accord with the whole spirit of the conclusions of this work given that the Liturgy of the Presanctified has never had the character of the main eucharistic unity being intended for the receiving of Holy Communion without a festive assembly. In this way, the ecclesiological character of the main Liturgy is preserved.

[149] Hefele-Leclercq, *Histoire des Conciles*, III, 1909, p. 216. Cf. J. Goar, *Euchologion sive Rituale Graecorum*, 1647, p. 16 (ed. 1960, p. 13).

[150] i.e. that of the Bishop. See Eusebius, *Eccl. Hist.* X.4.68.

[151] Characteristic is the comparison Eusebius makes between the Bishop and the presbyters when he writes that in the Bishop "Christ dwells in His fullness," while "those of second rank (= Presbyters) after him (= the Bishop) are given apportionments of the power of Christ and of the Holy Spirit according to the capacity of each" (*Eccl. Hist.* X.4.67). The distinction between whole ("fullness") and part should be noted.

GENERAL CONCLUSIONS

Keeping clear of the antithetical schemes in which modern church historiography has imprisoned the unity of the early Church, and starting from the central place occupied by the Eucharist in the life of the Church, we have looked in the sources from the first three Christian centuries for an answer to the fundamental question: what was the unity of the Church in the Divine Eucharist and the Bishop who led it, and how did this unity influence the formation of the early Catholic Church? We have summarized the basic conclusions of our research at the end of each part of this study. We shall now attempt to place them within the more general context of historical theology.

The maintenance and formation of the Church's unity in the Divine Eucharist and the Bishop had its preconditions and its developments as we have seen. It could not have been otherwise since the Church lives and moves in space and time as an historical reality. There was, however, perhaps no other historical fact so inseparably united with the unchangeable nature of the Church as was her unity in the Eucharist and in the Bishop. Hence no other fact had such a permanent and decisive effect on the Church's life in history, or gave her such fundamental and stable forms as did this unity.

Linked with the unity of the Church to the point of identity, as we have seen from the earliest historical documents, the Divine Eucharist was not slow to form the foundation on which the Catholic Church of the first three centuries was built and took shape. Through the complete identification of the eucharistic assembly with the "Church of God" which "is" or "sojourns" in a certain place, the basic principle was

247

laid down for the formation of early catholicism: inasmuch as the eucharistic assembly incarnates and reveals in history not a part of the one Christ but the one Lord Himself in His entirety, who takes up the "many" in Himself in perpetuity in order to make them One and bring them back through His sacrifice before the throne of the Father, what we have in the Eucharist is not a part of the Church, but the whole Church herself, the whole body of Christ. Thus, the ecclesiological fullness and "catholicity" of the Church sojourning in each place formed the first and the basic consequence of the unity of the Church in the Divine Eucharist. "Each single Church, gathered around the Bishop and culminating in his person, is not simply a part of the whole within the one, holy, catholic and apostolic Church; but inasmuch as she communes in the whole in the unity of the Holy Spirit, she is herself one, holy, catholic and apostolic Church, i.e. the "fullness" and the "body of Christ."[1]

As a direct historical consequence of this fact, the Eucharist was regarded as an act of the *whole* Church and not simply of certain of her orders or members. There was no such thing as an individual Eucharist in the service of private devotion or connected with only some of the members of the Church during the period we are looking at. Thus our research has shown the preservation of *one* eucharistic assembly only in each Church to be an indisputable historical reality of that period. There was more than one assembly, or more than one altar, only when a schism had arisen in which case the situation was no longer normal.

A fundamental and direct consequence of this ecclesiological character of the eucharistic assembly was the position and significance of the Bishop in the Church. It is known that the institution of episcopacy was interwoven with the whole formation of early catholicism. But contrary to what recent historiography has asserted, this interweaving was not provoked by external factors; it was bound up with the position of the Bishop in the Eucharist and through this with the nature of the Church regardless of heresies or other external dangers. As our study has shown, a Eucharist without the Bishop – at least once the Apostles were no longer there – was unthinkable. On the other hand, it was also unthinkable to have a Bishop without his place in the Eucharist. Hence, as has been shown, only the Bishop was originally ordained to lead the Eucharist and offer it in the name of the "whole Church" as the "president" of the eucharistic assembly. Only after the fourth century did the Bishop become primarily the "administrator" transferring to the Presbyter the ministry of the Eucharist and slowly and gradually becoming detached from that ministry often indeed to such a degree that he regarded the offering of the Eucharist as a secondary task. But during the historically crucial period of the first three centuries when the foundations of catholicism were laid, the Bishop was first and foremost the "priest," as being the only person who could offer the Eucharist by right of his ordination, while he was assisted in the affairs of church administration by the *synedrion* or council of Presbyters who received a special charism for this through their ordination. Being the leader of the one single eucharistic assembly and offering the Eucharist in its name, the Bishop was seated "in the place of God," and his throne was the living icon on earth of the heavenly throne of God given that the Eucharist on earth was nothing other than a true antitype of the worship of God in heaven. The Bishop offered to God through his hands the body of the Eucharist, in which the Church in that place was united, thus becoming the very body of Christ. All the members and "orders" of the Church consequently passed through him in the highest expression of their relationship with God in the Eucharist. The salvation of the members of the Church consequently passed through his hands. Now we see why anyone who does not go through the Bishop in his relationship to God is "worshipping the devil" (Ignatius). Hence, also the axiom formulated by Cyprian, that the Church is in the Bishop and that "where the Bishop is, there is the Church."[2] This axiom, which had such a decisive effect on the formation of the early Catholic

Church, was not the result of some legalistic view of the Church as Protestant historians have maintained. It was not the product of Rome with its legalistic spirit, in such a way that the "catholicization" of the Church and her "romanization" are to be identified historically, as both Roman Catholic and Protestant historians in recent times have accepted with one accord. This axiom was a direct and natural consequence of the mystical view of the Church as the body of Christ manifested historically in the Eucharist, and of the position of the Bishop in the eucharistic assembly. Since the Church was the body of Christ and because the eucharistic synaxis was this body, for this reason the head of this assembly automatically became the visible head of the Church in that place. In consequence, the Bishop's position in the Eucharist alone is the primary, complete and ecclesiological justification for the authority which the Canons ascribe to him.

But just as in each Church there was but one Eucharist "which was under the leadership of the Bishop," so there could not be but "one Bishop" in each Church. The ruling of the First Ecumenical Council in its 18th Canon, where it decrees "that there shall not be two Bishops in the same city," has both its historical and its ecclesiological roots in the unity in the Eucharist and the Bishop during the first three centuries. More than one Bishop in the same place meant more than one Eucharist, and in consequence more than one Church in that place. This was the basis historically for the principle of geographical boundaries to each Church. If it became unthinkable for a Church to exist without clearly defined geographical boundaries, if the name of each Bishop was attached inseparably and from earliest times to the name of a particular geographical area, this was not simply a matter of good organization but of ecclesiological principle. And if there was ecclesiological content to this canonical arrangement, historically at least we cannot see what this is to be attributed to if not the unbreakable connection of the eucharistic assembly in each place and the Bishop who led it with the very Church of God which was in that place.

It is to precisely the same reasons that the canonical principle of the absolute essential equality of all Bishops should be attributed historically. We do not know whether modern ideals of democracy are able to explain this principle satisfactorily. We do, however, know that such ideals would not be sufficient to explain such a basic canonical principle if the latter were not grounded in ecclesiological presuppositions. These ecclesiological presuppositions consist, as we have seen, in the fact that each of the Bishops, as head of his own eucharistic assembly, was the leader of a complete Church which needed no complement: "While the bond of concord exists and the mystery of the Catholic Church still remains undivided, each Bishop organizes his actions and his administration for himself, as he thinks best, being accountable to the Lord alone."[3] These words of Cyprian's, which undoubtedly expressed the consciousness of the Church in the period we are studying here, provide full clarification of the canonical and ecclesiological underpinning to the absolute equality of Bishops and to their whole position in the Church.

This relation of the Bishop to his Church and to the Lord did of course presuppose another equally basic principle of the early Church's organization: the connection of each of the Bishops with a particular Church. If in the early Church there was no such thing as a Bishop without his own Church, this should not be regarded as a fact devoid of ecclesiological import. For a Bishop who does not form the center of unity of a particular Church or who is dependent on another Bishop would be a defective Bishop. Hence, the prohibition of ordinations *in absoluto* goes back historically to the principle of the fullness of each Church.

Two questions arise, however. The first is this: if each Church and each Bishop was regarded by the early Church not as a *part* of a whole but as the whole itself, does this not mean that we have not one Church in the world, but several?

This question is indeed a serious one, but it is modern man's question. It has been said here repeatedly that only in modern times has the relationship of locality to universality been understood as an opposition. To pose this question in the form of a dilemma of having to choose between the local and the universal Church in the Church of the first three centuries is to betray historical methodology. The relation of the local to the universal Church was not a dilemma for that period. Neither Protestant provincialism nor Roman Catholic universalism is justified by the sources of that period. On the contrary, what seems paradoxical to modern man was for the early Church entirely natural: each Church was the full body of Christ, "the whole Church" as St Paul puts it, while all these full Churches together formed nothing other than *one* Church only in the whole world. This paradox was possible because the way the Church was seen at that period was primarily and principally mystical and sacramental. Because the Church was nothing other than Christ Himself, united in whom the "many" were saved, there could not but be only one Church in the world with Him as her head. But since on the other hand, this one Christ and His one body were not abstract concepts but a tangible reality manifested in place and time in a mystical way, most especially in the mystery of the Eucharist, that body could be sought only where these mystical and sacramental prerequisites were fulfilled. That, for the early Church, was precisely the one Eucharist in each place "which was under the leadership of the Bishop." Thus, because of the mystical and sacramental identity of each Church with one and the same body, the multiplicity of Churches led naturally to the recognition of one sole Church in the world. For this reason, each local Church did not constitute a reality different from "the Catholic Church throughout the world" in such a way as to be regarded as a *part* of her, but was completely identified with her. Thus, as the Church throughout the world was "one, holy, catholic and apostolic," so each Church was in essence and not by way of metaphor "one, holy, catholic and apostolic." Thus, we are not looking at two kinds of Church, the local and the Church throughout the world, but *one* Church, one Christ and His one body, sacramentally manifested in its fullness in that place where the faithful are united in the breaking of the one bread under the leadership of their Bishop. In a view of the Church such as this, the dilemma between universal and local Church clearly has no place.

If the relation of the one Church throughout the world to the episcopal Churches in different places was of this kind – as we have called it here, a relationship of the mystical identity of full circles and not a unity formed by adding together incomplete parts – how was the unity of the one Church throughout the world manifested in practice? It should be stressed at this point that although early Christianity inherited from Judaism the consciousness of being a people scattered to the ends of earth, it rejected any center for the visible expression of its worldwide unity such as for instance the Temple in Jerusalem was for the Jews. Have we given serious thought to why this did not happen in the history of the Church? If it was due to external causes (persecutions etc.), then why, once these causes were removed and the "Christian world" had been brought into being by Constantine, did the Church not think to build a "universal" church in parallel with the Bishops' cathedral churches in various places in which the Eucharist could be celebrated from time to time as an expression of the one body of the Church throughout all the world? If something of the kind had happened, this would have meant destroying the integrity of each Church in which case we should indeed have had a unity of parts. But as there was not in practice one universal Eucharist, so there was not one universal Bishop in the early Church because the two were bound up together. Therefore, on the universal level we do not have a fixed and permanent center for the expression of ecclesial unity in the Divine Eucharist and the Bishop, and it is in this that Roman Catholic ecclesiology since the First Vatican Council has deviated from the early Church. Instead of a permanent center of unity, a foundation was provided by the principle of the mutual recognition of each of the local Churches: the "common union" of the Churches as Eusebius characteristically calls it with reference to the second century. This recognition was essential, and was manifested through the "concession" of the Eucharist to Bishops visiting another Church, and the admission to communion of believers travelling from place to place on the basis of episcopal letters of recommendation. Disruption of this mutual recognition for whatever reason led to schism on the universal level, and occasioned the convocation of synods the purpose of which was to restore "communion." This was how the institution of local councils originally appeared, and these prepared the way historically for the appearance of the Ecumenical Council through which "the Bishops who are at the ends of the earth" affirmed that they "are in the mind of Christ" and that all the Churches under them, identified with each other, had but one head which is Jesus Christ.

The second question arising out of the relationship we have demonstrated between Eucharist, Bishop and Church is this: if the one Eucharist under the Bishop formed the manifestation in space of the whole body of Christ, how then are the many parish Eucharists under the same Bishop to be understood? Do we not have through these a proliferation of Churches within the same Church? As we have seen, this formed the great problem in history of the emergence of parishes. Our research here has established that as long as there still survived in the early Church the consciousness that the unity of the very Church of God was manifested through the one Eucharist under the leadership of the Bishop, the parishes that appeared for reasons of practical need were not regarded as self-contained eucharistic units within the diocese, but were dependent on the one episcopocentric Eucharist as its organic offshoots. Thus, whether through the *fermentum* or through other means, the living presence of the Bishop in the parishes' Eucharist did not cease to be regarded as indispensable. In consequence, the one, episcopocentric Eucharist was not essentially broken up by the appearance of the parishes. What actually happened may be described as a *spatial distribution of the synthronon of the Presbyterium* in order to serve needs. In other words, each of the thrones of the *synthronon*, without becoming a separate center of eucharistic unity – for in no parish did the presbyter ever sit on a eucharistic throne, the *synthronon* characteristically being found exclusively in cathedrals in the early Church – was as it were spatially detached from the one cathedral church while the Bishop's throne remained the only center of the Eucharist in each Church.

With the parishes, then, what appeared was not in essence a proliferation of Eucharists, but a mere extension of the one episcopocentric Eucharist into different parts of the diocese in such a way that the originally unified *synthronon* was not abolished or parcelled out into several self-contained eucharistic centers within one and the same Church. This fundamental fact compels the historian of the early Church to make a comparison which goes to the heart of the unity of the Church: while the spread of Christianity in rural areas and in the world generally gave rise to new complete Churches, the appearance of parishes simply led to the extension of the one Eucharist under the Bishop within the geographical boundaries of the diocese without creating new centers of eucharistic unity. Obviously, it could not have been otherwise, insofar as the consciousness still survived that in the "one Eucharist which is under the leadership of the Bishop" was incarnate the very Church of God sojourning in a particular place.

If we want to present church unity schematically as it took shape on the basis of unity in the Eucharist and in the Bishop, we could compare the episcopal dioceses throughout the world to full circles identified with each other in such a way that their centers (Bishops) meet in one head ("in the mind of Jesus Christ") and the parishes to *radii* within each of these circles. In this way, the "one, holy, catholic and apostolic Church" *does not form a unity of parts added together, but an organic unity* of complete Churches, identified with one another, in such a way as to form one body under one head.

Such was the unity of the Church of the first three centuries in the Divine Eucharist and the Bishop and its effect on the formation of the basic characteristics of the early Catholic Church.

In the wake of these conclusions which have been reached without reference to any of the modern theories about the unity of the Church, we are now able to place in the light of the Church of the first three centuries certain basic theories from among these which are closely bound up both with the subject of this study and with the whole theology of unity in our day.

First of all, if the conclusions of this study of the first three centuries are accepted, then the importance of the theory of *eucharistic ecclesiology* automatically comes to the fore.[4] As the study of the sources here has shown, it is not in fact possible to speak of the Church and her unity without referring first of all to the Divine Eucharist. "The Divine Eucharist is the center of Christians' unity with Christ in the body of the Church. For through it the Church reveals herself *par excellence* as the body of Christ and communion of the Holy Spirit";[5] and this, as we have seen, was the unchanging consciousness of the Church of the first three centuries. It is in consequence a *positive* element of "eucharistic ecclesiology" that prominence is given to the Eucharist in ecclesiology, a prominence which has not been sufficiently emphasized by our theology in the past.

Another positive element in "eucharistic ecclesiology" is its acceptance of the catholicity and ecclesiological fullness of each local Church.[6] As we have seen from examining the sources, this is true of *all* the texts of the first three centuries, and hence we always find in them "Catholic Churches" in the plural. This means that each local Church enjoys *self-sufficiency of grace and salvation* which is the purpose of the Church. This position reflects the basic understanding of the Orthodox Church that "in the Divine Eucharist is contained the *whole* body of Christ,"[7] humans' salvation being achieved precisely "through their incorporation into the body of Christ."[8]

Apart from these positive elements, however, the theory of eucharistic ecclesiology as taken to its ultimate conclusions by the above-mentioned theologians can lead to unacceptable and dangerous positions. Thus, while the view of the Eucharist as the element incarnating and expressing the Church *par excellence* is correct, the view that this is the *sole sine qua non* condition for the notion of the Church and her unity could not be accepted so unreservedly. From the purely methodological standpoint, it has already been noted[9] that there is a danger of one-sidedness if unity in the Eucharist is not characterized as a *part* only of the wider subject of the Church's unity. But also from the standpoint of the substantive evidence of the sources examined here, it has been underlined that in order to express the concept of the Church and her unity, in addition to the Eucharist other essential elements are required, such as right faith without which "even the Eucharist is an impossibility."[10] It is consequently a negative element in the extreme positions of eucharistic ecclesiology that through them dogmatic differences tend to become unimportant in the unity of the Church, on account of the axiom that every Church, inasmuch as she celebrates the Eucharist, "does not cease to remain in herself the Church of God, albeit isolated" and cut off from the others.[11] There was, rightly, a strong reaction against this position.[12] For as the present study has shown, to have the notion of the "Catholic Church", the Eucharist is not sufficient, but orthodoxy is also required; while the consciousness of the Church of the first three centuries, as expressed through Cyprian, was unable to recognize eucharistic fullness in a schismatic Church, even if she celebrated the Eucharist.[13] Of course, as was stressed at the appropriate place, this position of Cyprian's was not accepted in the West where Augustine's conception of schism ultimately prevailed. But the first three centuries, to which this study is confined, do not permit any conclusion other than this position of Cyprian's.

Judged from this viewpoint, any attempt at

"intercommunion" between Churches divided by heresy or schism is unthinkable according to the sources of the period examined here. Communion in the Eucharist presupposes full unity in all the basics, such as love and faith ("let us love one another, that with one mind we may confess..."), because eucharistic unity constitutes the culmination and full expression of the unity of the Church. In consequence, it is not this or that particular difference between the divided Churches which makes it impossible for them to commune in the Eucharist but *the division per se*. Eucharistic communion makes sense only in a fully united Church, and hence the term "intercommunion" has rightly been criticized as inept.[14] The precipitate tendency towards "intercommunion" in the modern ecumenical movement is due, theologically, to the absence of the ecclesiological view of the Eucharist emphasized here, and psychologically, to the tendency to accept schism as a natural fact endemic to the Church organism;[15] any feeling of sorrow or repentance for which is superfluous. By contrast, for those who look at the Eucharist through the prism of ecclesiology, the avoidance of communion with the heterodox, far from having any sense of self-satisfaction or arrogance, expresses a continuing experience of the tragedy of schism as expressed in the most existential way through the refusal of eucharistic communion.

Emphasized to the extreme, however, the axiom "where the Eucharist is, there is the Church" similarly destroys in the final analysis any notion of *canonical* unity in the Church leading in essence to the antithesis introduced by R. Sohm between Religion and Law. It is perhaps not fortuitous that N. Afanassieff, who was chiefly responsible for introducing the so-called "eucharistic ecclesiology," stresses that only love and not canons of law and rights can have a place in the unity of the Church, inasmuch as "in the pattern of eucharistic ecclesiology... power based on right does not exist... universal ecclesiology and eucharistic ecclesiology have different conceptions on the question of church government:

the first conceives this government as a matter of law and rights, and the second regards it as founded on grace."[16] Such an absolute view of the eucharistic character of the Church to the exclusion of canonical preconditions leads Fr A. Schmemann, too, to the view that we have ecclesiological fullness even in the parish, inasmuch as the Eucharist is celebrated there,[17] which conflicts with the conclusions of this study in which the eucharistic element is interwoven with the canonical, which is to say, the Eucharist with the Bishop. As we have seen, the integrity of the Eucharist and the integrity of the priesthood are joined together so inseparably that they are not thought of by the early Church as two different subjects. And we are rightly reminded in contemporary theological discussions that "the theology of priesthood and that of the Eucharist are identical and inseparable."[18] Besides, the extensive study of the historical literature in Part Three of the present work (on the emergence of the parish) make the conclusion unavoidable that the parish can on no account be regarded as a complete Church even though the Eucharist is celebrated in it.

Accepting the extreme position of the axiom "where the Eucharist is, there is the Church" will equally lead to a denial of the unity of the "one Catholic Church throughout the world" which, as we have seen, emerges from this work. The ecclesiological fullness of each "Catholic Church" in a place *is not unrelated to or independent of* her unity with the rest of the "Catholic Churches." As stressed above, *any Church which is cut off ceases to be a "Catholic Church."* This means that *whereas we have many "Catholic Churches" in the world, we have only one body* because "Christ is not divided." In consequence and in essence, the Divine Eucharist is one and so is the Church "even though the tabernacles of the gatherings are in various places" (Council of Antioch, 325). Hence, a Church which is not united with the rest of the Catholic Churches, i.e. with the *one body of Christ in all the world*, cannot continue to be the Church of God.

Identified as she is with the One whole Christ, each "Catholic Church," *in communion with the other Churches like her,* is not a part of a whole; *but nor can it be said that she can live cut off from the others.* For her wholeness and fullness *are not her exclusive and private possession.* It is the one Christ who Himself, however, lives and is incarnate *identically* in the other Churches too. In order for each Church to be the body of Christ, then, she cannot but be identified with the other Churches constituting with them *one sole Church* in the whole world. This is precisely what is implied by the thesis of this work according to which the unity of the Church throughout the world is a unity *in identity.* It is the identity of the Churches with the one Christ and with each other which means that *no local Church can be a "Catholic Church" if she is cut off from the rest.*

The view of the unity of the "one Catholic Church throughout the world" in modern theology, even modern Orthodox theology, as a *unity of parts* is certainly not compatible with the conclusions of our work. In consequence, it is not right to combat whatever errors there might be in "eucharistic ecclesiology" by borrowing schemes alien to the sources of the first three centuries such as that of "unity of parts" which was introduced under the influence of modern conceptions. *No impartial student of history* will be able to discover "one unified universal Church organized into one body" in the first three centuries. But while there was no such thing as a "unity of parts," the unity of the one Catholic Church throughout the world was not lacking. This unity existed and, without destroying the ecclesiological fullness of each "Catholic Church" by making her a *part* of a whole, it was manifested all the time, but most especially when outside conditions required it. This happened principally through the institution of the Holy Councils.

This major subject of the institution of Councils has in no way been underestimated in the present work. On the contrary, it has been clearly stated that it is so important as to be the subject of a special study since this institution has no place methodologically in the eucharistic unity to which the present study confines itself. Whenever any relation between eucharistic unity and Councils is observed in the sources, we do not fail to examine it in detail.[19] Another reason why it was not possible to incorporate the subject of Councils into the present work is that during the first three centuries which we are looking at, i.e. up to Cyprian, the institution of Councils is not yet firmly established at least in its its supreme form that of the Ecumenical Council. Only sporadic and haphazard convocations of local Councils appear, and for these – and this is the most important point for the historian – *there are no sources.*

From what has already been said above in connection with the so-called "eucharistic ecclesiology," it is evident that the "catholicity" of each episcopal Church *cannot be understood independently of her full unity with the rest of the Churches in the one body of Christ.* Cut off from the others, any such Church *ceases to be "catholic." This forms the theoretical basis for the necessity of the institution of Councils.* The realization of this necessity by the Church of the first three centuries led naturally to the convocation of Councils through which the *"common union"* was expressed (Eusebius' term for the Councils occasioned by the Paschal controversy). The institution of Councils, in consequence, arose during the first three centuries as the supreme way of verifying the *"common union"* of the local Churches in one body.

Of course, within the time frame of this work, that is up to Cyprian, there is no consolidation of the Council as an institution nor any theoretical description of it, and our silence on the subject is thus demanded by the sources. This, however, does not prevent the Church evolving as to her forms of administration. Hence in the fourth century, for reasons beyond the scope of this work, the institution of Councils became *fixed*, and besides this the *Ecumenical Council* now makes its appearance as the supreme manifestation of the conciliar system. Was this something revolutionary relative to the first three centuries? In other words, do the conclusions drawn in our study concerning the period up to Cyprian conflict with the establishment of the conciliar system from the fourth century onwards? The answer is negative, and here are the reasons why.

As was stressed above,[20] the Church right from the beginning lived with the consciousness of containing within herself *the entire world (oikoumenê)*. This "ecumenical" or universal spirit never left the Church during the first three centuries. As has also repeatedly been stressed, *"the common union"* was an *ecclesiological necessity* for each Church. Without this union, the catholicity of the local Church was inconceivable. Hence, the appearance of the Councils and their development during the fourth century into Ecumenical Councils, constituting "the Church's supreme collective authority, in both senses of the word,"[21] was a natural consequence of the consciousness of the "common union" of the Churches which became firmly established during the first three centuries.

As was natural, this consciousness of a "common union" of the Churches in the first three centuries, forcefully expressed through the Holy Councils, brought the Bishops of the Churches too into a relationship of profound communion and unity with each other. Just as the many Eucharists formed but one Eucharist, so the many Bishops formed but "one episcopate." It would consequently be correct in principle to speak of the *"collegiality"* of the Bishops at least from Cyprian's time. But the notion of *"collegiality,"* being expounded so extensively today by Roman Catholic theology[22] appears in many aspects questionable in the light of the conclusions of our study. The central point at issue in this case is the very notion of "collegiality," which presupposes the idea that the Churches in various places and their Bishops are *parts* of a *collective*[23] *organism*, complementing one another in a unity formed by *addition*. For modern exponents of the theory of "collegiality," the Bishops throughout the world constitute as a whole a "college" which is the antitype and successor of the college of the Twelve. Hence, it is not difficult, but is on the contrary imperative, for this college to have a head corresponding to that of the college of the Twelve, and this is the Bishop of Rome who occupies the place of Peter. Thus, although this theory of "collegiality" stresses the importance of the Council as institution, far from diminishing the position of the Bishop of Rome, it actually gives it ecclesiological support because he is now regarded as the indispensable figure who expresses the unity of the episcopate. Whether Peter was indeed the head of the Twelve and whether the Bishop of Rome has a right to regard himself as Peter's successor are certainly debatable problems, but they do not constitute the crucial and basic question raised by the theory of collegiality of Bishops from the viewpoint of the conclusions of our study. The principal question is whether, in the consciousness of the early Church in the first three centuries, the correspondence between the college of the Twelve and that of the Bishops was such as to make *each* of the Bishops a successor of only a *part* of the college of the Twelve and *all of them collectively* (i.e. *as a college*) successors of the Twelve as a whole. The answer to this question is that, as has been shown at length here, the college of the Twelve and the "throne of Peter" which was preeminent within it formed the foundation, not of one Church, but of *every* episcopal Church because *every* Bishop was understood as being a successor to *all* the Apostles – and to Peter. The unity of the Bishops in consequence was not "collective" or "collegial" in the sense of bringing together by addition an apostolic succession which was divided up among the various Bishops. Every one of the Bishops sat on the throne of Peter; his Church being regarded as fully apostolic and based on the foundation of *all* the Apostles. Hence, it was believed that not only was it impossible for any one of these Bishops to possess priesthood or any ecclesiologically acknowledged jurisdictions more fully than any other Bishop, but that all of them united together could not form a sum of parts complementing each other, but an *organic* unity grounded in their full identity with each other and with the one body of Christ. This crucial point, which expresses the fullness of the episcopal rank, continues despite the appearance of the theory of the collegiality of Bishops to be the source of all essential disagreement with the whole substance of Roman Catholic ecclesiology in the light of the consciousness of the first three centuries.

NOTES

[1] Metr. Dionysios of Servies and Kozani, "Encyclical for the Inauguration of the Holy Synod of Bishops of the Church of Greece," in *Oikodomi, Ecclesiastical and Literary Bulletin* 2, 1959, p. 126.

[2] Cyprian, *Epist.* 66, 8.

[3] Cyprian, *Epist.* 55 (52). 21.

[4] See above, p. 17f.

[5] I. Karmiris, "Body of Christ," p. 365.

[6] See analysis by A. Lanne, *op. cit.* p. 914, *et al.*

[7] I. Karmiris, "Body of Christ," p. 365f.

[8] *ibid.* p. 334.

[9] p. 17f.

[10] See above, p. 134.

[11] N. Afanassieff, "*Una Sancta*," p. 549.

[12] See above, p. 37, n. 49.

[13] p. 148f., above.

[14] See N. Nissiotis, "Worship," p. 215.

[15] See above, p. 9f.

[16] "The Church which Presides in Love," p. 107-8.

[17] "Towards a Theology of Councils, p. 179f.

[18] See Metropolitan Athenagoras of Thyateira, *Theological Research on Christian Unity* (in Greek), 1964, p. 82f.

[19] See p. 151f.

[20] p. 150f.

[21] I. Karmiris, *The Ecclesiology of the Three Hierarchs*, p. 139f.

[22] See above, p. 190, n. 331.

[23] Translator's note: the same term is used in Greek for the cognate words *collegial* and *collective*. In following the author's argument here, it will be helpful to bear in mind that at the root of both these English words is the Latin *conligere*, "to gather together" (*sc.* discrete objects).

In the bibliography below we have included only those of the works used which we consider the most basic. As not to add further to this already long list, we have avoided giving all the bibliography relating to the various aspects of our subject. Further bibliographical references may be found in the footnotes to the text.

ACHELIS, H., *Die ältesten Quellen des orientalischen Kirchenrechts. Die Canones Hyppolyti* (Texte und Untersuchungen 6, 4), 1891.

ADAM, K., *Das Wesen des Katholizismus*, 1927[4].

AFANASSIEFF, N., "La Doctrine de la Primauté à la Lumière de l'Ecclésiologie" in *Istina* (1957), No. 4, 401-420.

_____ "The Church which Presides in Love," in *The Primacy of Peter in the Orthodox Church* (ed. J. Meyendorff, A. Schmemann, N. Afanassieff, N. Koulomzine), 1963, pp. 57-110.

_____ "Una Sancta" in *Irénikon* 36 (1963), 436-475.

AGOURIDIS, S., *Time and Eternity (Eschatology and Mysticism) in the Theological Teaching of John the Theologian* (in Greek), 1959.

ALES, A. d', *La théologie de Saint Cyprien*, 1922.

ALIVIZATOS, H., " The Significance of the Episcopal Office According to Irenaeus" (in Greek) in *Nea Sion* 10 (1910), 336ff.

_____ *The Cause of the Disputes over Easter in the Second Century* (in Greek), 1911.

_____ *The Sacred Canons and the Laws of the Church* (in Greek), 1949[2].

_____ "On the Nature of the Church from an Orthodox Perspective" (in Greek), in *Theologia* 21 (1950), 26ff.

_____ *The Mind of the Church*, 1955.

_____ *The Greek Orthodox Church*, 1955.

ALTANER, B., *Patrology* (1958)

ALTENDORF, *Einheit und Heiligkeit der Kirche*, 1932.

ANDROUTSOS, Ch., *Dogmatics of the Orthodox Eastern Church* (in Greek), 1907 (1956²)

_____ *Symbolics from an Orthodox Perspective* (in Greek), 1930²

ARNOLD, A., *Der Ursprung des christlichen Abendmahl in Lichts der neuesten liturgiegeschichtlichen Forschung*, 1932.

ATHENAGORAS, Metropolitan of Thyateira and Great Britain, *Theological Research on Christian Unity* (in Greek), 1964.

AUDET, J. -P., *La Didachè: Instruction des Apôtres*, 1948.

BACKMANN, P., "Der erste Brief auf die Korinther," (*Kommentar zum. N.T. 7*), 1910².

BALANOS, D., *Patrology* (in Greek), 1931.

BARDY, G., *La Théologie de l'Église de Saint Clément de Rome à saint Irenee, 1945.*

_____ *La théologie de l'Église de saint Irénée au Concile de Nicée*, 1947.

_____ *La Question des Langues dans l'Église Ancienne*, 1948.

_____ "Le Sacerdoce Chrétien, du Ier au Ve Siècles," in *Le Prêtre d'hier et d'aujourd'hui (Unam Sanctam*, 1928), 1954.

BARTH, K., *Kirchliche Dogmatik* IV/1, 1953.

BATIFFOL, P., *L'Église Naissante et le Catholicisme*, 1909³.

_____ *Leçons sur la Messe*, 1920⁷

BAUER, W., *Rechtgläubigkeit und Ketzerei im ältesten Christentum*, 1964².

BAUERNFEIND, O., "Die Apostelgeschichte," (*Theolog. Handkommentar zum N.T.*, 5), 1939.

BAUR, F.C., "Die Christuspartei in der korinthischen Gemeinde, der Gegensatz des petrinischen und paulinischen Christentums in der ältesten Kirche," in *Tübinger Zeitschrift*, 1831, No. 4, pp. 61-206.

BEESON, C.H., *Hegemonius, Acta Archelai* (Die griechischen christlichen Schriftsteller, 16), 1906.

BEHM, J., *Die Handauflegung im Urchristentum nach Verwendung, Herkunft und Bedeutung*, 1911.

BENEVOT, P.M., *St Cyprian, The Lapsed – The Unity of the Catholic Church (Ancient Christian Writers* 25), 1957.

BEICKE, B.O., *Diakonie, Festfreude und Zelos in Verbindung mit der alterchristlichen Agapenfeier*, 1951.

BEST, E., *One Body in Christ*, 1955.

BETZ, J., *Die Eucharistie in der Zeit der griechischen Väter*, I/1, 1954.

———— "Eucharistie" in *L.T.K.*, III, 1959, 1143f.

BILLERBECK, P., STRACK, H.L., *Kommentar zum N.T. aus Talmud und Midrasch*, 1926.

BONIS, K., "St Ignatius the Godbearer and his Views on the Church" (in Greek), in *Orthodoxos Skepsis* 1 (1958), 10-12, 21-22, 39-41.

BOTTE, B.,

———— *Hippolyte de Rome, La Tradition Apostolique* (*Sources Chrétiennes* No. 11), 1946.

———— *La Tradition Apostolique de Saint Hippolyte* (Liturgiewissenschaftliche Quellen und Forschungen 39), 1963.

BOUSSET, W., *Kyrios Christos, Geschichte des Christusglaubens von den Anfangen des Christentums bis Irenaus*, 1913.

BRATSIOTIS, P.

———— "The Apostle Paul and the Unity of the Church" (in Greek), in *E.E.Th.S.* (1957-58), 1959,, pp. 151-163.

———— The Revelation of the Apostle John (in Greek), 1950.

———— "L'Apocalypse de Saint Jean dans le Culte de l'Église Grecque Orthodoxe," in *Revue d'Histoire and de Philosophie Religieuses*, 42 (1962), 116-121.

BRAUN, F.M., *Neues Licht auf die Kirche*, 1946.

BROSCH, J., *Charismen und Ämter in der Urkirche*, 1951.

BRUNNER, E., *Das Missverständniss der Kirche*, 1951.

BULTMANN, R., *Glauben und Verstehen*, II, 1958².

———— "The Transformation of the Idea of the Church in the History of Early Christianity," in *Canadian Journal of Theology* 1 (1955), 73-81.

———— *Theologie des Neuen Testaments*, 1958.

BUTLER, C., "Saint Cyprian and the Church," in *The Downside Review* 71 (1953), 263-66.

CAMELOT, P.-Th., "Saint Cyprien et la Primauté," in *Istina* (1957) 423ff.

CAMPBELL, J.V., "The Origin and Meaning of the Christian use of the Word *Ekklesia*," in *Journal of Theological Studies* 49 (1948), 130ff.

CAMPENHAUSEN, H. von, *Kirchliches Amt und geistliche Vollmacht in den ersten drei Jahrhunderten*, 1953.

CAPELLE, B., "Authorité de la Liturgie chez les Pères," in *Recherches Theolog. anc. et med.* 21 (1954), 5-22.

_____ *Travaux Liturgiques*, 1962

CASEL, O., *Die Liturgie als Mysterienfeier*, 1923⁵.

_____ *Das christliche Kultmysterium*, 1935².

_____ "Die Kirche als Braut Christi nach Scrift, Vaterlehre und Liturgie," in *Theologie der Zeit*, publ. Karl Rudolph, I, 1936, pp. 91-111.

CERFAUX, L., *La Théologie de l'Église Suivant Saint Paul*, 1948.

CHARKIANAKIS, S., *On the Infallibility of the Church in Orthodox Theology* (in Greek), 1965.

CHRISTOPHILOPOULOS, A., *Greek Church Law* (in Greek), I-III, 1952-1956.

CHRISTOU, P., *True Life According to the Teaching of Ignatius the Godbearer* (in Greek), 1951.

COLSON, J., *L'Évêque dans les Communautés Primitives*, 1951.

_____ *Les Fonctions Ecclésiales aux Deux Premiers Siècles*. 1956.

_____ *L'Épiscopat Catholique. Collegialité et Primauté dans les Trois Premiers Siècles de l'Église*, 1963.

CONGAR, Y., *The Mystery of the Church*, 1950.

_____ *Sainte Église. Études et Approches Ecclésiologiques*, 1963.

CONNOLLY, R.H., *Didascalia Apostolorum. The Syriac Version Translated and Accompanied by the Verona Fragment*, 1929.

_____ "The Eucharistic Prayer of Hippolytus" in *Journal of Theological Studies* 39 (1938), 350-369.

COPPENS, J., *L'Imposition des Mains et les Rites Connexes dans le N.T.*, 1925.

_____ "Le Fils d'Homme Daniélique et les Relectures de Dan. 7, 13 dans les Apocryphes et les Écrits du N.T.," in

Ephemerides Theologicae Lovanienses 37 (1961), 5-51.

CORWIN, V., *Saint Ignatius and Christianity in Antioch*, 1960.

CRAIG, C.T., *The One Church in the Light of the New Testament*, 1951.

CULLMANN, O., "Jésus, Serviteur de Dieu," in *Dieu vivant* 16 (1950), 17ff.

_____ *Urchristentum und Gottesdienst*, 1950.

_____ *Petrus Jünger – Apostel – Martyrer*, 1952.

_____ *Die Christologie des Neuen Testaments*, 1957.

DABIN, P., *La Sacerdoce Royale des Fidèles dans la Tradition Ancienne et Moderne*, 1950.

DANIÉLOU, J., "Μια Εκκλησια chez les Pères Grecs des Premiers Siècles," in *1054-1954 l'Église et les Églises*, I, 1954, pp. 129-139.

_____ *Théologie du Judéo-Christianisme*, 1958.

_____ *Message Évangélique et Culture Hellénistique aux IIe et IIIe siècles*, 1961.

DEISSMANN, A., *Die neutestamentliche Formel "in Christo Jesu" untersucht*, 1892.

DIECKMANN, H., *Die Verfassung der Urkirche, dargestellt auf Grund der Paulusbriefe und der Apostelgeschichte*, 1923.

DIX, G., *The Treatise on the Apostolic Tradition of Saint Hippolytus of Rome*, 1937.

_____ *A Detection of Aumbries*, 1942.

_____ "Ministry in the Early Church," in *Apostolic Ministry* (ed. Kirk), 1946.

_____ *The Shape of the Liturgy*, 1948.

_____ *Jew and Greek*, 1963.

DODD, C.H., *The Interpretation of the Fourth Gospel*, 1953.

DOELGER, F.J., *Sol Salutis, Gebet und Gesang in Christlichen Altertum. Rücksicht auf die Ostung im Gebet und Liturgie*, 1925.

DUCHESNE, L., *Liber Pontificalis*, I-II, 1886.

_____ *Origines du Culte Chrétien*, 1889.

_____ *Histoire Ancienne de l'Église*, I, 1906.

_____ *Fastes Épiscopaux de l'Ancienne Gaulle*, I, 1907[2].

DVORNIK, F., *The Idea of Apostolicity in Byzantium and the Legend of Saint Andrew*, 1958.

EHRHARDT, A., *The Apostolic Succession in the First Two Centuries of the Church*, 1953.

ELERT, W., *Abendmahl und Kirchengemeinschaft in der alten Kirche hauptsächlich des Ostens*, 1954.

ELFERS, H., *Die Kirchenordnung Hippolyts von Rom*, 1938.

EVDOKIMOV, P., *L'Orthodoxie*, 1959.

EVTAXIAS, I., *Stipulations Concerning Priestly Authority in the Canon Law of the Orthodox Eastern Church* (in Greek), I, 1872.

FEDERER, K., *Liturgie und Glaube. Eine theologiegeschichtliche Untersuchung*, 1950.

FEINE, P., *Theologie des Neuen Testaments*, 1934.

FLOROVSKY, G., "The Church: Her Nature and Task," in *The Universal Church in God's Design*, (World Council of Churches), 1948.

_____ "Le Corps du Christ Vivant," in *La sainte Église Universelle: Confrontation OEcuménique*, 1948.

_____ "The Doctrine of the Church and the Ecumenical Movement," in *The Ecumenical Review* 2 (1950), 152-161.

_____ "Orthodox Contribution," in *Ways of Worship* (ed. P. Edwall etc.), 1961.

_____ "Corpus Mysticum: The Eucharist and Catholicity," in *Church Service Society*, The Annual, 1936-1937, No. 9.

FOAKES JACKSON – KIRSOPP LAKE (ed.), *The Beginnings of Christianity*, I-IV, 1920-33.

FOERSTER, E., *R. Sohms Kritik des Kirchenrechtes*, 1942.

FRAINE, J. de, *Adam et son Lignage: Études sur la Notion de "Personalité Corporative" dans la Bible*, 1959.

FRIES, H., "Die Eucharistie und die Einheit der Kirche," in *Pro Mundi Vita. Festschrift zum eucharistischen Weltkongress*, 1960.

FUNK, F., *Patres Apostolici*, I, 1901.

GAECHTER, P., "Unsere Einheit mit Christus nach dem hl. Irenaus," in *Zeitschrift für katholische Theologie*, 58 (1934) 516ff.

GALTIER, P., "*Ad his qui sunt undique*," in *Revue d'Histoire Ecclésiastique* 44 (1949), 425ff.

GENOUILLAC, H., *L'Église Chrétienne au Temps de Saint*

Ignace d'Antioche, 1907.

GERKE, F., *Die Stellung des I. Clemensbriefes innerhalb der Entwicklung der altchristlichen Gemeinde-Verfassung und des Kirchenrechts*, 1931.

GEWIESS, J., *Die urapostolische Heilsverkündigung nach der Apostelgeschichte*, 1939.

GILLMANN, F., *Das Institut der Chorbischöfe im Orient; historische-kanonische Studie*, (Veröffentlichungen aus dem kirchenhistorischen Seminar, II, 1), 1903.

GOAR, F.J., *Euchologion sive Rituale Graecorum*, 1947 (new ed. 1960).

GOGUEL, M., *Les Premiers Temps de L'Église*, 1949.

_____ "Unité et Diversité du Christianisme Primitif," in *Revue d'Histoire et de Philosophie Religieuses* 19 (1939).

GOOSENS, W., *Les Origines de l'Eucharistie*, 1931.

GÖPFERT, A., *Die Katholizität. Eine dogmengeschichtliche Studie*, 1876.

GREENSLADE, S.L., *Schism in the Early Church* (no date)

GRENIER, A., *Manuel d'Archéologie Gallo-Romaine*, II, 1934.

GUARDINI, R., *Vom Sinn der Kirche*, 1955[4].

HAMEL, A., *Der Kirchenbegriff Hippolyts*, 1929.

_____ *Die Kirche bei Hippolyt von Rom*, 1951.

HAMER, J., *L'Église Est Une Communion*, 1962.

HANSSENS, J.M., *"De Concelebratione Eucharistica,"* in *Periodica*, 17 (1927), 143ff.; 21 (1932), 219ff.

_____ *La Liturgie d'Hippolyte* (*Orientalia Christiana Analecta* 155), 1959.

HARDEN, J.M., *The Ethiopic Didascalia Translated*, 1920.

HARNACK, A., *Lehrbuch der Dogmengeschichte*, I, 1894[3].

- *Entstehung und Entwicklung der Kirchenverfassung und des Kirchenrechts, in den zwei ersten Jahrhunderten*, 1910.

_____ *Mission und Ausbreitung des Christentums in den drei ersten Jahrhunderten*, II, 1924[4].

_____ *Das Wesen des Christentums*, 1950[2].

HATCH, E., *The Organization of the Early Christian Churches*, 1888.

HEFELE – LECLERCQ, *Histoire des Conciles*, II-III, 1909.

HEILER, F., *Urkirche und Ostkirche*, 1937.

_____ *Altkirchliche Autonomie und päpstliche Zentralismus,* 1941.

HEUSSI, K., *Kompendium der Kirchengeschichte,* 1949[10].

IMBART DE LA TOUR, *Les pariosses rurales du IVe au XIe siècle,* 1900.

IOANNIDIS, V., "The Kingdom of God in the New Testament Teaching" (in Greek), in *E.E.Th.S.,* 1956.

_____ "The Unity of the Church according to St Paul" (in Greek), in *Efcharisterion: Essays in Honor of Professor H. Alivizatos,* 1958, p. 173ff.

_____ *Introduction to the New Testament* (in Greek), 1960.

JALLAND, T.G., "The Doctrine of the Parity of Ministers" in Kirk (ed.), *The Apostolic Ministry,* 1946.

JANSSEN, H., *Kultur und Sprache. Zur Geschichte der alten Kirche im Spiegel der Sprachentwicklung, von Tertullian bis Cyprian,* (*Latinitas Christiana primaeva, Studia ad sermonem latinum pertinentia,* 8) 1938.

JEREMIAS, J., *Die Kindtaufe in der ersten vier Jahrhunderten,* 1958.

_____ *Die Abendmahlswörte Jesu,* 1949[2].

JOHNSON, A.R., *The One and the Many in the Israelite Conception of God,* 1942.

JUNGMANN, J., *Missarum Solemnia* I-II, 1952[3].

_____ "Fermentum," in *Colligere Fragmenta (Festschrift Alban Dold),* 1952, pp. 185-190.

_____ *The Early Liturgy to the Time of Gregory the Great,* 1959.

KAISER, M., *Die Einheit der Kirchengewalt nach dem Zeugnis des N.T. und der apostolischen Väter,* 1956.

KALLINIKOS, K., *The Church Building and the Rites Performed in it* (in Greek), 1921.

KALOGIROU, I., *The Unity in Ecumenicity of the Orthodox Church According to Basic Ecclesiological Principles* (in Greek), 1960.

_____ *On the Character of the Orthodox Catholic Church According to the Basic Soteriological Principles in the New Testament* (in Greek), 1961.

KARMIRIS, I., *Dogmatic and Credal Documents of the Or-*

thodox Catholic Church (in Greek), I, 1960²

_____ "The Body of Christ, which is the Church" (in Greek), in *Ekklesia* 39 (1962), 334-337, 364-67.

_____ *The Orthodox Doctrine of the Church* (in Greek), 1964.

_____ *Summary of the Dogmatics of the Orthodox Catholic Church* (in Greek), 1960.

_____ *The Ecclesiology of the Three Hierarchs.* Vol. I, *Beginning and Revelation of the Church* (in Greek), 1961.

KATTENBUSCH, F., "Der Quellort der Kirchenidee," in Harnack-Festgabe, 1921.

KELLY, J.N.D., *Early Christian Creeds*, 1952.

_____ *Early Christian Doctrines*, 1958.

KLEIN, J., *Grundlegung und Grenzen des kanonischen Rechtes*, 1947.

KOCH, H., *Cyprianische Untersuchungen*, 1926.

KONIDARIS, G. *The Formation of the Catholic Church up to the Beginning of the Fifth Century and the Three Hierarchs* (in Greek), 1955.

_____ *General Church History from Jesus Christ to Our Own Times* (in Greek), I, 1957², (abbreviated to G.C.H.).

_____ "The Importance of the Institution of the Church in the History and Life of Christianity According to Clement of Rome" (in Greek), in *Orthodox Skepsis* 1 (1958), 37ff.

_____ *New Research Towards Solving the Problems of the Sources of Church Polity in Early Christianity* (in Greek), 1956f.

_____ *On the Supposed Difference in Forms in the Polity of Early Christianity* (in Greek), 1959².

_____ *Ecclesiastical History of Greece* (in Greek), I, 1954-1960.

_____ *On the Regional and Chronological Limitations on the Use of the Term "the Bishops and the Deacons"* (in Greek), 1960.

_____ *The Historian, the Church and the Content of Tradition During the First Two Centuries* (in Greek, translated from German), 1961.

_____ "Warum die Urkirche von Antiochia den *proestota presbyteron* der Ortsgemeinde als "ho Episkopos" bezeichnete," in *Münchener theologische Zeitschrift* (1961), 269-84.

_____ *State and Civil Life in the Worship of Orthodox Christianity* (in Greek, translated from German), 1961.

_____ "Apostolic Succession" (in Greek), in *Threskeftiki kai Ethiki Enkyklopaideia* [Encyclopedia of Religion and Ethics], IV, 1964, cols. 1109-1121.

KOTSONIS, I., *The Place of the Laity in the Church Organization*, 1956.

_____ *The Canonical Viewpoint on Contact with the Heterodox*, 1957.

_____ *Interrelationships between the Pastors of the Church*, 1950.

KRÜGER, G., *Die Rechtsstellung der vorkonstantinischen Kirche*, 1935.

KÜNG, H., "Der Frühkatholizismus im N.T. als kontrovestheologisches Problem," in *Tübinger Theol. Quartalschrift*, 1962, pp. 385-424.

LABRIOLLE-REFOULE, *Tertullian, Traité de la Prescription Contre les Hérétiques* (Sources chrétiennes, 46), 1957.

LA PIANA, G., "The Roman Church at the End of the Second Century," in *The Harvard Theological Review* 18 (1925).

_____ "Foreign Groups in Rome During the First Centuries of the Empire," in *The Harvard Theological Review*, 20 (1927).

LATOURETTE, K.S., *A History of the Expansion of Christianity*, I, 1938.

LEBRETON, J., "Le Développement des Institutions à la Fin du IIe s. et au Début du IIIe s.," in *Recherches des Sciences religieuses*, 1934.

LECLERCQ, H., "Catholique," in *D.A.C.L.*, II/2, 1910.

LIETZMANN, H., *Messe und Herrenmahl*, 1926.

_____ *Geschichte der alten Kirche*, I, 1937.

LIGHTFOOT, J.B., *The Apostolic Fathers. Ignatius and Polycarp*, I, 1889.

LINTON, O., *Das Problem der Urkirche in der neueren Forschung*, 1932.

LOHMEYER, E., *Gottesknecht und Davidsohn*, 1945.

LOHSE, B., *Das Passafest der Quartadecimaner*, 1953.

LUBAC, H. de, *Catholicisme: Les Aspects Sociaux du Dogme*, 1947².

_____ *Corpus Mysticum*, 1949².

McGREGOR, G.H.C., "The Eucharist in the Fourth Gospel," in *New Testament Studies* 9 (1963).

MANSON, T.W., *The Teaching of Jesus*, 1955.

_____ *Ministry and Priesthood*, 1958.

MARTIMORT, A.G. (ed.), *L'Église en Prière: Introduction à la Liturgie*, 1961.

MERSCH, E., *La théologie du Corps mystique*, II, 1946².

_____ *Le Corps Mystique du Christ*, I-II, 1955³.

MEYENDORFF, J., "Sacraments et Hierarchie dans l'Église," in *Dieu Vivant* 26 (1954), p. 81.

_____ "L'Église et la Communauté des Fidèles dans l'Église Orthodoxe," in *L'Évêque et son Église, Cahiers de la Pierre-qui-vire*, 1955, pp. 94-103.

_____ *L'Église Orthodoxe, Hier et Aujourd'hui*, 1960 [ET *The Orthodox Church: Its Past and its Role in the World Today*, 1962).

MICHAELIS, W., *Das Ältestenamt*, 1953.

MICHEL, A., "Unité de l'Église," in *D.T.C.* 15 (1946) 2200-2215.

MICHEL, O., *Das Zeugnis des Neuen Testaments von der Gemeinde*, 1941.

MILASCH, N., *The Ecclesiastical Law of the Eastern Orthodox Church* (in Greek), 1906.

MINEAR, P., *Images of the Church in the New Testament*, 1960.

MÖHLER, J., *Die Einheit der Kirche*, 1824 (French translation: *L'Unité dans l'Église*, in Unam Sanctam No. 2)

MÖRSDORF, K., "Zur Grundlegung des Rechtes der Kirche," in *Münchener Theologische Zeitschrift* 3 (1952), 329-348.

_____ "Altkanonisches Sacramentsrecht? Eine Auseinandersetzung mit den Anschauungen Rudolph Sohms über die inneren Grundlagen des Decretum Gratiani," in *Studia Gratiana*, I, 1953, 485-502.

MOURATIDIS, K., *The Essence and Polity of the Church Ac-*

cording to the Teaching of John Chrysostom (in Greek), 1958.

_____ *Diversification, Secularisation and Recent Developments in the Law of the Roman Catholic Church* (in Greek), 1961.

MOUREAU, H., "Catholicité," in *D.T.C.*, II, 199ff.

MÜLLER, K., *Beiträge zur Geschichte der Verfassung der alten Kirche* (Abhandlungen d. Preuss. Akad. d. Wiss., Phil.-hist. Kl. 3), 1922.

_____ "Kirchenverfassung in christlichen Altertum," in *R.G.G.* III (1929), 968-988.

MUSSNER, F., *Christus, das All und die Kirche*, 1955.

MORAITIS, D., *The Liturgy of the Presanctified* (in Greek), 1950.

_____ *History of Christian Worship. Ancient Times (First to Fourth Century)*, (in Greek), 1964.

NAUTIN, P. *Lettres et Écrivains Chrétiens des IIe et IIIe Siècles*, 1961.

NEUENZEIT, *Das Herrenmahl. Studien zur Paulinischen Eucharistieauffassung*, 1958.

NISSIOTIS, N., "Worship, Eucharist, Intercommunion: An Orthodox Reflection," in *Studia Liturgica*, 2 (1963).

PAPADOPOULOS, Ch., *History of the Church of Alexandria* (in Greek), 1935.

_____ *On Chorepiscopi and Titular Bishops* (in Greek), 1935.

PEDERSEN, J., *Israel, its life and Culture*, 1926.

PEIFER, C., "Primitive Liturgy in the Formation of the New Testament," in *Bible Today* 1 (1962), 14-21.

PERLER, O., "L'Évêque, Représentant du Christ Selon les Documents des Premiers Siècles," in *L'Épiscopat et l'Église Universelle*, ed. Y. Congar and B.D. Dupuy, 1962, pp. 31-66.

PÉTRÉ, H., *Etheriae Peregrinatio* (*Sources Chrétiennes* No. 21), 1948.

PHILIPPIDIS, L., *History of the New Testament Period* (in Greek), 1958.

PHYTRAKIS, A., *Relics and Tombs of the Martyrs in the First Three Centuries* (in Greek), 1955.

_____ *Reactions Against the Veneration of Saints in the Ancient Church*, 1956.

PLOCHL, W., *Geschichte des Kirchenrechts*, I, 1953.

QUASTEN, J., *Patrology,* I-III, 1950-1960.

_____ *Momumenta eucharistica et liturgica vetustissima,* 1935-1937.

RAWLINSON, A.D.J., "Corpus Christi," in *Mysterium Christi* (ed. G.A. Bell and A. Deissmann, 1930, pp. 225ff.

RICHARDSON, C.C., "The Church in Ignatius of Antioch," in *Journal of Religion* 17 (1947), 428-443.

ROBINSON, J.A.T., *The Body,* 1952.

ROBINSON WHEELER, H., *The Hebrew Conception of Corporate Personality* (Werden und Wesen des A.T. Wissenschaft), 1936.

ROMANIDES, J., *The Ecclesiology of St Ignatius of Antioch,* 1956.

_____ *The Original Sin* (in Greek), 1957.

ROUGET, P., *Amen: Acclamation du Peuple Sacerdotal,* 1947.

RUCH, C., "La Messe d'après la s. Écriture," in *D.T.C.,* X, 795ff.

SCMAUS, M., *Katholische Dogmatik,* III/1, 1958.

SCHMEMANN, A., "Theology and Eucharist" (in Greek), in *Theology, Truth and Life,* (ed. Zoi Brotherhood), 1962.

_____ "Towards a Theology of Councils," in *St Vladimir's Seminary Quarterly* 6 (1962), 170-184.

- "Unity, Division, Reunion in the Light of Orthodox Ecclesiology," in *Theologia* 22 (1951), 242ff.

SCHMIDT, K.L., "Εκκλησια," in *T.W.N.T.,* I, 573-595.

SCHNACKENBURG, R., *Die Kirche im Neuen Testament,* 1961.

SCHNEIDER, C., *Geistesgeschichte des Christentums,* I, 1954.

SCHNEIDER, J. *Die Einheit der Kirche nach N.T.,* 1936.

SCHÜRER, E., *Geschichte des judischen Volkes im Zeitalter Jesu Christi* III, 1920.

SCHWEITZER, A., *Geschichte der Paulinischen Forschung,* 1911.

SCHWEIZER, E., "ΣΩΜΑ," in *T.W.N.T.,* VII, 1024f.

_____ "Der Menschensohn," in *Zeitschrift für die neutestamentliche Wissenschaft* 50 (1959) 185-209.

_____ "Die Kirche als Leib Christi in den Paulinischen Antilegomena," in *Theolog. Literaturzeitung* (1961), 241-246.

_____ *Gemeinde und Gemeindenordnung im N.T.*, 1959.

SEMMELROTH, O., *Die Kirche als Ursakrament*, 1953.

SESTON, W., "Note Sur les Origines Religieuses des Pariosses Rurales," in *Revue d'Histoire et de Philosophie Religieuses* 15 (1935) 243-254.

SJÖBERG, E., *Der verborgene Menschensohn in den Evangelien*, 1955.

SIOTIS, M., "Die klassische und die christliche Cheirotonie in ihrem Verhältnis," in *Theologia* 20 (1949), 21 (1950) and 22 (1951).

_____ *History and Revelation in New Testament Studies* (in Greek), 1953.

_____ *Divine Eucharist: New Testament Information about the Divine Eucharist in the Light of the Church's Interpretation* (in Greek), 1957.

_____ "Die Ecclesiologie als Grundlage der neutestamentlichen Auslegung in der griechisch-orthodoxen Kirche," 1961.

SOHM, R., *Kirchenrecht*, I, 1892.

SOIRON, T., *Die Kirche als der Leib Christi nach der Lehre des hl. Paulus*, 1951.

STEPHANIDIS, V., *Church History* (in Greek), 1948, (1959²).

STENDAHL, K., "Kirche: II. Im Urchristentums," in *Die Religion in Geschichte und Gegenwart*, 3 Aufl. III (1959), 1297-1304.

STONE, D.A., *A History of the Doctrine of the Holy Eucharist*, I, 1909.

SUNDKLER, B., "Jésus et les Païens" in *Revue d'Histoire et de Philosophie religieuses* 16 (1936).

SOTERIOU, G., *Christian and Byzantine Archaeology* (in Greek), I, 1942.

TELFER, W., *The Office of a Bishop*, 1962.

THEODOROU, A., *History of Dogmas* (in Greek), I/1, 1963.

TÖDT, H.E., *Der Menschensohn in der synoptischen Überlieferung*, 1959.

TREMBELAS, P., *Little Euchologion* (in Greek), I, 1950.

_____ *Dogmatics of the Orthodox Catholic Church* (in Greek), III, 1961.

_____ "The Divine Eucharist in its Connection with the

Other Mysteries and Sacramental Rites" (in Greek), in *Efcharisterion, Essays in Honor of Professor H. Alivizatos*, 1958, pp. 462-472.

_____ "Worship in Apostolic Times" (in Greek), in *Theologia* 31 (1960), 183ff.

_____ "Contributions to the History of Christian Worship," in *E.E.Th.S.* (1958-60), 1963, pp. 9-93.

TURNER, C.H., "Apostolic Succession: A. The Original Conception; B. The Problem of the Non-catholic Orders" in *Essays on the early History of the Church and Ministry* (ed. H.B. Swete), 1918.

TURNER, H.E.W., *The Pattern of Christian Truth: A Study in the Relations between Orthodoxy and Heresy in the Early Church*, 1954.

VELLAS, V., *Personalities of the Old Testament* (in Greek), I,1957².

VOLTZ, von der E., *Ignatius von Antiochien als Christ und Theologe*, 1894.

WEISS, J., *Der erste Korintherbrief* (Mayer 5) 1910⁹.

WILLIAMS, G., "The Role of the Layman in the Ancient Church," in *Greek, Roman and Byzantine Studies* 1 (1958), 9-42.

WOLFF, H.W., *Jesaja 53 im Urchristentum*, 1950³.

WOLFSON, H., *Philo*, II, 1947.

ZEIGLER, A.W., *Das Brot von unseren Felder. Ein Beitrag zur Eucharistielehre des hl. Irenäus* (Pro Mundi Vita, Festschrift zum eucharistischen Weltkongress 1960), 1960.

ZEILLER, J., "La Conception de l'Église aux Quatre Premiers Siècles," in *Revue d'Histoire ecclésiastique* 29 (1933), 582.

ZIMMERLI, W. – JEREMIAS, J., "ΠΑΙΣ," in *T.W.N.T.*, V, 636ff.

For further bibliography, see *inter alia* the following:

_____ *L'Épiscopat et l'Église Universelle* (*Unam Sanctam* 39), 1962.

_____ *Prêtres d'Hier et d'Aujourd'hui* (*Unam Sanctam* 28), 1954.

_____ *Études sur le sacrement de l'ordre* (*Lex Orandi* 22), 1957.

TABLE

Showing the changes introduced in the late fourth century into the sources from the first three centuries, in relation to the place of the Bishop and the Presbyter in the Divine Eucharist

Epistles of Ignatius		*Apostolic Tradition* of Hippolytus		*Didascalia* of the Apostles	
Text from beginning of second century	Text from end of fourth/ beginning of fifth century	Text from beginning of third century	Text from end of fourth/ beginning of fifth century	Text from beginning of third century	Text from end of fourth/beginning of fifth century
The Eucharist is " one, which is under the leadership of the Bishop" , with " the Bishop sitting in the place of God and the presbyters in the place of the council of the Apostles" (Magn. 6-7, Smyrn. 8, Philad. 4)	To the original text are added descriptions of the Presbyters as " priests" , i.e. those who offer the Eucharist: - " Let the rulers be obedient to Caesar... the deacons, to the presbyters, the high priests" (Philad. 4) - " the priests and deacons are good, but the high priest is better" (Philad. 9)	- The Bishop is ordained, *inter alia*, " to offer the gifts of the Holy Church" , whereas - the Presbyter, in order to " govern the people in purity of heart" (*Ap. Trad.* 3 and 8)	i) *Ap. Const.* VIII and *Epitome.* While the prayer for the ordination of a bishop remains the same, at the ordination of a presbyter the words are added: " that... he may also... perform the spotless sacred rites on behalf of Thy people" (*Ap. Const.* VIII.16.5 and *Epitome* 6) ii) *Canons of Hippolytus*: No special prayer for the ordination of a Presbyter; it refers you to that for the ordination of a Bishop, on the grounds that the only difference between Bishops and Presbyters is the right to ordain	- The Bishop " presides in the place of God Almighty" and " makes you partakers of the Holy Eucharist of God" , whereas - " the Presbyters form the " council of the Bishop" (*Did.* 9)	i) *Ap. Const.* 1-VI: to the functions of the Presbyters are added: " ... to offer, baptize, bless..." , and hence it called the Presbyters " priests" (*Const.* III.20.2 and II.27.3). ii) Ethiopic version of the Didascalia: " the Presbyter teaches, baptizes, blesses, censes; and offers the sacrifice" (*Eth. Didasc.* 17)
Cf. Justin, 1 *Apol.* 67	Cf. 1 i) Ambrosiaster, *Liber. Quest.* 101.5 and *Comm. in 1 Tim.* 3.10) ii) *Apost. Const.* VIII.16.3-5	Cf. Syriac *Didascalia* (below)	Cf. i) *Jerome Ep.* 146.1 and ii) *Chrysostom on 1 Tim.* 11.	Cf. i) Ignatius (genuine text), above. ii) *Ap. Trad.* (above)	Cf. i) First Ecum. Council Can. 18 ii) Councils of Ancyra Can. 1 and Neocaesarea Can.s 9 and 13.